THE ULTIMATE
CSS REFERENCE

BY **TOMMY OLSSON**
& PAUL O'BRIEN

The Ultimate CSS Reference

by Tommy Olsson and Paul O'Brien

Copyright © 2008 SitePoint Pty Ltd

Managing Editor: Simon Mackie   **Technical Director:** Kevin Yank

Technical Editor: Andrew Tetlaw   **Editor:** Georgina Laidlaw

Expert Reviewer: Natalie Downe   **Cover Design:** Simon Celen

Expert Reviewer: Roger Johansson   **Interior Design:** Xavier Mathieu

Printing History:

First Edition: February 2008

Published by SitePoint Pty Ltd

48 Cambridge Street Collingwood
VIC Australia 3066
Web: www.sitepoint.com
Email: business@sitepoint.com

ISBN 978–0–9802858–5–7
Printed and bound in the United States of America

About the Authors

Hailing from Hampshire in the UK, **Paul O'Brien** is a freelance web designer specializing in CSS layouts. After selling a successful packaging business back in 1998 he was all set for a quiet existence, dabbling with his hobby of web design. However, what started out as a hobby soon became a full-time occupation as the demand for well-coded CSS layouts started growing. Even when he's not working, he can be found giving out helpful advice in the SitePoint Forums where he has racked up nearly 20,000 posts, all of which are CSS-related.

Paul's other passion is karate, which he has studied continuously for 35 years. He currently holds the rank of Third Dan (Sandan) in Shotokan karate, so I wouldn't argue with him if I were you!

Tommy Olsson is a pragmatic evangelist for web standards and accessibility, who lives in the outback of central Sweden. Visit his blog at http://www.autisticcuckoo.net/.

About the Expert Reviewers

The always excitable **Natalie Downe** works for Clearleft, in Brighton, as a client-side web developer. An experienced usability consultant and project manager, her first loves remain front-end development and usability engineering. She enjoys Doing Things Right and occasionally dabbling in the dark art of Python and poking the odd API.

Roger Johansson is a web professional with a passion for web standards, accessibility, and usability. He spends his days developing web sites at Swedish web consultancy NetRelations, and his evenings and weekends writing articles for his personal sites, http://www.456bereastreet.com/ and http://www.kaffesnobben.com/.

About the Technical Editor

Andrew Tetlaw has been tinkering with web sites as a web developer since 1997 and has also worked as a high school English teacher, an English teacher in Japan, a window cleaner, a car washer, a kitchen hand, and a furniture salesman. At SitePoint he is dedicated to making the world a better place through the technical editing of SitePoint books and kits. He is also a busy father of five, enjoys coffee, and often neglects his blog at http://tetlaw.id.au/.

About the Technical Director

As Technical Director for SitePoint, Kevin Yank oversees all of its technical publications—books, articles, newsletters, and blogs. He has written over 50 articles for SitePoint, but is best known for his book, *Build Your Own Database Driven Website Using PHP & MySQL.* Kevin lives in Melbourne, Australia, and enjoys performing improvised comedy theater and flying light aircraft.

About SitePoint

SitePoint specializes in publishing fun, practical, and easy-to-understand content for web professionals. Visit http://www.sitepoint.com/ to access our books, newsletters, articles, and community forums.

The Online Reference

The online version of this reference is located at http://reference.sitepoint.com/css. The online version contains everything in this book, fully hyperlinked and searchable. The site also allows you to add your own notes to the content and to view those added by others. You can use these user-contributed notes to help us to keep the reference up to date, to clarify ambiguities, or to correct any errors.

Your Feedback

If you wish to contact us, for whatever reason, please feel free to email us at books@sitepoint.com. We have a well-manned email support system set up to track your inquiries. Suggestions for improvement are especially welcome.

Reprint Permissions

Do you want to license parts of this book for photocopying, email distribution, Intranet or Extranet posting or for inclusing in a coursepack? Please go to Copyright.com and type in this book's name or ISBN number to purchase a reproduction license.

Table of Contents

Chapter 1 **What Is CSS?** 1

    CSS Versions 4

    Linking CSS to a Web Document 5

        Media Queries 14

    Standards Mode, Quirks Mode, and Doctype Sniffing 17

    Summary 20

Chapter 2 **General Syntax and Nomenclature** 23

    Statements 25

    At-rules 25

    Rule Sets 26

    Selectors 26

    Declaration Blocks 28

    Declarations, Properties, and Values 28

        Keywords 29

        Lengths and Units 29

        Percentages 32

        Colors 33

        Numbers 37

        Strings 37

        URIs 38

        Initial Values 39

        Shorthand Properties 39

    CSS Comments 42

    CSS Identifiers 43

    CSS Escape Notation 43

CSS Syntax Errors 44

Summary 45

Chapter 3   At-rules Reference 47

@charset 48

@import 49

@media 51

@page 52

@font-face 54

@namespace 55

Chapter 4   Selector Reference 59

Universal Selector 60

Element Type Selector 62

Class Selector 63

ID Selector 65

Attribute Selector 67

CSS3 Attribute Selectors 71

Selector Grouping 72

Combinators 73

Descendant Selector 74

Child Selector 76

Adjacent Sibling Selector 77

General Sibling Selector 79

Pseudo-classes 80

:link 83

:visited 84

:active 85

:hover 86

:focus 87

:first-child 88

:lang(C) 89

CSS3 Pseudo-classes 90

Pseudo-elements 106

:first-letter 107

:first-line 110

:before 113

:after 114

::selection 115

Chapter 5   The Cascade, Specificity, and Inheritance

The Cascade, Specificity, and Inheritance 117

The Cascade 118

!important Declarations 124

Specificity 126

Inheritance 133

The CSS Property Value inherit 135

Summary 137

Chapter 6   CSS Layout and Formatting

CSS Layout and Formatting 139

The Viewport, the Page Box, and the Canvas 141

The CSS Box Model 142

Containing Block 147

Collapsing Margins 148

The Internet Explorer 5 Box Model 156

The Internet Explorer hasLayout Property 158

Formatting Concepts 163

Block Formatting 164

Inline Formatting 166

List Formatting 168

Table Formatting 168

Replaced Elements 175

Positioning 176

Relative Positioning 176

Absolute Positioning 178

Fixed Positioning 178

Stacking Contexts 179

Floating and Clearing 180

The Relationship Between display, position, and float 184

Summary 185

Chapter 7   **Box Properties** 187

Dimensions 187

height 188

min-height 190

max-height 192

width 194

min-width 196

max-width 198

Margins 200

margin-top 200

margin-right 202

margin-bottom 205

margin-left 207

margin 209

Padding 211

padding-top 212

padding-right 213

padding-bottom 215

padding-left 216

padding 218

Borders and Outlines 220

border-top-color 220

border-top-style 222

border-top-width 224

border-top 226

border-right-color 228

border-right-style 229

border-right-width 232

border-right 233

border-bottom-color 235

border-bottom-style 236

border-bottom-width 239

border-bottom 240

border-left-color 242

border-left-style 243

border-left-width 246

border-left 247

border-color 249

border-style 251

border-width 254

border 255

outline-color 258

outline-style 259

outline-width 260

outline 261

Chapter 8   Layout Properties 263

display 264

position 267

float 269

clear 271

visibility 273

top 275

right 276

bottom 277

left 278

z-index 279

overflow 280

clip 283

Chapter 9   List Properties 285

list-style-type 286

list-style-position 288

list-style-image 289

list-style 290

Chapter 10   Table Properties 291

table-layout 292

border-collapse 293

border-spacing 294

empty-cells 295

caption-side 297

Chapter 11   Color and Backgrounds 299

background-color 299

background-image 301

background-repeat 303

background-position 305

background-attachment 309

background 312

color 315

Chapter 12   Typographical Properties 317

font-family 318

font-size 320

font-weight 321

font-style 323

font-variant 324

font 325

letter-spacing 326

word-spacing 327

line-height 328

text-align 330

text-decoration 332

text-indent 334

text-transform 335

text-shadow 337

vertical-align 338

white-space 341

direction 343

unicode-bidi 344

Chapter 13   Generated Content 347
content 348
counter-increment 352
counter-reset 354
quotes 355

Chapter 14   User Interface Properties 357
cursor 358

Chapter 15   Paged Media Properties 361
page-break-before 362
page-break-inside 363
page-break-after 364
orphans 365
widows 366

Chapter 16   Vendor-specific Properties 367
Mozilla Extensions 371
    -moz-border-radius 372
    -moz-box-sizing 375
    The display Property Value: -moz-inline-box 377
Internet Explorer Extensions 379
    zoom 380
    filter 381
    behavior 387
    The expression Property Value 388
Summary 390

Chapter 17 Workarounds, Filters, and Hacks 391

Internet Explorer Conditional Comments 394

Workarounds and Filters 400

CSS Hacks 404

Summary 408

Chapter 18 Differences Between HTML and XHTML 409

MIME Types 411

Case Sensitivity 412

Optional Tags 413

Root Element Properties 415

Appendix A Alphabetic Property Index 417

What Is CSS?

Have you ever thought about what a web page is? I mean, what it *really* is? Some people think of a web page as a visual medium—an aesthetically pleasing experience which may or may not contain information that's of interest to the viewer. Other people think of a web page as a document that may be presented to readers in an aesthetically pleasing way. From a technical point of view, the document interpretation is more appropriate.

When we examine the elements of its construction, a web document can consist of up to three layers—content, presentation, and behavior—as illustrated in Figure 1.1.

The **content layer** is always present. It comprises the information the author wishes to convey to his or her audience, and is embedded within HTML or XHTML markup that defines its structure and semantics. Most of the content on the Web today is text, but content can also be provided through images, animations, sound, video, and whatever else an author wants to publish.

The **presentation layer** defines how the content will appear to a human being who accesses the document in one way or another. The conventional way to view a web page is with a regular web browser, of course, but that's only one of many possible access methods. For example, content can also be converted to synthetic speech for users who have impaired vision or reading difficulties.

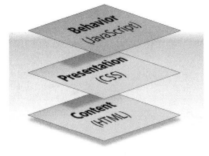

Figure 1.1: The three layers of a web document

The **behavior layer** involves real-time user interaction with the document. This task is normally handled by JavaScript. The interaction can be anything from a trivial validation that ensures a required field is filled in before an order form can be submitted, to sophisticated web applications that work much like ordinary desktop programs.

It's possible to embed all three layers within the same document, but keeping them separate gives us one valuable advantage: we can modify or replace any of the layers without having to change the others.

Certain versions of HTML and XHTML also contain **presentational element types**—that is, elements that specify the appearance of the content, rather than structure or semantics. For example, <b> and <i> can be used to control the presentation of text, and <hr> will insert a visible rule element. However, as these types of elements embed presentation-layer information within the content layer, they negate any advantage we may have gained by keeping the layers separate.

Cascading Style Sheets, or **CSS**, is the recommended way to control the presentation layer in a web document. The main advantage of CSS over presentational HTML markup is that the styling can be kept entirely separate from the content. For example, it's possible to store all the presentational styles for a 10,000-page web site in a single CSS file. CSS also provides far better control over presentation than do presentational element types in HTML.

By externalizing the presentation layer, CSS offers a number of significant benefits:

- All styling is kept in a limited number of style sheets. The positive impact this has on site maintenance can't be overestimated—editing one style sheet is obviously more efficient than editing 10,000 HTML files!

- The overall saving in bandwidth is measurable. Since the style sheet is cached after the first request and can be reused for every page on the site, it doesn't have to be downloaded with each web page. Removing all presentational markup from your web pages in favor of using CSS also reduces their size and bandwidth usage—by more than 50% in many documented cases. This benefits the site owner, through lower bandwidth and storage costs, as well as the site's visitors, for whom the web pages load faster.

- The separation of content from presentation makes it easier for site owners to reuse the content for other purposes, such as RSS feeds or text-to-speech conversion.

- Separate styling rules can be used for different output media. We no longer need to create a special version of each page for printing—we can simply create a single style sheet that controls how every page on the site will be printed.

Although CSS is designed to be independent of the markup language of the documents to which it is applied, in reality, it's used mainly with HTML and XML (including XHTML).

 HTML and XHTML

In this reference, when we mention HTML, we really mean HTML and/or XHTML, except where otherwise specified. The differences between the two markup languages are all documented in Differences Between HTML and XHTML (p. 409).

CSS Versions

The first CSS specification, CSS1,[1] became a World Wide Web Consortium (W3C)[2] recommendation in December 1996. It included properties for controlling typography, such as fonts, text alignment, spacing, margins, and list formatting. It allowed the designer to specify the dimensions of block-level boxes and to surround boxes with borders. Yet, when it came to layout and design, CSS1 didn't have much to offer: you could specify foreground and background colors and background images, and you could float a box to the left or to the right and make text flow around it.

CSS2 came out in 1998, and contained a lot of the features that designers had been longing for. Boxes could be made to behave like HTML table cells, or they could be positioned in different ways; more powerful selectors (p. 59) were available; style sheets could be imported into other style sheets; style rules could be specific to certain output media; and so on. Vast improvements had also been made in the areas of paged media (printing), and the generation of content from the style sheet.

As it turned out, some parts of CSS2 were very difficult to implement, so the W3C decided to revise the specification and adapt it to real-world situations. Most of the special features for paged media were removed. The creation of generated content (p. 347) was restricted to the `:before` and `:after` pseudo-elements, and restrictions were placed on how generated content could be styled.

The name of the revised version was "Cascading Style Sheets, Level 2 Revision 1"—CSS2.1 for short.[3]

> ### References to CSS2 Mean CSS2.1
>
> Today, references to CSS2 usually mean CSS2.1, since the original CSS2 was never really implemented by any browser.
>
> In this reference, we'll use the term CSS2 when we refer to Level 2 of the CSS specification (as opposed to CSS1 or CSS3). Unless we explicitly state otherwise,

---

[1] http://www.w3.org/TR/CSS1
[2] http://www.w3.org/
[3] http://www.w3.org/TR/CSS21/

What Is CSS?

> this term refers to CSS2.1, which is the latest—and current—revision of the CSS2 specification.

The work on CSS3[4] has been going on for years, but seems to advance very slowly. CSS3 is divided into modules, and the idea is that each module can become a recommendation independently from the others. No module has reached that stage, but some parts of the CSS3 specification have already been implemented by browsers.

Some features in the CSS3 working drafts that have already been implemented include multi-column output of text,[5] rounded corners on borders,[6] opacity control,[7] HSL/HSLA/RGBA colors,[8] and text shadows[9] (a part of CSS2 that was removed in CSS2.1).

The CSS3 selectors module[10] will be released separately from the rest of CSS3. Some of those selectors are already implemented in modern browsers.

Linking CSS to a Web Document

We can use any of three methods to specify CSS styling rules for elements in an HTML document, but only one method to specify CSS rules for XML documents. We can use all four methods with XHTML documents that are served as XML. XHTML served as HTML is HTML as far as browsers are concerned, so only the three HTML methods can be used in that case. See Differences Between HTML and XHTML (p. 409) for details about the different ways in which you can serve XHTML.

The methods are:

- Place the rules in a separate, external style sheet that's referenced by a `link` element or an `@import` rule in a style element (HTML, XHTML).

---

4 http://www.w3.org/Style/CSS/current-work
5 http://www.w3.org/TR/css3-multicol/
6 http://www.w3.org/TR/css3-background/#the-border-radius
7 http://www.w3.org/TR/css3-color/#transparency
8 http://www.w3.org/TR/css3-color/
9 http://www.w3.org/TR/css3-text/#text-shadow
10 http://www.w3.org/TR/css3-selectors/

- Place the rules within an separate, internal style sheet within a `style` element (HTML, XHTML).
- Place the rules in inline CSS specified in a `style` attribute of a markup tag (HTML, XHTML).
- Place the rules in a separate, external style sheet referenced by a processing instruction (or PI) (XML).

Separate style sheets—both external and internal—can be targeted to one or more output media. External style sheets can be specified as **alternative**, which means that they're not applied by default, but can be enabled by users in browsers that support alternative style sheets.

We specify the output media using the predefined media types shown in Table 1.1.

Table 1.1: Media Types

Media Type	Description
`"all"`	applies to all media
`"Braille"`	Braille/tactile feedback devices
`"embossed"`	paged Braille printers
`"handheld"`	handheld devices
`"print"`	paged media and print preview mode on the screen
`"projection"`	projected presentation (used by Opera in full-screen mode)
`"screen"`	color computer screens
`"speech"`	speech synthesizers (see the note below)
`"tty"`	media with a fixed-pitch character grid
`"tv"`	television-type devices

Using one or more external style sheets is generally considered to be the best practice, as it enforces the desirable separation between content and presentation.

Should each style sheet be specific to one output medium, or should you have a single style sheet and use `@media` at-rules (p. 51) to specify styles for different output media? The answer to that question depends, primarily, on how differently the content will be presented in different media. Style sheets for `"screen"` and `"projection"` media can often be combined, while style sheets for `"print"` or `"handheld"` usually benefit from being kept separate.

An internal style sheet can sometimes be justified on a page which has presentational needs that are very different from the rest of the site. It could also be used, along with one or more external style sheets, for styling special elements that only occur on one page.

Using an Internal Style Sheet During Development

It can be useful to keep your CSS in an internal style sheet during the initial development phase, to avoid problems that can arise when style sheets are cached by the browser. Once the design is completed, you can move the CSS to an external style sheet.

Inline styles should normally be avoided, since they tie presentation to content in the same unfortunate way as do presentational HTML elements such as the deprecated <font> and <center> elements.

About Aural Style Sheets

Aural style sheets (`media="speech"`) are not formally specified in CSS2.1. The specification reserves the speech media type, but says nothing about which properties apply to it and which don't. Therefore, aural style sheets will not be covered in this reference.

Referencing an External Style Sheet Using a `link` Element or `@import` At-rule

Here's an example of an external style sheet reference that uses a `link` element:

```
<link rel="stylesheet" type="text/css" href="/style.css"
    media="screen">
```

The link element, which must reside within the head element of an HTML document, links an external style sheet to the document. Multiple, comma-separated media types can be specified in the media attribute, for example, media="screen,projection". If it's omitted, this attribute defaults to media="screen", according to the HTML4 specification, but in reality, browsers seem to apply media="all" if the attribute is omitted.

Here's an example of a style sheet reference that uses an @import at-rule (p. 49):

```
<style type="text/css">
  @import url(/style.css);
</style>
```

The style element, like the link element, must reside within the head element.

Relative URIs in the href attribute or @import rule are relative to the HTML document that contains the link. (When @import is used inside an external style sheet, relative URIs are relative to the importing style sheet.)

The link element can also be used to link to an *alternative* style sheet:

```
<link rel="alternate stylesheet" type="text/css"
    href="/contrast.css" media="screen" title="High contrast">
```

This alternative style sheet, which is disabled by default, can be enabled by the user if the browser supports alternative style sheets. All style sheets with the same title attribute will be enabled or disabled as a group. Alternative style sheets are mutually exclusive, so enabling one group will automatically disable all other groups.

Watch Out for Alternative Spelling

The CSS specifications use the term "alternate" instead of "alternative." The keyword used in the rel attribute must also be "alternate".

A style sheet that's linked with `rel="stylesheet"` but lacks a `title` attribute, like the first example in this section, is known as a **persistent style sheet**. It will always be applied—even if an alternative style sheet is enabled by the user.

A style sheet that's linked with `rel="stylesheet"`, and for which a `title` attribute has been specified, is known as a **preferred style sheet**. It will be applied unless the user has enabled an alternative style sheet.

Let's take a look at a more complex example:

```
<link rel="stylesheet" type="text/css"
    href="/base.css" media="all">

<link rel="stylesheet" type="text/css"
    href="/def_layout.css" media="screen" title="Default">

<link rel="stylesheet" type="text/css"
    href="/def_colour.css" media="screen" title="Default">

<link rel="alternate stylesheet" type="text/css"
    href="/alt_layout.css" media="screen" title="Custom">

<link rel="alternate stylesheet" type="text/css"
    href="/alt_colour.css" media="screen" title="Custom">

<link rel="stylesheet" type="text/css"
    href="/print.css" media="print">
```

Here, **base.css** is a persistent style sheet, as it doesn't have a `title` attribute; it will always be applied for all media types, since it has the attribute `media="all"`.

By default, **def_layout.css** and **def_colour.css** will also be applied for screen media, since they're preferred style sheets.

If the user selects **Custom** style sheets in the browser, as depicted in Figure 1.2, **def_layout.css** and **def_colour.css** will be disabled, and **alt_layout.css** and **alt_colour.css** will be enabled.

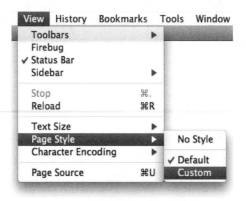

Figure 1.2: Selecting alternative style sheets in Firefox

When printing, or in print preview, **print.css** will be applied since it has the attribute `media="print"`. Note that **base.css** will also be applied since it specifies `media="all"`. The other four style sheets will not be applied here, however, since they specify only screen media.

We can use the alternative style sheet feature to offer multiple viewing options from which the user can make a selection. In Eric Meyer's Complex Spiral Demo,[11] the user is able to select from one of many available alternative style sheets, as depicted in Figure 1.3.

---

[11] http://meyerweb.com/eric/css/edge/complexspiral/demo.html

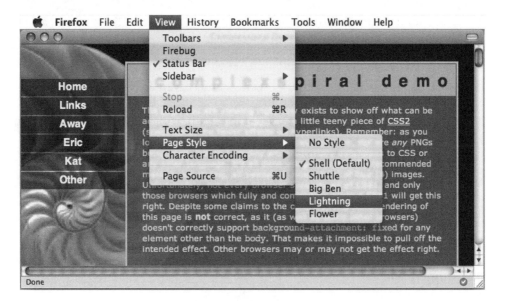

Figure 1.3: Alternative style sheets in the Complex Spiral Demo

Using an Internal Style Sheet

The `style` element, which must reside within the `head` element of an HTML document, specifies an internal style sheet which will only apply to elements in the enclosing document:

```
<style type="text/css" media="screen,projection">
  ⋮ CSS rules...
</style>
```

The `type` attribute is required, and should have the value `"text/css"` which denotes CSS styles. As in the case of external style sheets, the `media` attribute defaults to `"screen"` if you omit it, according to the HTML4 specification, but in reality, browsers seem to apply `media="all"` if the attribute is omitted.

Pre-HTML4 browsers don't support the `<style>` element—they'll render the element's content as text. As a special case, an SGML comment surrounding the content in its entirety will be ignored in CSS-compatible browsers. Note, however, that this applies only to HTML. It doesn't apply to XHTML served as XML—there, such a comment will be treated as a comment, effectively hiding all the CSS.

What Is CSS?

The practice of commenting out the content of `<style>` elements is archaic and unnecessary, since very few pre-HTML4 browsers are in regular use these days. It's harmless in HTML, but must be avoided in XHTML—even if served as text/html—to ensure that such a document will still work when served as XML.

Here's an example of an internal style sheet in HTML, which is hidden from ancient browsers:

```
<style type="text/css" media="screen,projection">
<!--
  : CSS rules...
-->
</style>
```

Using Inline Styles

The following inline CSS will make the font size of an unordered list 120% of what it would normally be. It will also make the text and the list bullet points dark green:

```
<ul style="font-size:120%; color:#060">
  : list items...
</ul>
```

Using `style` attributes creates a strong coupling between the content and the presentation, which is usually undesirable.

Inline CSS is more limited than internal or external style sheets. It's not possible to specify a media type, so style attributes will apply for all media types. Also, you can't specify inline CSS rules for pseudo-classes (p. 80) or pseudo-elements (p. 106).

If you use inline CSS, the HTML specification[12] states that you must declare the style language. You can do so using a HTTP header or an equivalent `<meta>` element:

```
<meta http-equiv="Content-Style-Type" content="text/css">
```

---

[12] http://www.w3.org/TR/html401/present/styles.html#default-style

In reality, browsers don't care because the HTML specification also states that the style content type defaults to `"text/css"` if it's not specified in a `<meta>` element or a `Content-Style-Type` HTTP header.

Yes, it may seem that the statements "you must declare the style language" and "the style content type defaults to `"text/css"` if not specified" are mutually exclusive, but the intent was only to provide a safety net. The specification recommends that authoring tools automatically generate the style sheet language information in order to avoid forcing user agents to rely on the default value. The effectiveness of this recommendation remains to be seen.

Referencing an External Style Sheet Using an XML PI

In XML documents, including XHTML served as XML, an external style sheet can be referenced using a processing instruction (PI). Such processing instructions are normally part of the XML prologue, coming after the XML declaration, but before the doctype declaration (if there is one) and the root element's start tag.

This example shows an XML prologue with a persistent style sheet (**base.css**), a preferred style sheet (**default.css**), and an alternative style sheet (**custom.css**):

```
<?xml version="1.0" encoding="utf-8"?>
<?xml-stylesheet type="text/css" href="/base.css"?>
<?xml-stylesheet type="text/css" href="/default.css"
    title="Default"?>
<?xml-stylesheet type="text/css" href="/custom.css"
    title="Custom" alternate="yes"?>
```

Watch Out for Alternative Spelling

The CSS specifications use the term "alternate" instead of "alternative." The attribute name in a PI must be `alternate`.

Differences Between the Methods

In addition to the differences that exist in the ways the style sheets or CSS rules are specified in the markup, there are a few other differences that we may need to consider, depending on which method we choose:

- An external style sheet can't contain SGML comments (`<!--` … `-->`) or HTML tags (including `<style>` and `<style>`). Nor can it use SGML character references (such as `&#169;`) or character entity references (such as `&copy;`). If you need to use special characters in an external style sheet, and they can't be represented through the style sheet's character encoding, specify them with CSS escape notation (p. 43).

- The content type of the `style` element type in HTML is CDATA, which means that character references (numeric character references or character entity references) in an internal style sheet aren't parsed. If you need to use special characters in an internal style sheet, and they can't be represented with the document's character encoding, specify them with CSS escape notation (p. 43). In XHTML, the content type is #PCDATA, which means that character references are parsed, but only if the document's served as XML.

- Unlike in `style` elements, character references are parsed in `style` attributes, even in HTML.

Media Queries

Media queries is a CSS3 extension to media types that allows us far greater control over rendering across different devices than do media types alone. Used in conjunction with a media type, a media query is a logical expression, evaluating to `true` or `false`, that tests one or more features of the output device to which the CSS is to be applied. Media queries can be used in `<link>` tags, XML processing instructions, the `@import` at-rule, and the `@media` at-rule. The CSS associated with the media query expression is only applied if the expression evaluates to `true`.

A logical expression can consist of either a media feature, or a media feature followed by a colon (`:`) and a value—similar to a normal property/value pair. A logical expression in a media query must be enclosed in parentheses (…). Let's look at a some examples:

```
<link rel="stylesheet" type="text/css" href="/style.css"
    media="all and (color)">

<?xml-stylesheet media="all and (color)" rel="stylesheet"
    href="example.css" ?>
```

```
@import url(/style.css) all and (color);

@media all and (color) {
    one or more rule sets...
}
```

In the above examples, we can see media queries used in the `media` attribute of a `<link>` tag and an XML processing instruction, and with the optional media type list in `@import` and `@media` at-rules. In all three examples, the media query uses the expression `all and (color)` to indicate that the CSS should be applied to all output media that are capable of representing color.

Here's another example that applies to hand-held devices, but only if the viewport width is at least 20em:

```
@media handheld and (min-width:20em) {
    one or more rule sets...
}
```

You can use multiple expressions in a media query if you join them with the `and` keyword. The following example applies the CSS if the output device is a screen-based device with a width between 800 and 1280 pixels:

```
@import url(/style.css) screen and (min-width:800px)
    and (max-width:1280px);
```

You can also use multiple, comma-separated media queries in a single at-rule:

```
@import url(/style.css) screen and (color), projection and (color);
```

The comma acts like an "or" keyword, so the above example will apply the CSS to color-screen or projection devices.

As you've seen in these examples, many of the media features can be prefixed with `min-` or `max-` to express boundary constraints. These prefixes should be thought of as "greater than or equal to" and "less than or equal to," respectively. The W3C chose to use these prefixes instead of a syntax involving < and > characters, due to the special meaning those characters have in HTML and XML.

Media features generally apply only for certain media types. It's meaningless to query color capabilities for `"speech"` media, or to specify a width in pixels for `"tty"` media—these kinds of logical expressions will always evaluate to `false`.

The media features in Table 1.2 are listed in the latest W3C recommendation for media queries, dated 6 June 2007.[13]

Table 1.2: Media Features

Feature	Value	Min/Max	Description
color	integer	yes	number of bits per color component
color-index	integer	yes	number of entries in the color lookup table
device-aspect-ratio	integer/integer	yes	aspect ratio
device-height	length	yes	height of the output device
device-width	length	yes	width of the output device
grid	integer	no	true for a grid-based device
height	length	yes	height of the rendering surface
monochrome	integer	yes	number of bits per pixel in a monochrome frame buffer
resolution	resolution ("dpi" or "dpcm")	yes	resolution
scan	"progressive" or "interlaced"	no	scanning process of "tv" media types
width	length	yes	width of the rendering surface

---

[13] http://www.w3.org/TR/css3-mediaqueries/

The `device-width` and `device-height` features refer to the dimensions of the output device (that is, the screen size).

The `width` and `height` features, on the other hand, refer to the dimensions of the rendering surface, which is the viewport (for example, the browser window) for screen media, or the page box for print media.

Resolutions are specified using a number immediately followed by one of the units `dpi` (dots per inch) or `dpcm` (dots per centimeter).

Aspect ratios are specified as the quotient of two integers representing width/height: for example, 16/9 or 1280/1024.

Currently, support for media queries is limited. Opera 9 has partial support,[14] as does Safari 3. Support for media queries is also appearing in browsers for other devices, such as Opera Mini 4, Opera for the Nintendo Wii,[15] iPhone, and the Nokia S60 browser. Apple suggests using media queries as a way of targeting the iPhone browser,[16] since, confusingly, that browser does not support the `"handheld"` media type.

Standards Mode, Quirks Mode, and Doctype Sniffing

Some of the early browser implementations of CSS were fraught with problems—they only supported parts of the specification, and in some cases, the implementation of certain CSS features didn't comply with the specification.

Today's browsers generally provide excellent support for the latest CSS specification, even incorporating features that aren't yet in the official specification, but will likely appear in the next version.

Due to the implementation deficiencies in early browsers, many old style sheets were written to work with the then-contemporary browsers rather than to comply

---

[14] http://www.opera.com/docs/specs/css/
[15] http://www.opera.com/docs/specs/?platform=wii#css
[16] http://tinyurl.com/2tyr6z

with the CSS specification. This presented a dilemma for browser vendors releasing new versions of their products that had better support for the CSS standard. While they wanted to do the right thing with properly written CSS, and display web pages according to CSS standards, this had the potential to make a mess of millions of existing web pages whose CSS didn't comply with the CSS specification.

The solution was to have the browser make an educated guess as to whether the current document seemed to be modern or old-school, and then choose the appropriate rendering mode. The basis for this guesswork was the presence, or absence, of an SGML document type declaration (or doctype declaration) in the markup. A **doctype declaration** contains the name of the document's root element, and usually, a reference to the document type definition (DTD), which contains the syntactic rules for the markup language used in the document. Web browsers had so far ignored the doctype declaration, which was mainly intended for markup validators.

The process by which a browser chooses a rendering mode based on the doctype declaration is known as **doctype sniffing** (or **doctype switching**), and was first implemented in Microsoft Internet Explorer 5 for Mac OS. Today, doctype sniffing is also used in Opera (7 and later), Firefox and other Gecko-based browsers, Safari, Internet Explorer 6 and 7, and Konqueror (3.2 and later).

If the browser decides that the document is modern, it'll render it in **standards mode**. This means that, as a rule, CSS is applied in accordance with the CSS2 specification.

If the browser decides that the document is old-school, it'll render it in **quirks mode**. This mode applies CSS in the quirky way that suited predecessors of that browser, or even of other browsers. The exact implementations of quirks mode differ between browsers.

Opera (7.5 and later), Firefox, and Safari also have a third mode, called **almost standards mode**,[17] in which the layout of images in table cells is implemented as in quirks mode, rather than in accordance with the CSS2 specification. In every

---

[17] http://developer.mozilla.org/en/docs/Gecko%27s_Almost_Standards_Mode

other respect, this mode is equivalent to standards mode. Almost standards mode was added so that the old-school method of aligning images split across table cells is more likely to render as the authors intended, and not to fall apart. This mode corresponds to standards mode in Internet Explorer 6 and 7, Internet Explorer 5 for Mac OS and OS X, Konqueror, and Opera versions prior to 7.5. These browsers do not implement vertical alignment in table cells in compliance with the CSS2 specification, so their standards mode is really an almost standards mode.

Doctype sniffing is only undertaken for documents served with a MIME type of text/html. The specification of any XML MIME type, including application/xhtml+xml, automatically triggers standards mode (see MIME Types (p. 411) for more details).

How Does it Work?

So how does doctype sniffing work? Which declarations trigger standards mode, quirks mode, and almost standards mode? The document type definition reference, for HTML and XHTML, consists of the string PUBLIC followed by a **formal public identifier** (FPI), optionally followed by a **formal system identifier** (FSI), which is the URL for the DTD.

Here's an example of a doctype declaration that contains both an FPI and an FSI:

```
<!DOCTYPE html PUBLIC "-//W3C//DTD HTML 4.01//EN"
    "http://www.w3.org/TR/html4/strict.dtd">
```

This example contains only the FPI:

```
<!DOCTYPE html PUBLIC "-//W3C//DTD HTML 4.01 Transitional//EN">
```

Doctype sniffing works by detecting which of these parts are present in the doctype declaration. If an FPI is present, but an FSI isn't, browsers generally choose quirks mode, since this was the common way of writing doctype declarations in the old days. Browsers also choose quirks mode if the doctype declaration is missing altogether—which used to be very common—or is malformed.

If both an FPI and a correct FSI are present, browsers with two layout modes choose their standards mode. Browsers with three layout modes will examine the DTD reference before committing to a choice. Generally, the DTDs for HTML 4.0 Strict, HTML 4.01 Strict, and XHTML 1.0 Strict trigger standards mode. The corresponding Transitional DTDs trigger almost standards mode for a text/html MIME type.

Internet Explorer 6 uses a very primitive form of doctype sniffing, which presumes that the doctype declaration is the very first line in the document. An SGML comment before the doctype declaration will trigger quirks mode, as will an XML declaration before an XHTML doctype—even XHTML 1.0 Strict. The following declaration will trigger quirks mode in IE6 (but not IE7) if served as text/html:

```
<?xml version="1.0" encoding="utf-8"?>
<!DOCTYPE html PUBLIC "-//W3C//DTD XHTML 1.0 Strict//EN"
    "http://www.w3.org/TR/xhtml1/DTD/xhtml1-strict.dtd">
```

For more detailed information about doctype sniffing, including a table of which doctypes trigger specific rendering modes in different browsers, see http://hsivonen.iki.fi/doctype/.

Summary

Using cascading style sheets is the recommended way to control the presentation of web pages. It allows the presentation layer to remain separate from the content and behavior layers, which makes site maintenance much easier and reduces bandwidth usage.

One or more external style sheets can be attached to an HTML page via `link` elements or `@import` rules. A page can also include internal style sheets within `style` elements. XML pages can be linked to external style sheets via processing instructions. Finally, styling can be specified for an HTML element via its `style` attribute, but this approach isn't recommended.

An external or internal style sheet can be applied for one or more output media.

A style sheet or group of style sheets can be persistent, preferred, or alternative, and chosen as such by the user through a browser that supports alternative style sheets.

Some browsers apply CSS rules in two or three different modes: standards mode, almost standards mode, and quirks mode. The choice of rendering mode is made through the process of doctype sniffing.

For all intents and purposes, the current CSS specification is CSS2.1. Some modern browsers implement a few features from the CSS3 working drafts, but currently those features cannot be relied upon for anything other than experimental use.

General Syntax and Nomenclature

In this section, we'll describe the building blocks of a CSS style sheet and the correct syntax for each part. We'll also define the unavoidable jargon we'll use throughout this reference. When everyone uses the same term for the same thing, communication is usually easier and less error prone.

CSS syntax is not rigid: whitespace can usually be added freely between tokens, and line breaks have no semantic value.

CSS is case insensitive in all matters under its control. However, some things lie outside the control of CSS and these may or may not be case sensitive, depending on external factors such as markup language and operating system.

Element type names, for instance, are case insensitive for HTML but case sensitive for XML (including XHTML served as XML). Font names, with the exception of the generic font family CSS keywords, may be case sensitive on some operating systems.

Disambiguating the Nomenclature

In order to name the various items that make up CSS syntax, let's consider the example in Figure 2.1.

```
      ● ● ○                    sample.css
    1   /* A sample style sheet */
    2   @import url(base.css);
    3
    4   h2 {
    5       color: #666;
    6       font-weight: bold;
    7   }
    8

Line:    8  Column:   1   ○ CSS        ○ ▼  Soft Tabs:  2  CSS: h2
```

Figure 2.1: Sample CSS syntax

The example begins with a comment (p. 42):

```
/* A sample style sheet */
```

The comment is followed by two statements (p. 25). The first statement is an at-rule (p. 25):

```
@import url(base.css);
```

The second statement is a rule set (p. 26):

```
h2 {
  color: #666;
  font-weight: bold;
}
```

The rule set consists of a selector (p. 26) (the text before the left curly brace, {) and a declaration block (p. 28) (delimited with the curly braces, {}). The block contains two declarations (p. 28) separated by semicolons:

```
color: #666;
font-weight: bold;
```

Each declaration includes a property name and a value, separated by a colon.

Statements

A CSS style sheet is composed from a list of statements. A statement is either an at-rule (p. 25) or a rule set (p. 26). The following example has two statements; the first is an at-rule that is delimited by the semicolon at the end of the first line, and the second is a rule set that is delimited by the closing curly brace, }:

```
@import url(base.css);
h2 {
    color: #666;
    font-weight: bold;
}
```

At-rules

An **at-rule** is an instruction or directive to the CSS parser. It starts with an **at-keyword**: an @ character followed by an identifier (p. 43). An at-rule can comprise a block delimited by curly braces, {}, or text terminated by a semicolon, ;. An at-rule's syntax will dictate whether it needs a block or text—see At-rules Reference (p. 47) for more information.

Parentheses, brackets, and braces must appear as matching pairs and can be nested within the at-rule. Single and double quotes must also appear in matching pairs.

Here's an example of an at-rule that requires a block—the `@media` (p. 51) at-rule:

```
@media print {
    body {
        font-size: 12pt;
    }
}
```

Here's an example of an at-rule terminated by a semicolon—the `@import` (p. 49) at-rule:

```
@import url(base.css);
```

Rule Sets

A **rule set** (also called a rule) comprises a selector (p. 26) followed by a declaration block (p. 28); the rule set applies the declarations listed in the declaration block to all elements matched by the selector.

Here's an example of a rule set:

```
h2 {
  color: #666;
  font-weight: bold;
}
```

Selectors

A **selector** comprises every part of a rule set (p. 26) up to—but not including—the left curly brace {. A selector is a pattern, and the declarations (p. 28) within the block that follows the selector are applied to all the elements that match this pattern. In the following example rule set, the selector is h2:

```
h2 {
  color: #666;
  font-weight: bold;
}
```

This selector—which is comprised of a single simple selector—will match all elements of type h2 in an HTML document. A **simple selector** can either be an element type selector (p. 62) or the universal selector (p. 60), (*), optionally followed by attribute selectors (p. 67), ID selectors (p. 65), or pseudo-classes (p. 80).[1] A selector can comprise a number of simple selectors separated by combinators (p. 73),

---

[1] Note that in CSS3, simple selectors are defined slightly differently than they are in CSS2.1. See Selector Reference (p. 59) for details.

but it can contain only one pseudo-element (p. 106), which must be appended to the last simple selector in the chain.

Here's a more complex selector:

```
h2+p.warning:first-line {
  color: #666;
  font-weight: bold;
}
```

This selector consists of two simple selectors separated by an adjacent sibling combinator (p. 77) (the + character), and a pseudo-element (:first-line). The first simple selector (h2) is a type selector. The second simple selector contains a type selector (p) and an attribute selector (p. 67)—in this case, a special form of attribute selector called a class selector (p. 63), which will match HTML class attributes containing the word "warning."

As such, the selector above would match the first line of text within any p element that has a class attribute value of "warning" and is an adjacent sibling to an h2 element.

Finally, two or more selectors can be grouped, separated by commas (,); the declaration block that follows applies to both selectors. Consider these two rules:

```
#main ol {
  margin-left: 2em;
}
#main ul {
  margin-left: 2em;
}
```

They can be grouped like this:

```
#main ol, #main ul {
  margin-left: 2em;
}
```

You can read about selectors in detail in the selector reference section (p. 59).

General Syntax and
Nomenclature

Declaration Blocks

Declaration blocks begin with a left curly brace, {, and end with a right curly brace, }. They contain zero or more declarations (p. 28) separated by semicolons:

```
h2 {
  color: #666;
}
```

A declaration block is always preceded by a selector (p. 26). We can combine multiple rules that have the same selector into a single rule. Consider these rules:

```
h2 {
   color: #666;
}
h2 {
   font-weight: bold;
}
```

They're equivalent to the rule below:

```
h2 {
   color: #666;
   font-weight: bold;
}
```

Although the last semicolon within a declaration block is optional, it's good practice to include it, as it'll help you avoid syntax errors in the future. As you start to add declarations to a block, it's all too easy to forget the semicolon.

Declarations, Properties, and Values

A declaration is made up of a property name and a value, separated by a colon; whitespace characters can appear around any of these elements. A declaration must appear within a declaration block (p. 28), like so:

```
h2 {
   color: #666;
}
```

There's a large collection of property names that we can use in our style rules. Syntactically, they are in fact CSS identifiers (p. 43), and must be specified correctly, otherwise the declaration will be ignored. Property values can be specified in various forms, depending on the property in question—each property has its own syntactic and semantic requirements and restrictions. Values can be expressed as keywords (p. 29), strings (p. 37), colors (p. 33), numbers (p. 37), lengths (p. 29), percentages (p. 32), and URIs (p. 38).

Keywords

Many CSS property values can be specified as keywords. A keyword is an identifier (p. 43), and it mustn't be surrounded by quotation marks. So the correct syntax is `background-color: yellow;`, whereas `background-color: "yellow";` is an error.

See the definition of each property for information about which keywords, if any, it allows.

Lengths and Units

The value type for many CSS properties is specified as `<length>`.[2] A **length** is a measurement comprising a numeric value and a unit only—whitespace can't appear between the number and the unit.

The numeric value can be either an integer or a real number. If the numeric value is 0, the unit can be omitted (after all, zero pixels is the same measurement as zero millimeters).[3] But if the value isn't zero, the unit must be specified.[4]

The units in which length is measured can be either relative or absolute, but an absolute unit is useful only if the physical properties of the output medium are known.

---

[2] http://www.w3.org/TR/CSS21/syndata.html#length-units
[3] It could even be argued that the unit *should* be omitted if the number is 0.
[4] The `line-height` property can take a non-zero, unit-less value, but it's not a value of the type `<length>`.

Relative Units Explained

The three possible relative units are listed in Table 2.1.

Table 2.1: Relative Units

Unit	Description
em	the current font size
ex	the x-height of the current font
px	pixels

The em and ex units depend on the font size that's applied to the element.

A measurement of 1em is defined as being equal to the font size, however that may be defined. When we specify a font size in em, 1em is equal to the inherited font size—that is, the size the text would have had if we hadn't changed it. As such, font-size:1.2em; makes the text 1.2 times larger than the parent element's text.

This unit's name is a centuries-old legacy from the typographic world, where an M-square or "mutton square" was a blank, square type whose sides' length was equal to the width of an uppercase M—usually the widest character—in that font.

The ex unit is equal to the x-height of the current font, which is normally the height of a lowercase x, as depicted in Figure 2.2. Interestingly, an x-height is defined even for fonts that don't include a lowercase x.

Figure 2.2: Font size and x-height

In CSS, pixels are considered to be a relative unit because they don't correspond to a fixed physical measure. The CSS2.1 specification provides a lengthy definition of pixel measurements,[5] but the bottom line is that a pixel is relative to the viewing distance. A **standard pixel** is 0.26mm (1/96 inch) square.

On an LCD computer monitor, or similar device, a pixel is usually the smallest area that can be rendered. On high-resolution output devices, such as laser printers or photosetters, pixels must be rescaled by the user agent so that, for example, a one-pixel border is approximately as wide on paper as it is on a computer screen. As such, pixel measurements are relative to the device on which the document is reproduced.

Note that px units must not be used for a tty media type (for instance, character-grid devices).

Pixels and Accessibility

The classification of pixels as relative units has nothing to do with the concept of relative units as it's defined in the Web Content Accessibility Guidelines (WCAG) 1.0,[6] where "relative" means that web page elements can scale easily to meet the needs of the user—for example, changing the text size in the browser, or changing the size of the browser window. In WCAG terms, pixels are absolute, as you can't change the size of a pixel from within your browser.

Absolute Units Explained

Table 2.2 identifies the five absolute units that are available to us.

Table 2.2: Absolute Units

Unit	Description
mm	millimeters
cm	centimeters
in	inches

---

[5] http://www.w3.org/TR/CSS21/syndata.html#length-units
[6] http://www.w3.org/TR/WAI-WEBCONTENT/

Unit	Description
pt	points
pc	picas

Millimeters and centimeters are defined in the SI standard.[7] Inch measurements are now used mainly in the United States. One inch measures 25.4mm.

A point is an old typographic measurement, but multiple standards were used for points in print, and the Didot point used in continental Europe was slightly larger than the point used in Britain and America. In CSS, one point is defined as 1/72 inch (0.353mm), just as it is in PostScript.

A pica is equal to 12 points, just as it is in typography, which translates into 1/6 inch or 4.23mm in CSS.

Physical (absolute) units shouldn't normally be used for on-screen display. A font size specified as 7pt may be readable (albeit barely) at nine pixels on a 96dpi Windows system, but it will display at an illegible seven pixels on an older 72dpi Mac system.

In a similar vein, pixels shouldn't usually be used when you're specifying styles for print media. Although user agents are expected to rescale pixels if necessary, pixels don't make sense on high-resolution devices.

Percentages

A percentage is an integer, or a decimal number, followed by a percentage character (%). Whitespace characters mustn't appear between the number and the %. For example, here's a width declaration that uses a percentage value:

```
#example {
  width: 50%;
}
```

---

[7] http://www.bipm.org/en/publications/brochure/

A percentage value is, by its nature, relative to something else. The interpretation of percentages differs between CSS properties, so you'll have to use the reference to find the specific property you're dealing with, and to identify what its stated percentage value means. In some cases, the interpretation of percentage values can be quite unexpected; for example, vertical padding refers to a percentage of the width—not height—of the containing block.

Colors

Color values can be represented in several different ways in CSS.

Hexadecimal Notation

Hexadecimal RGB (red, green, blue) notation is perhaps the most common format. It consists of a # character followed by three or six hexadecimal digits. When six digits are provided, the first pair represents the red value, the second pair represents the green value, and the last pair represents the blue value: #rrggbb. A value with three digits represents the corresponding six-digit value where each digit occurs twice; thus #09f is the same as #0099ff (red=00, green=99, blue=ff).

Decimal Notation

We can also write a color value with decimal functional notation—rgb(0, 160, 255) or rgb(0%, 63%, 100%)—where the order of the arguments is red, green, and blue. Using the first form, 255 corresponds to 100%. Values outside the valid range (0–255 or 0%–100%) are automatically changed to the corresponding limit.

CSS3 makes a few extra functional notations available:

- rgba(0, 160, 255, 0.2) for RGBA colors; the fourth argument is the alpha opacity and accepts a value from 0 to 1
- hsl(240, 100%, 50%) for HSL colors (hue, saturation, luminosity)
- hsla(240, 100%, 50%, 0.2) for HSLA colors (hue, saturation, luminosity, alpha)

At the time of writing, these three notations were supported only by the Gecko[8] and WebKit[9] rendering engines.

Keywords

Colors can also be represented by the keywords listed in Table 2.3.

Table 2.3: Color Keywords

Keyword	Color Value
aqua	#00ffff
black	#000000
blue	#0000ff
fuchsia	#ff00ff
gray	#808080
green	#008000
lime	#00ff00
maroon	#800000
navy	#000080
olive	#808000
orange (added in CSS 2.1)	#ffa500
purple	#800080
red	#ff0000

---

[8] Gecko is used by Firefox, Mozilla, and Camino, among others.
[9] WebKit is used by Safari.

Keyword	Color Value
silver	#c0c0c0
teal	#008080
white	#ffffff
yellow	#ffff00

Color Keyword Compatibility

Support for color keywords differs between browsers so, to be on the safe side, it's best to use the numeric or functional notation. The use of keywords for colors is also disallowed by the Web Content Accessibility Guidelines (WCAG) 1.0.[10]

Finally, you can use the keywords listed in Table 2.4 to specify system colors—various colors that are used by the operating system and/or window manager, and can be applied when you want to create a "native application" look and feel.

Table 2.4: System Colors

Keyword	Description
Background	the desktop background color
ButtonFace	the face color for 3D elements
ButtonHighlight	the highlight color for 3D elements
ButtonShadow	the shadow color for 3D elements
ButtonText	the text color on buttons
CaptionText	the color of captions, scrollbar arrows, etc.

General Syntax and Nomenclature

---

[10] http://www.w3.org/TR/WCAG10-CSS-TECHS/#style-colors

Keyword	Description
GrayText	the color of disabled text
Highlight	the color of selected items in a control
HighlightText	the text color in selected items
InactiveBorder	the border color of an inactive window
InactiveCaption	the caption color of an inactive window
InactiveCaptionText	the color of text in an inactive caption
InfoBackground	the background color in tooltips
InfoText	the text color in tooltips
Menu	the menu background color
MenuText	the menu text color
Scrollbar	the color of the scrollbar "trough"
ThreeDDarkShadow	the dark shadow color for 3D display elements
ThreeDFace	the face color for 3D display elements
ThreeDHighlight	the highlight color for 3D display elements
ThreeDLightShadow	the light shadow color for 3D display elements
ThreeDShadow	the dark shadow color for 3D display elements
Window	the window background color
WindowFrame	the color of the window frame

Keyword	Description
WindowText	the color of text in windows

Note that even though the keywords are case insensitive, they're presented here as they are in the CSS2.1 specification, for maximum readability.

System Color Keyword Compatibility

The support for these keywords is even less reliable than that provided for the "regular" color keywords. You should test your document extensively—in different browsers and different operating systems—if you use them.

Numbers

A number can be specified either as an integer or a real number (one that contains a decimal point), and can have an initial - or + to indicate its sign. Numbers can only be specified in decimal notation. For example, here's a `line-height` declaration that uses a number value:

```
#example {
  line-height: 1.5;
}
```

Strings

A string value must be enclosed in double or single quotes. So, to include a quote inside a string, you'll need to escape it with a backslash character, like so:

```
ol#breadcrumbs:before {
  content: "You are \"here\": ";
}
html {
  font-family: 'Grey\'s Bold',serif;
}
```

Of course, it's often easier to use the opposite quotation character around the string—if you need a double quote inside the string, surround the whole string with single quotes, and vice versa:

```css
ol#breadcrumbs:before {
  content: 'You are "here": ';
}
html {
  font-family: "Grey's Bold",serif;
}
```

If you want a string to contain characters that can't easily be typed from the keyboard, characters that can't be expressed in the style sheet's character encoding, or non-printable characters, you can represent those characters using CSS escape notation (p. 43).

Note also that a string value in CSS can't contain a literal new line. If you need to include a new-line character inside a string value, use a character escape (\a).

URIs

URI values are expressed with a functional notation that, for historical reasons, is named url.[11] A URI is expressed using the following syntax: url(*URI*). For example, here's a background-image declaration that specifies the URI of an image file:

```css
#example {
  background-image: url(images/bg.gif);
}
```

The argument for *URI* is a string that may be enclosed in quotes; if you choose to use quotes, they may be double or single quotes.[12] Certain characters appearing in an unquoted URI value—whitespace characters, single and double quotes, parentheses, and commas—must be escaped with a backslash. In some types of

---

[11] In the beginning, web addresses were called Uniform Resource Locators (URL). Later, something called Uniform Resource Name (URN) was added. A Uniform Resource Identifier (URI) is a URL or a URN.

[12] Some browsers, like Internet Explorer 5 for Mac, don't support single quotes in url(*URI*) syntax.

URIs, you can also replace these characters with URI escape sequences; for example, you can use %20 to replace a space character.

> ### Relative URIs
>
> Relative URIs are relative to the style sheet, not to the HTML document that links to the style sheet.

Initial Values

The default value for a property, when it's not specified explicitly or inherited, is called the **initial value**. The initial value of each property is defined in the CSS specification.

Browsers have user agent style sheets that define the default rendering of the various HTML element types. In some cases, the rules in those built-in style sheets define values other than the initial values from the CSS specification. For example, links are usually underlined, even though the initial value for the `text-decoration` property is `none`.

You can read more about these topics in The Cascade, Specificity, and Inheritance (p. 117).

Shorthand Properties

Some properties can be combined into **shorthand notation**—a notation that allows us to specify values for related properties in a single declaration.

Shorthand for Box Properties

One form of shorthand notation allows us to specify values for two, three, or four sides of a box simultaneously, like this:

```
margin: 1em 2em 3em 4em;
```

That declaration is equivalent to these:

General Syntax and Nomenclature

```
margin-top: 1em;
margin-right: 2em;
margin-bottom: 3em;
margin-left: 4em;
```

The TRouBLe Mnemonic

Note the order in which these properties occur in the shorthand notation. They appear in a clockwise order, starting at the top: Top, Right, Bottom, Left. Remembering this order keeps you out of TRouBLe.

This form of shorthand notation can take one, two, three, or four values. If four values are specified, they're assigned to the appropriate sides in TRouBLe order. If only two or three values are specified, the "missing" side is assigned the same value as the one opposite it. If only a single value is specified, it's applied to all four sides. Take a look at this declaration:

```
margin: 1em 2em 3em;
```

That's equivalent to these:

```
margin-top: 1em;
margin-right: 2em;
margin-bottom: 3em;
margin-left: 2em; /* same as margin-right */
```

In the same vein, consider this declaration:

```
margin: 1em 2em;
```

It's the same as these:

```
margin-top: 1em;
margin-right: 2em;
margin-bottom: 1em; /* same as margin-top */
margin-left: 2em; /* same as margin-right */
```

This form of shorthand notation is used for the properties: margin (p. 209), padding (p. 218), border-width (p. 254), border-color (p. 249), and border-style (p. 251).

Shorthand for Other Properties

A somewhat different form of shorthand notation allows us to specify a number of related properties at once. For example, we can combine multiple background-related properties into one `background` declaration:

```
background: #fff url(bg.png) no-repeat fixed right top;
```

This declaration is equivalent to the following:

```
background-color: #fff;
background-image: url(bg.png);
background-repeat: no-repeat;
background-attachment: fixed;
background-position: right top;
```

Unlike the shorthand for box-related properties, when we're combining related properties, the order of the values is usually not relevant. That said, be sure to check each property for the required syntax.[13]

If a value is omitted, the *initial value* (p. 39) will be assigned to the corresponding property. Look at this declaration:

```
background: url(bg.png);
```

It's the same as these:

```
background-color: transparent; /* initial value */
background-image: url(bg.png);
background-repeat: repeat; /* initial value */
background-attachment: scroll; /* initial value */
background-position: 0% 0%; /* initial value */
```

Omitted values aren't ignored, so attempts to mix shorthand and standard declarations like the following are doomed to fail (they're also likely to confuse anyone who's looking at the code):

---

[13] We prefer to use the order in the CSS2.1 specification.

```
background-color: #fff;
background: url(bg.png);
```

The background color will not be white (#fff), since the first declaration provided here is overwritten by the implicit declaration background-color: transparent; in the shorthand property.

This form of shorthand notation is used by the properties: border (p. 255), border-top (p. 226), border-right (p. 233), border-bottom (p. 240), border-left (p. 247), outline (p. 261), background (p. 312), font (p. 325), and list-style (p. 290). See the relevant reference pages for the syntax details of each property.

CSS Comments

In CSS, a comment starts with /* and ends with */. Comments can span multiple lines, but may not be nested:

```
/* This is a single-line comment */

/* This is a comment that
   spans multiple lines */
```

According to the CSS2 specification,[14] comments that appear between tokens won't have any effect on the styles' rendering. In practice, however, we find comments causing errors in some older browsers in certain situations.

Comment Syntax

The // comment syntax used in C++ is not allowed. Neither are SGML comments that take the form <!---->, except in one situation: they may appear in internal style sheets—style sheets placed within the HTML source using the <style> tag—in order to hide the CSS statements from pre-HTML4 user agents. However, this use of comments is now redundant and can be disregarded. See Linking CSS to a Web Document (p. 5) for further information.

---

[14] http://www.w3.org/TR/CSS21/syndata.html#comments

CSS Identifiers

CSS identifiers are the labels used in property (p. 28) names, keyword values (p. 29), and at-rule (p. 25) names, as well as in element type names, classes, and IDs within selectors (p. 26). In the following example, `fieldset`, `border`, and `none` are all CSS identifiers:

```
fieldset {
  border: none;
}
```

According to the CSS2 specification,[15] they can contain the characters a to z and 0 to 9, ISO 10646 characters (equivalent to Unicode) U+00A1 and higher, the hyphen (-), and the underscore (_); they can't start with a digit, nor with a hyphen followed by a digit. Identifiers can also contain escaped characters (p. 43).

CSS Escape Notation

If you need to use characters that aren't easily inserted with a keyboard, or can't be represented through the style sheet's character encoding, specify them in an external style sheet using CSS Escape Notation. Representing escaped characters in CSS is quite different from the process we use in HTML.

The character escape sequence consists of a backslash character (\) followed by between one and six hexadecimal digits that represent a character code from the ISO 10646 standard (which is equivalent to Unicode, for all intents and purposes). Any character other than a hexadecimal digit will terminate the escape sequence.

If a character following the escape sequence is also a valid hexadecimal digit, you must either include six digits in the escape, or use a whitespace character to terminate the escape.

---

[15] http://www.w3.org/TR/CSS21/syndata.html#value-def-identifier

For example, if we wanted to output the string value `"»back"` (producing a chevron immediately adjacent to the word "back"), we'd need to use either `"\0000bbback"` or `"\bb back"` (0x00bb is the ISO 10646 code for the chevron character).

This also means that one whitespace character after an escape sequence will always be ignored—even if it appears after an escape sequence that uses six digits. If you want to include a whitespace character as part of the string, you'll need to double the whitespace.

Let's modify our previous example. If we wanted to output the string value `"»`
`back"` (displaying a chevron, followed by a space, followed by the word "back"), we'd need to use either `"\0000bb  back"` or `"\bb  back"`. In both cases, two spaces appear between the escape sequence and the word "back."

CSS Syntax Errors

According to the CSS2.1 specification,[16] a user agent should ignore the invalid parts of a style sheet. In general, a user agent should ignore:

- a statement that's an at-rule with an invalid at-keyword
- a statement that's a rule set with an invalid selector
- a statement that's a rule set with grouped selectors, one or more of which is invalid
- a declaration with an invalid property name or value
- a declaration with an unsupported property or value

However, in practice, the behavior of browsers varies, either because of browser bugs, or the incomplete implementation of CSS standards. See Workarounds, Filters, and Hacks (p. 391) for some examples of inconsistent browser behavior.

---

[16] http://www.w3.org/TR/CSS21/syndata.html#parsing-errors

Summary

A CSS style sheet contains statements—rule sets and at-rules—as well as comments delimited by /* and */.

A rule set, or rule, consists of a selector (or group of selectors) and a declaration block delimited by curly braces. A declaration block contains zero or more semicolon-separated declarations, each comprising a property, a colon separator, and a value.

Each property has its own syntax requirements, and some properties have shorthand equivalents.

Different properties take values of different types. Length is one of the most common types; it's made up of a number and a unit, but if the number is zero, the unit can be omitted. Percentage values are relative to some aspect of the document or display, and you need to look at the definition of each property to see how, if at all, percentages apply.

Some properties accept special keyword values, which must not be enclosed in quotes. String values, on the other hand, must be enclosed in single or double quotes. URIs are expressed using the url() notation.

Color values can be expressed in a few different ways, each one providing a value for the red, green, and blue channels. They can be expressed using a # character followed by three or six hexadecimal digits, or via the rgb() notation, which requires three comma-separated numerical values between 0 and 255, or three percentages. CSS3 introduces even more methods for expressing color values.

Special characters can be specified using CSS escape notation—a backslash followed by a hexadecimal value. A whitespace character after a character escape is ignored.

All keywords within the control of CSS are case insensitive, but other values may be case sensitive, depending on the markup language and the operating system of the web server. A CSS parser should ignore the invalid or unsupported parts of a style sheet.

General Syntax and
Nomenclature

Chapter

At-rules Reference

At-rules are instructions or directives to the CSS parser. They can be used for a variety of purposes.

The `@charset` (p. 48) at-rule can be used to specify the character encoding of an external style sheet. It must appear before anything else in the file.

The `@import` (p. 49) at-rule allows us to import one style sheet into another. All `@import` at-rules must appear before any rules.

The `@media` (p. 51) at-rule lets us target rules to the media types we specify.

The `@page` (p. 52) at-rule can be used to specify margins for paged media. You can set different margins for left- and right-hand pages when you're printing double-sided pages, as well as for the first page.

The `@font-face` (p. 54) at-rule allows us to specify custom fonts.

The `@namespace` (p. 55) at-rule in CSS3 lets us declare an XML namespace, as well as an optional prefix with which that namespace can be specified.

@charset

`@charset "encoding";`

SPEC			
CSS2			
BROWSER SUPPORT			
IE5.5+	FF1.5+	Saf3	Op9.2+
BUGGY	FULL	NONE	FULL

We use the `@charset` at-rule to specify the character encoding of an external style sheet. The at-rule must be followed by a quoted string value and a semicolon; the string must contain a valid encoding name from the IANA registry.[1]

Example

This example indicates that the style sheet will use the ISO-8859-15 character encoding:

`@charset "ISO-8859-15";`

For obvious reasons, if it's present, an `@charset` rule must be the very first thing in the CSS file. The only item that can precede it is a Unicode byte order mark (BOM).[2]

You'll rarely need to use an `@charset` rule in your style sheets. A user agent can deduce the character encoding of a CSS style sheet in four different ways, and if all of those fail, it uses a default.

For an external style sheet, a user agent will look for the following items:

- a `charset` attribute in a Content-Type HTTP header (or similar) sent by the web server
- a Unicode byte order mark, or an `@charset` at-rule
- a `charset` attribute specified in the `<link>` tag from which the HTML document links to the style sheet
- the encoding of the referring document or style sheet

This list defines the items in order of descending priority, and the first one that's found will determine the style sheet's encoding. If none are found, the user agent will assume the character encoding is UTF-8.

---

1 http://www.iana.org/assignments/character-sets
2 http://en.wikipedia.org/wiki/Byte_Order_Mark

> ## 💡 Using Special Characters
>
> You can refer to characters that can't be represented by the style sheet's encoding using CSS escape notation (p. 43).

Compatibility

Internet Explorer			Firefox			Safari			Opera
5.5	6.0	7.0	1.0	1.5	2.0	1.3	2.0	3.0	9.2
Buggy	Buggy	Buggy	Buggy	Full	Full	None	None	None	Full

In Internet Explorer versions up to and including 7, an `@charset` rule will *not* fail if the encoding is specified without quotes, even though it should.

In Firefox 1.0, an `@charset` rule will work only if it's specified without quotes, on which it should actually fail.

Other Relevant Stuff

> ⬡ CSS Escape Notation (p. 43)

@ @import

```
@import { URI | string } [ media type,… ] ;
```

SPEC
CSS1

BROWSER SUPPORT			
IE5.5+	FF1+	Saf1.3+	Op9.2+
BUGGY	FULL	FULL	FULL

The `@import` at-rule is a mechanism for importing one style sheet into another. It should be followed by a URI value and a semicolon, but it's possible to use a string value instead of the URI value. Where relative URIs are used, they're interpreted as being relative to the importing style sheet.

Example

Here are examples of the most common usage forms:

```
@import url("/css/main.css");
@import "local.css";
```

You can also specify one or more media types to which the imported style sheet applies—simply append a comma-separated list of media types to the URI.

Here's an example of a media type specification:

```
@import url(/css/screen.css) screen, projection;
```

The @import rules in a style sheet must precede all rule sets. An @import rule that follows one or more rule sets will be ignored. As such, the example below shows an *incorrect* usage; because it appears after a rule set, the following @import rule will be ignored:

```
html {
  background-color: #fff;
  color: #000;
}

/* The following rule will be ignored */
@import url("other.css");
```

Compatibility

Internet Explorer			Firefox			Safari			Opera
5.5	6.0	7.0	1.0	1.5	2.0	1.3	2.0	3.0	9.2
Buggy	Buggy	Buggy	Full	Full	Full	Full	Full	Full	Full

The media type specification feature isn't supported by Internet Explorer versions up to and including 7. In the example above, IE would attempt to request the file **./url(/css/screen.css) screen, projection**—that is, a file named **screen.css) screen, projection** in a subdirectory named **css** in a subdirectory named **url(** below the directory containing the importing style sheet.

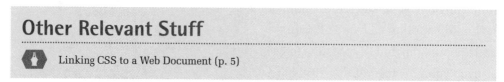

Other Relevant Stuff

Linking CSS to a Web Document (p. 5)

@ @media

```
@media media type,… {
ruleset
}
```

SPEC			
CSS2			
BROWSER SUPPORT			
IE5.5+	FF1+	Saf1.3+	Op9.2+
FULL	FULL	FULL	FULL

You can use the @media at-rule to specify that one or more rule sets in a style sheet will apply only to certain media types. The at-rule must be followed by a comma-separated list of media types and a block that contains rules.

It's up to you to decide whether you prefer to use separate style sheets for different media, or to use a single style sheet with @media rules.

Example

This rule set will be applied only when the document is printed or viewed in print preview mode:

```
@media print {
  body {
    padding: 1in;
    border: 0.5pt solid #666;
  }
}
```

In the expanded example below, the first set of rules will be applied only for screen and projection media (Opera uses the latter in its full-screen mode). The second set of rules will be applied only when the document is printed or viewed in print preview mode:

```
@media screen, projection {
  html {
    background: #fffef0;
    color: #300;
  }
  body {
    max-width: 35em;
    margin: 0 auto;
  }
}

@media print {
  html {
    background: #fff;
    color: #000;
  }
  body {
```

```
    padding: 1in;
    border: 0.5pt solid #666;
  }
}
```

Compatibility

Internet Explorer			Firefox			Safari			Opera
5.5	6.0	7.0	1.0	1.5	2.0	1.3	2.0	3.0	9.2
Full	Buggy	Buggy	Full	Full	Full	Full	Full	Full	Full

An `@media` rule won't fail in Internet Explorer 6 or 7 if a media type is omitted, though it should.

Other Relevant Stuff

 Linking CSS to a Web Document (p. 5)

Media Queries (p. 14)

@page

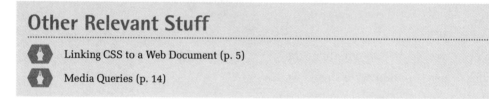

	SPEC
	CSS2

BROWSER SUPPORT			
IE7	FF2	Saf3	Op9.2+
NONE	NONE	NONE	FULL

```
@page  [ :left | :right | :first ]  {
margin ruleset
}
```

You can use the `@page` at-rule to specify margin values for the page box in style sheets for paged media such as the print media type.

In its simplest form, the at-rule is followed by a block of `margin` declarations:

```
@page {
  margin: 1in 1.5in;
}
```

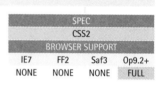

Example

This example sets default page margins:

```
@page {
  margin: 1in 1.5in;
}
```

You can specify different margins for all left-hand pages, all right-hand pages, or for the first page, by inserting a page selector between the at-rule and the block. The page selector is one of three pseudo-classes. Let's look at an example that shows how these pseudo-classes can be used:

```css
@page {
  margin: 2.5cm; /* default for all pages */
}

@page :left {
  margin-left: 5cm; /* left pages only */
}

@page :right {
  margin-right: 5cm; /* right pages only */
}

@page :first {
  margin-top: 8cm; /* extra top margin on the first page */
}
```

Compatibility

Internet Explorer			Firefox			Safari			Opera
5.5	6.0	7.0	1.0	1.5	2.0	1.3	2.0	3.0	9.2
None	None	None	None	None	None	None	None	None	Full

This at-rule is currently only supported by Opera 9.2 and later versions.

@ @font-face

```
@font-face {
font descriptors
}
```

SPEC			
CSS2, 3			
BROWSER SUPPORT			
IE5.5+	FF2	Saf3	Op9.2
PARTIAL	NONE	NONE	NONE

The @font-face at-rule allows you to define custom fonts. It was first defined in the CSS2 specification, but was removed from CSS2.1. Currently, it's a draft recommendation for CSS3. The at-rule contains one or more property declarations, like those in a regular CSS rule set, which are called **font descriptors**. You can specify up to 24 different properties, but it's beyond the scope of this reference to explain them all—you can read about them at the W3C Web Fonts page.[3]

Example

This at-rule declares the font family called Example Font, which is used in the statement that follows:

```
@font-face {
  font-family: "Example Font";
  src: url("http://www.example.com

  ➥    /fonts/example");
}
h1 {
  font-family: "Example Font",
  ➥    sans-serif;
}
```

The font descriptors allow you to define fonts, and to influence the browser's selection of fonts when no matching font is found on the client system. This matching can be performed not only on the font name, but on many other font characteristics as well.

In the simplest usage scenario, @font-face allows you to specify a font-family name, and the URI to a source file for the font, which can be downloaded by the user agent if needed. You can then use the font-family name in other font-family declarations where required.

Compatibility

Internet Explorer			Firefox			Safari			Opera
5.5	6.0	7.0	1.0	1.5	2.0	1.3	2.0	3.0	9.2
Partial	Partial	Partial	None	None	None	None	None	None	None

---

[3] http://www.w3.org/TR/css3-webfonts/

Internet Explorer versions 5.5 and later offer a partial implementation for the browser's WEFT (Web Embedding Fonts Tool) technology,[4] but this only works with EOT (Embedded OpenType Font) files.

Some experimental support[5] is provided for the `@font-face` at-rule in nightly builds of WebKit.[6]

Other Relevant Stuff

  `font-family` (p. 318)

sets the font family for text content

 # @namespace

`@namespace  [ prefix ] URI;`

SPEC
CSS3

BROWSER SUPPORT			
IE7	FF2+	Saf3	Op9.2+
NONE	FULL	NONE	FULL

The `@namespace` at-rule declares an XML namespace and, optionally, a prefix with which we can refer to it. `@namespace` rules must follow all `@charset` and `@import` rules, and precede all other at-rules and rule sets in a style sheet.

The scope of an `@namespace` rule is the style sheet in which it's declared—it doesn't extend to imported style sheets.

If no prefix is specified in the `@namespace` rule, the rule defines the default namespace.

Example

The first example below declares a default namespace; the second declares that the prefix svg can be used to refer to elements from the SVG namespace, `"http://www.w3.org/2000/svg"`:

```
@namespace
"http://www.w3.org/1999/xhtml";
@namespace svg
"http://www.w3.org/2000/svg";
```

At-rules Reference

---

[4] http://www.microsoft.com/typography/web/embedding/weft3/
[5] http://webkit.org/blog/124/downloadable-fonts/
[6] Web Kit is used by Safari.

If a prefix is specified, you can refer to elements in that namespace by prepending the prefix and a vertical bar, |, to the element selector, like so:[7]

```
@namespace "http://www.w3.org/1999/xhtml";
@namespace foo "http://example.com/ns/foo";

table {
  ⋮ declarations
}
foo|bar {
  ⋮ declarations
}
```

In the example above, the `table` selector matches `table` elements in the XHTML namespace, while the `foo|bar` selector matches `bar` elements in the namespace referred to by the prefix `foo`.

> ### 📓 Namespaces
>
> The namespace URI is the most important component of a namespace declaration. Consider this style sheet:
>
> ```
> @namespace foo "http://example.com/ns/foo";
> foo|bar {
>   ⋮ declarations
> }
> ```
>
> The `foo|bar` selector in the above example would match the `<xyz:bar>…</xyz:bar>` element in this markup fragment because the namespace URI in the markup matches the namespace URI in the at-rule:
>
> ```
> <abc xmlns:xyz="http://example.com/ns/foo">
>   <xyz:bar>…</xyz:bar>
> </abc>
> ```
>
> However, it would *not* match the `<foo:bar>…</foo:bar>` element in this markup fragment, since that element's in another namespace (that is, the URI doesn't match):
>
> ```
> <abc xmlns:foo="http://example.com/ns/xyz">
>   <foo:bar>…</foo:bar>
> </abc>
> ```

---

[7] It would have been more intuitive to use a colon separator than the vertical bar, but the colon character is already used for other purposes in selectors—more about this in Pseudo-classes (p. 80).

Thus, it's not the prefix, but the corresponding namespace URIs in the markup and at-rule, that must match.

Compatibility

Internet Explorer			Firefox			Safari			Opera
5.5	6.0	7.0	1.0	1.5	2.0	1.3	2.0	3.0	9.2
None	None	None	None	None	Full	None	None	None	Full

This at-rule isn't widely supported.

Chapter

Selector Reference

A selector is a pattern; it's the part of a CSS rule that matches a set of elements in an HTML or XML document. The declarations that appear in the block that follows the selector are applied to all elements that match this pattern, unless they're overridden by another rule in the cascade (p. 117).

As is discussed briefly in Selectors (p. 26), a selector can contain a chain of one or more simple selectors separated by combinators. A pseudo-element (p. 106)—for example, :first-line—can also be included after the last simple selector in the chain.

A simple selector contains either an element type selector (p. 62), such as h1, or the universal selector (p. 60), *. The universal selector can be considered to be implied (and can therefore be omitted) if it isn't the only component of the simple selector.

A simple selector can also contain class selectors (p. 63)—for example, .warning, ID selectors (p. 65)—for example, #menu, attribute selectors (p. 67)—for example, [`type="submit"`], and pseudo-classes (p. 80)—for example, `:hover`. These act like modifiers on a type selector (or the universal selector), and qualify the selector, as if to say "but only if ..."

📖 The CSS3 Difference

The terminology used in the CSS3 specification[1] differs from that used for CSS2. In CSS3, the term "simple selectors" is used to refer to the various components: type selectors, the universal selector, attribute or ID selectors, and pseudo-classes. The selector component that CSS2 calls a "simple selector" is referred to as "a sequence of simple selectors" in CSS3. In this reference, we'll use the CSS2 terminology, which should be familiar to most readers.

Universal Selector

SPEC			
CSS2			
BROWSER SUPPORT			
IE5.5+	FF1+	Saf1.3+	Op9.2+
BUGGY	FULL	FULL	FULL

```
* {
declaration block
}
```

The universal selector matches any element type. It can be implied (and therefore omitted) if it isn't the only component of the simple selector. The two selector examples shown here are equivalent:

Example

This rule set will be applied to every element in a document:

```
* {
  margin: 0;
  padding: 0;
}
```

```
*.warning {
  : declarations
}
.warning {
  : declarations
}
```

---

[1] http://www.w3.org/TR/css3-selectors/#changesFromCSS2

It's important not to confuse the universal selector with a wildcard character—the universal selector doesn't match "zero or more elements." Consider the following HTML fragment:

```
<body>
  <div>
    <h1>The <em>Universal</em> Selector</h1>
    <p>We must <em>emphasize</em> the following:</p>
    <ul>
      <li>It's <em>not</em> a wildcard.</li>
      <li>It matches elements regardless of <em>type</em>.</li>
    </ul>
    This is an <em>immediate</em> child of the division.
  </div>
</body>
```

The selector div * em will match the following em elements:

- "Universal" in the h1 element (* matches the `<h1>`)
- "emphasize" in the p element (* matches the `<p>`)
- "not" in the first li element (* matches the `<ul>` or the `<li>`)
- "type" in the second li element (* matches the `<ul>` or the `<li>`)

However, it won't match the `<em>immediate</em>` element, since that's an immediate child of the div element—there's nothing between `<div>` and `<em>` for the * to match.

Compatibility

Internet Explorer			Firefox			Safari			Opera
5.5	6.0	7.0	1.0	1.5	2.0	1.3	2.0	3.0	9.2
Buggy	Buggy	Buggy	Full	Full	Full	Full	Full	Full	Full

Internet Explorer versions up to and including 6 exhibit the star HTML selector (p. 400) bug: selectors that should fail, don't. A descendant selector, such as * html, shouldn't match any elements, because the html element is the top-most parent element and, as such, it can't be a descendant of any other element. However, Internet Explorer versions 5.5 and 6 ignore the universal selector at the beginning of this selector.

When the universal selector is immediately adjacent to an element type selector, Internet Explorer versions 6 and 7 will interpret the combination as a descendant selector (p. 74) instead of failing as they should.

In Internet Explorer 6 and 7, this selector will also select some inappropriate SGML elements such as the doctype declaration and comments.

In Opera 9.2, this selector will also match any recognized processing instructions.

 # Element Type Selector

SPEC
CSS1

BROWSER SUPPORT			
IE7+	FF1+	Saf1.3+	Op9.2+
FULL	FULL	FULL	FULL

```
E {
declaration block
}
```

While the universal selector matches any element, an element type selector matches elements with the corresponding element type name. Type selectors are case insensitive in HTML (including XHTML served as text/html), but are case sensitive in XML (including XHTML served as XML).

Compatibility

Example

Consider this example selector:

```
ul {
  : declarations
}
```

A type selector like the above ul matches all the elements within an HTML or XML document that are marked up as follows:

```
<ul> … </ul>
```

Internet Explorer			Firefox			Safari			Opera
5.5	6.0	7.0	1.0	1.5	2.0	1.3	2.0	3.0	9.2
Partial	Partial	Full	Full	Full	Full	Full	Full	Full	Full

Internet Explorer versions up to and including 6 don't support the abbr element, and the type selector abbr is ignored by those browsers. However, Dean Edwards has produced a simple workaround:[2] if the "html" namespace prefix is used in the

---

[2] http://dean.edwards.name/my/abbr-cadabra.html

selector `html\:abbr`, Internet Explorer 6 and earlier versions can be made to recognize the element and apply the declarations. In the following example, we group two element type selectors (see Selector Grouping (p. 72))—one for IE6, and one for all other browsers that support the `abbr` element:

```
html\:abbr, abbr {
    cursor: help;
    font-style: italic;
}
```

{} Class Selector

SPEC			
CSS1			
BROWSER SUPPORT			
IE7+	FF1+	Saf1.3+	Op9.2+
FULL	FULL	FULL	FULL

```
.className {
declaration block
}
```

Selecting elements on the basis of their class names is a very common technique in CSS. The attribute selector syntax `[class~="warning"]` is rather awkward, but thankfully there's a simpler and shorter form for it: the class selector.

Here's a simple example that selects all elements with a `class` attribute that contains the value `"warning"`:

Example

The following selector will match all `p` elements with a `class` attribute that contains the value `"intro"`:

```
p.intro {
    : declarations
}
```

```
.warning {
    : declarations
}
```

This example also illustrates the use of an implied universal selector—it's equivalent to `*.warning`. Note that whitespace characters can't appear after the period, or between an element type selector, or explicit universal selector, and the period. For example, the following selector will match all `p` elements with a `class` attribute that contains the value `"warning"`:

Selector Reference

```
p.warning {
  : declarations
}
```

A simple selector may contain more than one attribute selector and/or class selector; in such cases, the selector pattern matches elements whose attributes contain *all* the specified components. Here's an example:

```
div.foo.bar {
  : declarations
}
div.foo.bar[title^="Help"] {
  : declarations
}
```

The first example selector above matches `div` elements whose `class` attribute value contains both the words `"foo"` and `"bar"`. The second example selector matches `div` elements whose `class` attribute values contains both the words `"foo"` and `"bar"`, and whose `title` attribute values begin with the string `"Help"`.

Compatibility

Internet Explorer			Firefox			Safari			Opera
5.5	6.0	7.0	1.0	1.5	2.0	1.3	2.0	3.0	9.2
Buggy	Buggy	Full	Full	Full	Full	Full	Full	Full	Full

In Internet Explorer 6, the class selector doesn't work if the class name starts with a hyphen or an underscore.

In Internet Explorer up to and including version 6, only the last class selector is honored; all others in a chain of class selectors are ignored. For example, a selector like `.x.y.z` will match all elements with a `class` attribute that contains the value `"z"`, but will not restrict the match to elements that also have the `class` attribute values `"x"` and `"y"`, which it should.

In Internet Explorer versions up to and including 6, if an ID selector that's combined with a class selector is unmatched, all subsequent ID selectors that use the same ID and are combined with a class selector, are also treated as unmatched.

{} ID Selector

SPEC			
CSS1			
BROWSER SUPPORT			
IE7+	FF1+	Saf1.3+	Op9.2+
FULL	FULL	FULL	FULL

```
#ID {
declaration block
}
```

An ID selector matches an element that has a specific `id` attribute value. Since `id` attributes must have unique values, an ID selector can never match more than one element in a document.

Example

This example selector matches any element whose `id` attribute value is equal to `"breadcrumbs"`:

```
#breadcrumbs {
  ⋮ declarations
}
```

📓 ID, Please!

By **ID attribute**, the CSS specification[3] doesn't necessarily refer to an attribute whose name is `id`. An ID attribute is one whose type is declared as ID in the document type definition (DTD), or similar, for the markup language. In HTML (and XHTML), this selector matches the `id` attribute, but in XML it would apply to any attribute for which a type of ID was specified.

Since attribute types are declared in a DTD or schema—information that user agents don't normally read—ID selectors shouldn't be used for XML other than XHTML, unless you know that user agents have built-in knowledge about ID attributes.

In its simplest form, an ID selector looks like this:

```
#navigation {
  ⋮ declarations
}
```

This selector matches any element whose `id` attribute value is equal to `"navigation"`. In this selector, which is equivalent to `*#navigation`, the universal selector is implied. The universal selector is often omitted in cases like this.

---

[3] http://www.w3.org/TR/CSS21/selector.html#id-selectors

Of course, it's possible to use a type selector with an ID selector, but it's rarely necessary, since an ID uniquely identifies an element. Here's an example that only matches an unordered list element with an `id` attribute value that's equal to `"navigation"`:

```
ul#navigation {
   ⋮ declarations
}
```

Whitespace characters shouldn't appear between the type selector and the ID selector.

Compatibility

Internet Explorer			Firefox			Safari			Opera
5.5	6.0	7.0	1.0	1.5	2.0	1.3	2.0	3.0	9.2
Buggy	Buggy	Full	Full	Full	Full	Full	Full	Full	Full

In Internet Explorer 6, an ID selector is ignored unless it's the last ID selector in the simple selector.

In Internet Explorer versions up to and including 6, if an ID selector that's combined with a class selector is unmatched, all subsequent ID selectors that use the same ID and are combined with a class selector, are also treated as unmatched.

Attribute Selector

SPEC			
CSS2			
BROWSER SUPPORT			
IE7+	FF1+	Saf2+	Op9.2+
BUGGY	FULL	FULL	BUGGY

```
[ { attribute | attribute { = | |= | ~= } attribute
value } ] {
declaration block
}
```

An attribute selector will match
elements on the basis of either the
presence of an attribute, or the exact or
partial match of an attribute value.
Attribute selectors were introduced in
CSS2, and CSS3 added a few more
(p. 71).

Example

This selector matches all **input** elements
with a **type** attribute that's equal to
"**submit**" (in other words, **submit** buttons):

```
input[type="submit"] {
    ⋮ declarations
}
```

Attribute selectors are delimited by
square brackets; the simplest form of an
attribute selector consists of an attribute name surrounded by square brackets:

```
[href] {
    ⋮ declarations
}
```

This example selector matches any element that has an **href** attribute. It also contains
an implied universal selector, and is equivalent to ***[href]**.

Here's another example:

```
a[href] {
    ⋮ declarations
}
```

This selector matches any **a** element that has an **href** attribute, so it matches a
hypertext link, but not a named anchor.

Attribute selectors can also specify a value, or a partial value, to match. The values
must be strings (p. 37), in which case they're surrounded by single or double quotes,
or identifiers (p. 43), without quotes. All the examples below use strings.

Case Sensitivity

The value specified in an attribute selector is case sensitive if the attribute value in the markup language is case sensitive. Thus, values for `id` and `class` attributes in HTML are case sensitive, while values for `lang` and `type` attributes are not.

XHTML, when served as XML, is always case sensitive; see Differences Between HTML and XHTML (p. 409) for more on this.

It's not always easy to remember which HTML attributes are case sensitive and which aren't. It's usually best to assume that everything is case sensitive, but don't rely on it!

We can use the = operator to have an attribute selector match elements that have specific values:

```
input[type="submit"] {
   ⋮ declarations
}
```

This selector matches any input element that has a `type` attribute with a value equal to `"submit"`.

 Default Attributes

Attribute selectors can only match attributes and values that exist in the document tree, and there's no guarantee that a default value specified in a DTD (or similar) can be matched. For instance, in HTML, the default value for a form element's `method` attribute is `"get"`, but you can't rely on a selector like `form[method="get"]` to select a form element with the start tag `<form action="comment.php">`.

Attribute Selectors for IDs

Note that `[id="foo"]` isn't equivalent to `#foo`. Although both selectors would match the same element in HTML, there's a significant difference between their levels of specificity (p. 126).

We can use the |= operator to cause an attribute selector to match elements which have an attribute containing a hyphenated list of words that begin with a specific value:

```
[hreflang|="en"] {
  ⋮ declarations
}
```

This example selector matches any element that has an hreflang attribute containing a value of "en", whether or not that value is followed by a hyphen and more characters. In other words, it matches hreflang attribute values of "en", "en-US", "en-GB", and so on. This selector syntax was intended to allow language subcode matches.[4]

📖 Hyphen or No Hyphen?

All supporting browsers allow a hyphen to appear in the value in a selector like [hreflang|="en"]. It's unclear whether or not this is illegal, because the CSS specification doesn't contains any guidelines to help us deal with this situation.

We can use the ~= operator to make an attribute selector match elements that have an attribute that contains a list of space-separated words, one of which is the specified value:

```
[class~="warning"] {
  ⋮ declarations
}
```

This selector matches any HTML element with a class attribute that contains a space-separated list of words, one of which is "warning". So it matches <p class="warning"> and <strong class="important warning"> and <div class="warning highlight">, but not <p class="my-warning"> or <ul class="warnings">.

Compatibility

Internet Explorer			Firefox			Safari			Opera
5.5	6.0	7.0	1.0	1.5	2.0	1.3	2.0	3.0	9.2
None	None	Buggy	Full	Full	Full	Buggy	Full	Full	Buggy

---

[4] See also the :lang pseudo-class (p. 89).

Browsers differ in their treatment of minimized attributes in HTML. For example, the following HTML `input` element has a minimized `disabled` attribute:

```
<input type="text" name="email" disabled>
```

The selector `input[disabled="disabled"]` should match the element above, and represents the correct way to write the selector. However, most browsers fail to match it correctly. In Firefox 2 and earlier versions, and Safari 2 and earlier versions, the selector `input[disabled=""]` matches the element above. In Opera 9.2, the selector `input[disabled="true"]` matches the element above. Internet Explorer 7 doesn't seem to recognize attribute selectors for minimized attributes at all.

In Internet Explorer 7:

- If the closing square bracket of an attribute selector,], is immediately followed by an element type selector, the rule is parsed as if there's a descendant combinator—that is, a space—between the selectors, instead of failing as it should.
- Some DOM attributes, such as `className`, are treated like HTML attributes.

Safari versions up to and including 3 will always ignore the case of HTML attribute values, even for attributes that are, in fact, case sensitive.

Firefox versions up to and including 2, will ignore the case of some attributes that should be compared in a case-sensitive manner: for example, the `id` and `for` attributes.

{} CSS3 Attribute Selectors

```
[attribute { ^= | $= | *= } attribute value] {
declaration block
}
```

SPEC			
CSS3			
BROWSER SUPPORT			
IE7	FF1+	Saf1.3+	Op9.2+
NONE	BUGGY	FULL	BUGGY

CSS3 defines three more attribute selector variations. These new selectors give us the ability to make partial matches to attribute values—we can match strings at the start, end, or anywhere within an attribute value.

We can use the ^= operator to cause an attribute selector to match elements that have an attribute containing a value that starts with the specified value:

Example

This example will match a elements with an href attribute that contains the string "example.com":

```
a[href*="example.com"] {
    : declarations
}
```

```
a[href^="http:"] {
   : declarations
}
```

This example matches a elements that have an href attribute value which starts with the characters "http:".

Using the $= operator, an attribute selector can match elements that have an attribute which contains a value ending with the specified value:

```
img[src$=".png"] {
   : declarations
}
```

This example matches img elements with a src attribute value that ends with the characters ".png".

Finally, we can use the *= operator to make an attribute selector match elements that have an attribute which contains the specified value:

```
div[id*="foo"] {
  : declarations
}
```

This example matches `div` elements whose `id` attribute value contains the characters `"foo"`.

Compatibility

Internet Explorer			Firefox			Safari			Opera
5.5	6.0	7.0	1.0	1.5	2.0	1.3	2.0	3.0	9.2
None	None	None	Buggy	Buggy	Buggy	Full	Full	Full	Buggy

Internet Explorer 7 doesn't support the partial matching of attribute values.

Safari versions up to and including 3 will always ignore the case of HTML attribute values, even for attributes that are, in fact, case sensitive.

Firefox versions up to and including 2, will ignore the case of some attributes that should be compared in a case-sensitive manner: for example, the `id` and `for` attributes.

Selector Grouping

We can group selectors using a comma (`,`) separator. The following declaration block will apply to any element that matches either of the selectors in the group:

```
td, th {
  : declarations
}
```

We can think of the comma as a logical OR operator, but it's important to remember that each selector in a group is autonomous. A common beginner's mistake is to write groups like this:

```
#foo td, th {
  : declarations
}
```

A beginner might think that the above declaration block will be applied to all `td` and `th` elements that are descendants of the element with an ID of `"foo"`. However, the selector group above is actually equivalent to this:

```
#foo td {
  ⋮ declarations
}
th {
  ⋮ declarations
}
```

To achieve the true goal, write the selector group as follows:

```
#foo td, #foo th {
  ⋮ declarations
}
```

> **No Trailing Comma Needed**
>
> Don't leave a comma after the last selector in the group!

Combinators

A selector can contain more than one simple selector. Between the simple selectors, we must include a combinator—something that explains the relationship between the selectors. There are three different combinators in CSS2, and one extra in CSS3; when we use them, they change the nature of the selector to reflect one of the following types:

- descendant selector (p. 74)
- child selector (p. 76)
- adjacent sibling selector (p. 77)
- general sibling selector (p. 79)

{} Descendant Selector

```
E F {
declaration block
}
```

	SPEC		
	CSS1		
BROWSER SUPPORT			
IE5.5+	FF1+	Saf1.3+	Op9.2+
BUGGY	FULL	FULL	FULL

The descendant selector matches all elements that are descendants of a specified element. The first simple selector within this selector represents the **ancestor element**—a structurally superior element, such as a parent element, or the parent of a parent element, and so on. The second simple selector represents the descendant element we're trying to match. If you're a little unclear about the terms ancestor element and descendant element, have a look at CSS Layout and Formatting (p. 139) for a complete explanation.

Example

Take a look at this example of the descendant selector in action:

```
ul li {
  : declarations
}
```

This selector matches all `li` elements that are descendants of a `ul` element—that is, every `li` element that has a `ul` element as its ancestor.

The combinator we use in a descendant selector is a whitespace character: a space, horizontal tab, carriage return, line feed, or form feed. Since whitespace characters are allowed around all combinators, you can include more than one whitespace character between the simple selectors in a descendant selector.

Consider the following HTML fragment:

```
<ul>
  <li>Item 1</li>
  <li>
    <ol>
      <li>Sub-item 2A</li>
      <li>Sub-item 2B</li>
    </ol>
  </li>
</ul>
```

We'll try to match elements in the above fragment using the selector below:

```
ul li {
    : declarations
}
```

This descendant selector will match all four li elements in the example HTML, because each of those elements has a ul element as its ancestor.

We can also use descendant selectors to match the li elements within the ol in the example above:

```
ul * li {
    : declarations
}
ul * * li {
    : declarations
}
ul * ol li {
    : declarations
}
ul li * li {
    : declarations
}
ul ol li {
    : declarations
}
ul li li {
    : declarations
}
ul li ol li {
    : declarations
}
```

However, there's no way we can use descendant selectors to match only the list items in the unordered list. To do that, we'd need a child selector (p. 76).

Compatibility

Internet Explorer			Firefox			Safari			Opera
5.5	6.0	7.0	1.0	1.5	2.0	1.3	2.0	3.0	9.2
Buggy	Buggy	Buggy	Full	Full	Full	Full	Full	Full	Full

In Internet Explorer 5.5 and 6, this combinator doesn't work after a :hover pseudo-class (p. 86).

In Internet Explorer 6 and 7, if there's only a comment—without any additional whitespace—between two simple selectors, that comment is incorrectly treated as a descendant selector, when in fact it should fail.

 # Child Selector

```
E>F {
declaration block
}
```

SPEC			
CSS2			
BROWSER SUPPORT			
IE7+	FF1+	Saf1.3+	Op9.2+
BUGGY	FULL	FULL	FULL

This selector matches all elements that are the immediate children of a specified element. The combinator in a child selector is a greater-than sign (>). It may be surrounded by whitespace characters, but if it is, Internet Explorer 5 on Windows will incorrectly treat it as a descendant selector (p. 74). So the best practice is to eschew whitespace around this combinator.

Example

Here's an example of the child selector at work:

```
ul>li {
  ⋮ declarations
}
```

This selector matches all li elements that are the immediate children of a ul element—that is, all li elements that have a ul element as a parent.

Consider this HTML fragment:

```
<ul>
  <li>Item 1</li>
  <li>
    <ol>
      <li>Subitem 2A</li>
      <li>Subitem 2B</li>
    </ol>
  </li>
</ul>
```

Let's try to match elements in the above fragment with the selector below:

```
ul>li {
  ⋮ declarations
}
```

The child selector above will only match the two `li` elements that are children of the `ul` element. It will not match the subitems, because their parent is the `ol` element.

Compatibility

Internet Explorer			Firefox			Safari			Opera
5.5	6.0	7.0	1.0	1.5	2.0	1.3	2.0	3.0	9.2
None	None	Buggy	Full	Full	Full	Full	Full	Full	Full

In Internet Explorer 7, this selector fails if a comment appears between the combinator and the simple selector that follows it.

If one of the simple selectors is missing, Internet Explorer 7 acts as if there were a universal selector in its place, instead of failing as it should.

{} Adjacent Sibling Selector

	SPEC
	CSS2

BROWSER SUPPORT			
IE7+	FF1+	Saf1.3+	Op9.2+
BUGGY	FULL	FULL	BUGGY

```
E+F {
declaration block
}
```

The adjacent sibling selector selects all elements that are the adjacent siblings of a specified element. Sibling elements must have the same parent element, and "adjacent" means "immediately following," so there can be no elements between the sibling elements. The combinator in an adjacent sibling selector is a plus character (+), as shown in this example:

Example

This selector matches all `p` elements that appear immediately after `h2` elements:

```
h2+p {
  : declarations
}
```

```
h2+p {
  : declarations
}
```

Applying the above selector to this block of HTML may make things clearer:

```
<h2>Heading</h2>
<p>The selector above matches this paragraph.</p>
<p>The selector above does not match this paragraph.</p>
```

The first paragraph matches the adjacent sibling selector h2+p, because the p element is an adjacent sibling to the h2 element. The second paragraph doesn't match the selector. Although it's a sibling of the h2 element, it's not adjacent to that element.

If we apply the above selector to the following HTML block, the paragraph isn't matched—it's not a sibling to the heading, since they don't have the same parent:

```
<h2>Heading</h2>
<div>
  <p>The selector above does not match this paragraph.</p>
</div>
```

If we apply the selector to the HTML block below, the paragraph is matched by the selector even though it appears not to be adjacent to the heading:

```
<h2>Heading</h2>
Lorem ipsum dolor sit amet.
<p>The selector above matches this paragraph.</p>
```

The selector matches the paragraph in this case because the node between them is a text node rather than an element node. So if you look at element nodes only, the heading and the paragraph are adjacent siblings.

Element Nodes and Text Nodes

A browser builds an internal document structure, called the **Document Object Model** (DOM), from a web page. This model consists of nodes of different types. The relationship between the nodes can be visualized as an upside-down tree, which is why the model is often referred to as the DOM tree.

The two main types of nodes in this tree are element nodes and text nodes. Element nodes correspond to HTML elements, while text nodes correspond to the textual contents of element nodes. For instance, a fragment like Important! will create one element node for the em element, and that element node will contain a text node with the text Important!.

See CSS Layout and Formatting (p. 139) for more information about the DOM.

Compatibility

Internet Explorer			Firefox			Safari			Opera
5.5	6.0	7.0	1.0	1.5	2.0	1.3	2.0	3.0	9.2
None	None	Buggy	Full	Full	Full	Full	Full	Full	Buggy

In Internet Explorer 7, this selector fails if a comment appears between the combinator and the simple selector that follows it.

If one of the simple selectors is missing, Internet Explorer 7 acts as if there were a universal selector in its place, instead of failing as it should.

In Internet Explorer 6 and 7, this selector will also select some inappropriate SGML elements such as the doctype declaration and comments.

In Opera 9.2, this selector will also match any recognized processing instructions.

General Sibling Selector

	SPEC
	CSS3
BROWSER SUPPORT	

IE7+	FF1+	Saf3	Op9.2+
BUGGY	FULL	NONE	FULL

```
E~F {
declaration block
}
```

The general sibling selector is available in CSS3, and the combinator used in this selector is a tilde character (~).

The selector matches elements that are siblings of a given element. This example will match a p element if it's a sibling of an h2 element:

Example

This selector matches all p elements that are siblings to h2 elements:

```
h2~p {
  : declarations
}
```

```
h2~p {
  : declarations
}
```

The elements don't have to be adjacent siblings, but they have to have the same parent, and the h2 element has to occur before the p element in the document source. Let's apply the above selector to some more examples:

```
<h2>Heading</h2>
<p>The selector above matches this paragraph.</p>
<p>The selector above matches this paragraph.</p>
```

Here, both paragraphs match the sibling selector h2~p, because the p elements are siblings to the h2 element.

The paragraph below isn't a sibling to the heading—they don't have the same parent—so our selector won't match this paragraph:

```
<h2>Heading</h2>
<div>
   <p>The selector above does not match this paragraph.</p>
</div>
```

Only the second paragraph above is matched by the sibling selector h2~p—even though they're siblings—because the first p element occurs before the h2 element:

```
<p>The selector above does not match this paragraph.</p>
<h2>Heading</h2>
<p>The selector above matches this paragraph.</p>
```

Compatibility

Internet Explorer			Firefox			Safari			Opera
5.5	6.0	7.0	1.0	1.5	2.0	1.3	2.0	3.0	9.2
None	None	Buggy	Full	Full	Full	None	None	None	Full

In Internet Explorer 7, this selector fails if a comment appears between the combinator and the simple selector that follows it.

If one of the simple selectors is missing, Internet Explorer 7 acts as if there were a universal selector in its place, instead of failing as it should.

Pseudo-classes

A pseudo-class is similar to a class in HTML, but it's not specified explicitly in the markup. Some pseudo-classes are dynamic—they're applied as a result of user interaction with the document.

A pseudo-class starts with a colon (:). No whitespace may appear between a type selector or universal selector and the colon, nor can whitespace appear after the colon.

CSS1 introduced the :link (p. 83), :visited (p. 84), and :active (p. 85) pseudo-classes, but only for the HTML a element. These pseudo-classes represented the state of links—unvisited, visited, or currently being selected—in a web page document. In CSS1, all three pseudo-classes were mutually exclusive.

CSS2 expanded the range of pseudo-classes and ensured that they could be applied to any element. :link and :visited now apply to any element defined as a link in the document language. While they remain mutually exclusive, the :active pseudo-class now joins :hover (p. 86) and :focus (p. 87) in the group of dynamic pseudo-classes. The :hover pseudo-class matches elements that are being designated by a pointing device (for example, elements that the user's hovering the cursor over); :active matches any element that's being activated by the user; and :focus matches any element that is currently in focus (that is, accepting input).

CSS2 also introduced the :lang (p. 89) pseudo-class to allow an element to be matched on the basis of its language, and the :first-child (p. 88) pseudo-class to match an element that's the first child element of its parent.

CSS3 promises an even greater range of powerful pseudo-classes (p. 90).

Remember that pseudo-classes, like ID selectors (p. 65) and attribute selectors (p. 67), act like modifiers on type selectors (p. 62) and the universal selector (p. 60): they specify additional constraints for the selector pattern, but they don't specify other elements. For instance, the selector li:first-child matches a list item that's the first child of its parent; it *doesn't* match the first child of a list item.

A simple selector can contain more than one pseudo-class if the pseudo-classes aren't mutually exclusive. For example, the selectors a:link:hover and a:visited:hover are valid, but a:link:visited isn't because :link and :visited are mutually exclusive. An element is either an unvisited link or a visited link.

The order of declaration is very important for the dynamic pseudo-classes `:hover`, `:focus`, and `:active`, depending on what you wish to achieve. The most commonly desired behavior for links is as follows:

```
a:link {
    : declarations
}
a:visited {
    : declarations
}
a:focus {
    : declarations
}
a:hover {
    : declarations
}
a:active {
    : declarations
}
```

 Dynamic Pseudo-class Mnemonics

Several mnemonics have been devised to help us remember this order, including "LoVe Frogs HAppy," "Las Vegas Fights Hell's Angels," and—for the *Star Wars* fans—"Lord Vader, Former Handle Anakin."

The `:link` and `:visited` pseudo-classes should generally come first.[5] Next should be `:focus` and `:hover`—they're specified now so that they override and apply to both visited and unvisited links. If `:focus` precedes `:hover`, the hover effect will apply to links with keyboard input focus. The `:active` pseudo-class should always come last, since we usually want to indicate clearly any links that have been activated.

This isn't the only useful order, nor is it in any way the "right" order. The order in which you specify your pseudo-classes will depend on the effects you want to show with different combinations of states. It's possible, for instance, that you might want to have different hover or focus effects on visited and unvisited links. In that case, you could combine pseudo-classes: `a:link:hover`.

---

[5] For a discussion about the pros and cons of different pseudo-class orders, see http://meyerweb.com/eric/thoughts/2007/06/11/who-ordered-the-link-states/.

If you want to apply special styling to the hover state of a link that also has keyboard input focus, use `a:focus:hover`.

{} `:link`

	SPEC		
	CSS1		
BROWSER SUPPORT			
IE7+	FF1+	Saf1.3+	Op9.2+
FULL	FULL	FULL	FULL

```
:link {
declaration block
}
```

This pseudo-class matches link elements that are determined to be unvisited.

In CSS1, this pseudo-class applied only to `a` elements that had an `href` attribute (that is, a hypertext link). In CSS2, the document language can define elements as hyperlink anchors. It's up to the user agent to decide which links it considers to be visited and unvisited.

Example

This example will set the font color of all unvisited HTML links to #cccccc:

```
a:link {
  color: #cccccc;
}
```

The two pseudo-classes `:link` and `:visited` are mutually exclusive: a link is either visited or unvisited. As such, a selector like `a:link:visited` should never match any element.

Compatibility

Internet Explorer			Firefox			Safari			Opera
5.5	6.0	7.0	1.0	1.5	2.0	1.3	2.0	3.0	9.2
Buggy	Buggy	Full	Full	Full	Full	Full	Full	Full	Full

Neither Internet Explorer 5.5 nor 6 supports the chaining of pseudo-classes; only the last pseudo-class is honored in these browsers.

{} :visited

```
:visited {
declaration block
}
```

SPEC			
	CSS1		
BROWSER SUPPORT			
IE7+	FF1+	Saf1.3+	Op9.2+
FULL	FULL	FULL	FULL

This pseudo-class matches link elements that are determined to have been visited.

In CSS1, this pseudo-class applied only to a elements that had an href attribute (that is, a hypertext link). In CSS2, the document language can define elements as hyperlink anchors. It's up to the user agent to decide which links it considers to be visited and unvisited.

Example

This rule will set the font color of all visited HTML links to #cccccc:

```
a:visited {
  color: #cccccc;
}
```

The two pseudo-classes :link and :visited are mutually exclusive: a link is either visited or unvisited. As such, a selector like a:link:visited should never match any element.

Compatibility

Internet Explorer			Firefox			Safari			Opera
5.5	6.0	7.0	1.0	1.5	2.0	1.3	2.0	3.0	9.2
Buggy	Buggy	Full	Full	Full	Full	Full	Full	Full	Full

Neither Internet Explorer 5.5 nor 6 supports the chaining of pseudo-classes; only the last pseudo-class is honored in these browsers.

:active

```
:active {
declaration block
}
```

	SPEC		
	CSS1		
	BROWSER SUPPORT		
IE5.5+	FF1+	Saf1.3+	Op9.2+
BUGGY	FULL	FULL	FULL

This pseudo-class matches any element that's in the process of being activated. It would apply, for instance, for the duration of a mouse-click on a link, from the point at which the mouse button's pressed down until the point at which it's released again. The pseudo-class does *not* signify a link to the active, or current, page—that's a common misconception among CSS beginners.

Example

This rule will set the font color of an active HTML link to #cccccc:

```
a:active {
  color: #cccccc;
}
```

Compatibility

Internet Explorer			Firefox			Safari			Opera
5.5	6.0	7.0	1.0	1.5	2.0	1.3	2.0	3.0	9.2
Buggy	Buggy	Buggy	Full	Full	Full	Full	Full	Full	Full

Internet Explorer 5.5 and 6 incorrectly apply this pseudo-class to links that have keyboard input focus—a state that should be matched by :focus, which those browsers do not support.

Internet Explorer versions up to and including 7:

- Apply :active only to HTML a elements that have an href attribute.
- Ignore :active unless it's the last part of a pseudo-class chain.

:hover

SPEC			
CSS2			
BROWSER SUPPORT			
IE7+	FF1+	Saf1.3+	Op9.2+
FULL	FULL	FULL	FULL

```
:hover {
    declaration block
}
```

The :hover pseudo-class matches any element that's being designated by a pointing device. The term **designated** refers to the process during which the cursor is hovered over the box generated by the element.

Example

This rule will apply a border to any img element over which the cursor is hovered:

```
img:hover {
    border: 5px solid #F2F2F2;
}
```

Compatibility

Internet Explorer			Firefox			Safari			Opera
5.5	6.0	7.0	1.0	1.5	2.0	1.3	2.0	3.0	9.2
Buggy	Buggy	Full	Full	Full	Full	Full	Full	Full	Full

In Internet Explorer versions up to and including 6:

- :hover is applied only to HTML a elements that have an href attribute.

- :hover is counted as two classes/pseudo-classes in the specificity calculation.

- :hover is ignored if it's not in the last simple selector.

Neither Internet Explorer 5.5 nor 6 supports the chaining of pseudo-classes; only the last pseudo-class is honored in these browsers.

In Internet Explorer 7:

- The element sometimes remains in the hover state if the cursor is moved from the element while the mouse button is pressed; the hover state sometimes doesn't apply when it should.

- :hover doesn't match elements with negative z-index property values.

:focus

```
:focus {
declaration block
}
```

	SPEC		
	CSS2		
BROWSER SUPPORT			
IE7	FF1+	Saf1.3+	Op9.2+
NONE	FULL	FULL	FULL

This pseudo-class matches any element that has keyboard input focus. **Keyboard input focus** describes any element that's ready to receive user input. It can apply to a form control, for instance, or to a link if the user navigates using the keyboard.

Example

This rule applies a border around any text `textarea` element that has focus:

```
textarea:focus {
  border: 2px solid blue;
}
```

Compatibility

Internet Explorer			Firefox			Safari			Opera
5.5	6.0	7.0	1.0	1.5	2.0	1.3	2.0	3.0	9.2
None	None	None	Full	Full	Full	Full	Full	Full	Full

Internet Explorer 7 and earlier versions don't support this pseudo-class; however, Internet Explorer 5.5 and 6 incorrectly apply the pseudo-class `:active` to links that have keyboard input focus—a state that should be matched by this pseudo-class.

:first-child

```
:first-child {
declaration block
}
```

SPEC			
CSS1			
BROWSER SUPPORT			
IE7+	FF1+	Saf1.3+	Op9.2+
BUGGY	BUGGY	BUGGY	BUGGY

This pseudo-class matches an element only if it's the first child element of its parent element. For instance, `li:first-child` matches the first list item in an `ol` or `ul` element. It doesn't match the first child of a list item.[7]

For example, let's take the CSS selector mentioned above:

Example

This example selector matches the first list item in an `ol` or `ul` element:

```
li:first-child {
    : declarations
}
```

```
li:first-child {
    : declarations
}
```

And let's apply it to the following markup:

```
<ul>
  <li>This item matches the selector li:first-child.</li>
  <li>This item does not match that selector.</li>
  <li>Neither does this one.</li>
</ul>
```

Only the first list item element is matched.

Note that this pseudo-class only applies to elements—it doesn't apply to anonymous boxes (p. 164) generated for text.

Compatibility

Internet Explorer			Firefox			Safari			Opera
5.5	6.0	7.0	1.0	1.5	2.0	1.3	2.0	3.0	9.2
None	None	Buggy	Buggy	Buggy	Buggy	Buggy	Buggy	Buggy	Buggy

---

[7] To perform that match, you can use `li>*:first-child`.

In Internet Explorer 7 some SGML constructs, such as comments, are counted as elements.

Internet Explorer 7, Firefox versions up to and including 2, Safari versions up to and including 3, and Opera 9.2 continue to select an element as the first child even when another element is dynamically inserted before it.

Internet Explorer 7 and Firefox select the first SGML construct on the page (usually the doctype), even though it's not a child of another element.

Opera 9.2 selects the root element, `html`, even though it isn't a child of another element.

 # :lang(C)

```
:lang(language code) {
declaration block
}
```

SPEC			
CSS2			
BROWSER SUPPORT			
IE7	FF1+	Saf3+	Op9.2+
NONE	FULL	BUGGY	FULL

If you specify a language using this pseudo-class, it'll match any element for which the same language is specified. The argument is matched in a similar way to the |= operator in attribute selectors (p. 67)—it can be an exact match, or a match to a hyphen-separated substring.

Example

The following rule set will be applied to elements whose language specification is `"fr"` (French), `"fr-be"` (French/Belgium), `"fr-ca"` (French/Canada), and so on:

```
:lang(fr) {
  declarations
}
```

The document language specifies how the language of an element is set. In HTML, the language doesn't have to be set explicitly on the element—it can be inherited. As such, this pseudo-class differs from the [lang|=xx] attribute selector, which only matches elements that have a lang attribute.

Compatibility

Internet Explorer			Firefox			Safari			Opera
5.5	6.0	7.0	1.0	1.5	2.0	1.3	2.0	3.0	9.2
None	None	None	Full	Full	Full	None	None	Buggy	Full

In Safari 3, this selector only matches elements on which the attribute is set explicitly—not those for which it's inherited.

Other Relevant Stuff

{} Attribute Selector (p. 67)

selects elements based on attribute values

CSS3 Pseudo-classes

CSS3 provides many more pseudo-classes than CSS2. Though browser support for them is varied, it *is* improving.

:nth-child(N)

```
:nth-child( { number expression | odd | even } ) {
declaration block
}
```

SPEC			
CSS3			
BROWSER SUPPORT			
IE7	FF2	Saf3	Op9.2
NONE	NONE	NONE	NONE

This pseudo-class matches elements on the basis of their positions within a parent element's list of child elements. The pseudo-class accepts an argument, *N*, which can be a keyword, a number, or a number expression of the form *an+b*. For more information, see Understanding :nth-child Pseudo-class Expressions (p. 95).

Example

This example selector will match odd-numbered table rows:

```
tr:nth-child(odd) {
  ⋮ declarations
}
```

If *N* is a number or a number expression, *N* matches elements that are preceded by *N* siblings in the document tree.

The following example selectors are equivalent, and will match odd-numbered table rows:

```
tr:nth-child(2n+1) {
  ⋮ declarations
}
tr:nth-child(odd) {
  ⋮ declarations
}
```

This example selector will match the first three rows of any table:

```
tr:nth-child(-n+3) {
  ⋮ declarations
}
```

This example selector will match any paragraph that's the first child element of its parent element:

```
p:nth-child(1) {
  ⋮ declarations
}
```

This is, of course, equivalent to the selector `p:first-child` (p. 88).

Compatibility

Internet Explorer			Firefox			Safari			Opera
5.5	6.0	7.0	1.0	1.5	2.0	1.3	2.0	3.0	9.2
None	None	None	None	None	None	None	None	None	None

This pseudo-class is currently supported only by the Konqueror web browser.[8]

---

[8] http://www.konqueror.org/

:nth-last-child(N)

```
:nth-last-child( { number expression | odd | even } )
{
declaration block
}
```

SPEC			
CSS3			
BROWSER SUPPORT			
IE7	FF2	Saf3	Op9.2
NONE	NONE	NONE	NONE

This pseudo-class matches elements on the basis of their positions within a parent element's list of child elements. The pseudo-class accepts an argument, *N*, which can be a keyword, a number, or a number expression of the form *a*n+*b*. For more information, see Understanding :nth-child Pseudo-class Expressions (p. 95).

Example

This example selector will match the last row of any table:

```
tr:nth-last-child(1) {
  declarations
}
```

If *N* is a number or a number expression, *N* matches elements that are followed by *N* siblings in the document tree.

This example selector will match the last four list items in any list, be it ordered or unordered:

```
li:nth-last-child(-n+4) {
  declarations
}
```

This selector will match any paragraph that's the last child element of its parent element:

```
p:nth-last-child(1) {
  declarations
}
```

This is, of course, equivalent to the selector `p:last-child` (p. 98).

Compatibility

Internet Explorer			Firefox			Safari			Opera
5.5	6.0	7.0	1.0	1.5	2.0	1.3	2.0	3.0	9.2
None	None	None	None	None	None	None	None	None	None

This pseudo-class is currently supported only by the Konqueror web browser.[9]

:nth-of-type(N)

```
:nth-of-type( { number expression | odd | even } )
{
declaration block
}
```

SPEC			
CSS3			
BROWSER SUPPORT			
IE7	FF2	Saf3	Op9.2
NONE	NONE	NONE	NONE

This pseudo-class matches elements on the basis of their positions within a parent element's list of child elements of the same type. This pseudo-class accepts an argument, *N*, which can be a keyword, a number, or a number expression of the form *a*n+*b*. For more information, see Understanding :nth-child Pseudo-class Expressions (p. 95).

Example

The following example selector matches the first child paragraph in a `div` element:

```
div>p:nth-of-type(1) {
  ⋮ declarations
}
```

If *N* is a number or a number expression, *N* matches elements that are preceded by *N* siblings with the same element name in the document tree.

The following example selector matches the second, fifth, eighth, and so on, paragraphs in a `div` element, ignoring any children that aren't paragraphs:

```
div>p:nth-of-type(3n-1) {
  ⋮ declarations
}
```

---

[9] http://www.konqueror.org/

The following example selectors will allow the application of different CSS styles to the odd- and even-numbered image elements that are children of the element whose `id` attribute value matches `"gallery"`:

```
#gallery>img:nth-of-type(odd) {
   ⋮ declarations
}
#gallery>img:nth-of-type(even) {
   ⋮ declarations
}
```

Compatibility

Internet Explorer			Firefox			Safari			Opera
5.5	6.0	7.0	1.0	1.5	2.0	1.3	2.0	3.0	9.2
None	None	None	None	None	None	None	None	None	None

This pseudo-class is currently supported only by the Konqueror web browser.[10]

---

[10] http://www.konqueror.org/

:nth-last-of-type(N)

	SPEC
	CSS3
	BROWSER SUPPORT

```
:nth-last-of-type( { number expression | odd |
even } ) {
declaration block
}
```

IE7	FF2	Saf3	Op9.2
NONE	NONE	NONE	NONE

This pseudo-class matches elements on the basis of their positions within a parent element's list of child elements of the same type. This pseudo-class accepts an argument, *N*, which can be a keyword, a number, or a number expression of the form *a*n+*b*. For more information, see Understanding :nth-child Pseudo-class Expressions (p. 95).

If *N* is a number or a number expression, *N* will match elements that are followed by *N* siblings with the same element name in the document tree.

Example

The following example selector will match the last three image elements that are children of the element whose **id** attribute value matches "**gallery**":

```
#gallery>img:nth-of-type(-n+3) {
  ⋮ declarations
}
```

The following example selector matches the penultimate term in a definition list:

```
dt:nth-last-of-type(2) {
  ⋮ declarations
}
```

Compatibility

Internet Explorer			Firefox			Safari			Opera
5.5	6.0	7.0	1.0	1.5	2.0	1.3	2.0	3.0	9.2
None	None	None	None	None	None	None	None	None	None

This pseudo-class is currently supported only by the Konqueror web browser.[11]

Understanding :nth-child Pseudo-class Expressions

CSS3 provides four powerful pseudo-classes that allow the CSS designer to select multiple elements according to their positions in a document tree. Using these

---

[11] http://www.konqueror.org/

pseudo-classes can be a little confusing at first, but it's easy once you get the hang of it. The pseudo-classes are:

- :nth-child(N) (p. 90)
- :nth-last-child(N) (p. 92)
- :nth-of-type(N) (p. 93)
- :nth-last-of-type(N) (p. 95)

The argument, *N*, can be a keyword, a number, or a number expression of the form *an+b*.

These pseudo-classes accept the keywords odd, for selecting odd-numbered elements, and even, for selecting even-numbered elements.

If the argument *N* is a number, it represents the ordinal position of the selected element. For example, if the argument is 5, the fifth element will be selected.

The argument *N* can also be given as *an+b*, where *a* and *b* are integers (for example, 3n+1).

In that expression, the number *b* represents the ordinal position of the first element that we want to match, and the number *a* represents the ordinal number of every element we want to match after that. So our example expression 3n+1 will match the first element, and every third element after that: the first, fourth, seventh, tenth, and so on. The expression 4n+6 will match the sixth element and every fourth element after that: the sixth, tenth, fourteenth, and so on. The keyword value odd is equivalent to the expression 2n+1.

If *a* and *b* are equal, or if *b* is zero, *b* can be omitted. For example, the expressions 3n+3 and 3n+0 are equivalent to 3n—they refer to every third element. The keyword value even is equivalent to the expression 2n.

If *a* is equal to 1, it can be omitted. So, for example, 1n+3 can be written as n+3. If *a* is zero, which indicates a non-repeating pattern, only the element *b* is required to indicate the ordinal position of the single element we want to match. For example, the expression 0n+5 is equivalent to 5, and as we saw above, it'll match the fifth element.

Both *a* and *b* can be negative, but elements will only be matched if *N* has a positive value. If *b* is negative, replace the + sign with a - sign.

If your head's spinning by now, you're not alone, but hopefully Table 4.1 will help put things into perspective. The expression represents a linear number set that's used to match elements. Thus, the first column of the table represents values for n, and the other columns display the results (for *N*) of various example expressions. The expression will match if the result is positive and an element exists in that position within the document tree.

Table 4.1: Result Sets for Pseudo-class Expressions

n	2n+1	4n+1	4n+4	4n	5n-2	-n+3
0	1	1	4	-	-	3
1	3	5	8	4	3	2
2	5	9	12	8	8	1
3	7	13	16	12	13	-
4	9	17	20	16	18	-
5	11	21	24	20	23	-

Thus the expression 4n+1 will match the first, fifth, ninth, thirteenth, seventeenth, twenty-first, and so on, elements if they exist, while the expression -n+3 will match the third, second, and first elements only.

The difference, then, between the nth- and nth-last- pseudo-classes is that nth- pseudo-classes count from the top of the document tree down—they select elements that have *N* siblings *before* them; meanwhile, the nth-last- pseudo-classes count from the bottom up—they select elements that have *N* siblings *after* them.

{} :last-child

```
:last-child {
declaration block
}
```

	SPEC		
	CSS3		
	BROWSER SUPPORT		
IE7	FF1+	Saf1.3+	Op9.2
NONE	BUGGY	BUGGY	NONE

This pseudo-class is analogous to the :first-child pseudo-class (p. 88) that was included in CSS2. It matches an element that's the last child element of its parent element, and as such, the pseudo-class is equivalent to :nth-last-child(1) (p. 92).

Example

This selector will match any paragraph that's the last child element of its parent element:

```
p:last-child {
  : declarations
}
```

Compatibility

Internet Explorer			Firefox			Safari			Opera
5.5	6.0	7.0	1.0	1.5	2.0	1.3	2.0	3.0	9.2
None	None	None	Buggy	Buggy	Buggy	Buggy	Buggy	Buggy	None

In Firefox versions up to and including 2, this selector continues to select the same element even after another element is dynamically inserted before it.

In Safari versions up to and including 3, this selector will match all elements that are child elements—not just the last child element.

:first-of-type

```
:first-of-type {
declaration block
}
```

	SPEC		
	CSS3		
BROWSER SUPPORT			
IE7	FF2	Saf3+	Op9.2
NONE	NONE	BUGGY	NONE

This pseudo-class matches the first child element of the specified element type, and is equivalent to :nth-of-type(1) (p. 93).

Compatibility

Example

This selector matches the first **p** element that's a child of a **div** element:

```
div>p:first-of-type {
  ⋮ declarations
}
```

Internet Explorer			Firefox			Safari			Opera
5.5	6.0	7.0	1.0	1.5	2.0	1.3	2.0	3.0	9.2
None	None	None	None	None	None	None	None	Buggy	None

In Safari 3, this selector continues to select the same element even after another element of the same type is dynamically inserted before it.

:last-of-type

```
:last-of-type {
declaration block
}
```

	SPEC		
	CSS3		
BROWSER SUPPORT			
IE7	FF2	Saf3+	Op9.2
NONE	NONE	BUGGY	NONE

This pseudo-class matches the last child element of the specified element type, and is equivalent to :nth-last-of-type(1) (p. 95).

Example

This selector matches the last **p** element that's a child of a **div** element:

```
div>p:last-of-type {
  ⋮ declarations
}
```

Compatibility

Internet Explorer			Firefox			Safari			Opera
5.5	6.0	7.0	1.0	1.5	2.0	1.3	2.0	3.0	9.2
None	None	None	None	None	None	None	None	Buggy	None

In Safari 3, this selector will match all siblings of the same type.

 # :only-child

	SPEC
	CSS3
	BROWSER SUPPORT

```
:only-child {
declaration block
}
```

IE7	FF1.5+	Saf1.3+	Op9.2
NONE	BUGGY	BUGGY	NONE

This pseudo-class matches an element if it's the only child element of its parent.

Compatibility

Example

The following selector will match a list item element if it's the only list item in its parent ol or ul element:

```
li:only-child {
    declarations
}
```

Internet Explorer			Firefox			Safari			Opera
5.5	6.0	7.0	1.0	1.5	2.0	1.3	2.0	3.0	9.2
None	None	None	None	Buggy	Buggy	Buggy	Buggy	Buggy	None

In Firefox 1.5 and 2, this selector will continue to match an element even after sibling elements are inserted dynamically before or after it.

In Safari versions up to and including 3, this selector behaves exactly like :first-child.

:only-of-type

```
:only-of-type {
declaration block
}
```

	SPEC		
	CSS1		
	BROWSER SUPPORT		
IE7	FF2	Saf3	Op9.2
NONE	NONE	NONE	NONE

This pseudo-class matches an element that's the only child element of its type.

Compatibility

Example

This selector will match an img element that's the only child img element of its parent element:

```
img:only-of-type {
  : declarations
}
```

Internet Explorer			Firefox			Safari			Opera
5.5	6.0	7.0	1.0	1.5	2.0	1.3	2.0	3.0	9.2
None	None	None	None	None	None	None	None	None	None

This pseudo-class is currently supported only by the Konqueror web browser.[12]

:root

```
:root {
declaration block
}
```

	SPEC		
	CSS3		
	BROWSER SUPPORT		
IE7	FF1+	Saf1.3+	Op9.2
NONE	FULL	FULL	NONE

This pseudo-class matches an element that's the root element of the document. In HTML documents, this selector matches the html element.

Example

In an HTML document, this selector will match the html element:

```
:root {
  : declarations
}
```

---

[12] http://www.konqueror.org/

Compatibility

Internet Explorer			Firefox			Safari			Opera
5.5	6.0	7.0	1.0	1.5	2.0	1.3	2.0	3.0	9.2
None	None	None	Full	Full	Full	Full	Full	Full	None

This pseudo-class is currently only supported by Firefox and Safari.

{} :empty

```
:empty {
declaration block
}
```

	SPEC		
	CSS3		
	BROWSER SUPPORT		
IE7	FF1+	Saf3+	Op9.2
NONE	BUGGY	FULL	NONE

This pseudo-class matches elements that have no children. Element nodes and non-empty text nodes are considered to be children; empty text nodes, comments, and processing instructions don't count as children. A text node is considered empty if it has a data length of zero; so, for example, a text node with a single space isn't empty.

Example

The selector p:empty will match the first paragraph, but not the second or third, in this example:

```
<p></p>
<p> </p>
<p>Hello, World!</p>
```

Compatibility

Internet Explorer			Firefox			Safari			Opera
5.5	6.0	7.0	1.0	1.5	2.0	1.3	2.0	3.0	9.2
None	None	None	Buggy	Buggy	Buggy	Buggy	Buggy	Full	None

In Firefox versions up to and including 2:

▨ The selector body:empty always matches the body element.

▨ The selector continues to match an element even after content has been added dynamically.

In Safari versions up to and including 2, when it appears in an internal style sheet (using `<style>` tags), this selector will always match. If this selector is used within an external style sheet, it works as designed.

 # :target

```
:target {
declaration block
}
```

SPEC			
CSS3			
BROWSER SUPPORT			
IE7	FF1+	Saf1.3+	Op9.2
NONE	FULL	BUGGY	NONE

This pseudo-class matches an element that's the target of a fragment identifier in the document's URI. The fragment identifier in a URI comprises a # character followed by an identifier name that matches the value of an `id` attribute of an element within the document.

Compatibility

Example

For example, if the URI was `http://www.example.com/index.html#section2`, the following selector would match the element that had an `id` attribute of `"section2"`:

```
:target {
  : declarations
}
```

Internet Explorer			Firefox			Safari			Opera
5.5	6.0	7.0	1.0	1.5	2.0	1.3	2.0	3.0	9.2
None	None	None	Full	Full	Full	Buggy	Buggy	Buggy	None

In Safari versions up to and including 3, this rule isn't applied when the user navigates using the back and forward buttons.

:enabled

SPEC
CSS3

BROWSER SUPPORT			
IE7	FF1.5+	Saf3+	Op9.2+
NONE	FULL	FULL	FULL

```
:enabled {
declaration block
}
```

This pseudo-class matches user interface elements that are enabled. An element is enabled when it can be activated or can gain focus—this usually means the element can be selected, clicked on, or accept text input.

Compatibility

Example

The following example will apply the rule to all **input** elements that are currently enabled:

```
input:enabled {
  declarations
}
```

Internet Explorer			Firefox			Safari			Opera
5.5	6.0	7.0	1.0	1.5	2.0	1.3	2.0	3.0	9.2
None	None	None	None	Full	Full	None	None	Full	Full

This pseudo-class is currently only supported in Safari 3, Firefox 1.5 and up, and Opera 9.2 and up.

:disabled

SPEC
CSS3

BROWSER SUPPORT			
IE7	FF1.5+	Saf3+	Op9.2+
NONE	FULL	FULL	FULL

```
:disabled {
declaration block
}
```

This pseudo-class matches user interface elements that are disabled. An element is disabled when it can't be activated or accept focus—this often means the element can't be selected, be clicked on, or accept text input, although it could do so if it was in an enabled state.

Example

The following rule will apply to all **input** elements that are currently disabled:

```
input:disabled {
  declarations
}
```

Compatibility

Internet Explorer			Firefox			Safari			Opera
5.5	6.0	7.0	1.0	1.5	2.0	1.3	2.0	3.0	9.2
None	None	None	None	Full	Full	None	None	Full	Full

This pseudo-class is currently only supported in Safari 3, Firefox 1.5 and up, and Opera 9.2 and up.

 # :checked Pseudo-class

SPEC			
CSS3			
BROWSER SUPPORT			
IE7	FF1+	Saf3+	Op9.2+
NONE	FULL	FULL	FULL

```
:checked {
declaration block
}
```

This pseudo-class matches elements like checkboxes or radio buttons that are checked or toggled to the "on" state. In HTML, this state corresponds to the `selected` and `checked` attributes.

Example

The following rule will apply to the element that has an `id` of `"confirm"` (for example, a checkbox) when that element has been checked:

```
#confirm:checked {
  : declarations
}
```

Compatibility

Internet Explorer			Firefox			Safari			Opera
5.5	6.0	7.0	1.0	1.5	2.0	1.3	2.0	3.0	9.2
None	None	None	Full	Full	Full	None	None	Full	Full

This pseudo-class is currently only supported in Safari 3, Firefox 1.0 and up, and Opera 9.2 and up.

{} :not(S)

```
:not(simple selector) {
declaration block
}
```

SPEC			
CSS3			
BROWSER SUPPORT			
IE7	FF1+	Saf1.3+	Op9.2
NONE	FULL	FULL	NONE

This pseudo-class is also known as the **negation pseudo-class**. The argument it takes can be any simple selector, but it can't contain either the negation pseudo-class or a pseudo-element. This pseudo-class matches elements that aren't matched by the specified selector.

Example

The following selector matches all elements except `table` elements:

```
:not(table) {
  : declarations
}
```

For example, the selector,

`input:not([type="submit"])`, matches all `input` elements, except `input` elements with a `type` value of `"submit"`—that is, HTML submit buttons.

Compatibility

Internet Explorer			Firefox			Safari			Opera
5.5	6.0	7.0	1.0	1.5	2.0	1.3	2.0	3.0	9.2
None	None	None	Full	Full	Full	Full	Full	Full	None

This pseudo-class is currently only supported by Firefox and Safari.

Pseudo-elements

Pseudo-elements match virtual elements that don't exist explicitly in the document tree. Pseudo-elements can be dynamic, inasmuch as the virtual elements they represent can change, for example, when the width of the browser window is altered. They can also represent content that's generated by CSS rules.

In CSS1 and CSS2, pseudo-elements start with a colon (:), just like pseudo-classes. In CSS3, pseudo-elements start with a double colon (::), which differentiates them from pseudo-classes.

CSS1 gave us :first-letter (p. 107) and :first-line (p. 110); CSS2 gave us generated content and the :before (p. 113) and :after (p. 114) pseudo-elements; and CSS3 added ::selection (p. 115).

:first-letter

```
:first-letter {
declaration block
}
```

SPEC			
CSS1			
BROWSER SUPPORT			
IE5.5+	FF1+	Saf1.3+	Op9.2+
BUGGY	BUGGY	FULL	BUGGY

The :first-letter pseudo-element is mainly used for creating common typographical effects like drop caps. This pseudo-element represents the first character of the first formatted line[13] of text in a block-level element, an inline block, a table caption, a table cell, or a list item.

Example

The following example selector will match the first letter of a p element:

```
p:first-letter {
  declarations
}
```

No other content (for example, an image) may appear before the text.

Certain punctuation characters, like quotation marks, that precede or follow the first character should be included in the pseudo-element. Despite the name, this pseudo-element will also match a digit that happens to be the first character in a block.

If the element is a list item, :first-letter applies to the first character of content after the list item marker unless the property list-style-position is set to inside, in which case the pseudo-element may be ignored by the user agent. If an element includes generated content created with the :before (p. 113) or :after (p. 114) pseudo-elements, :first-letter applies to the content of the element *including* the generated content (p. 347).

---

[13] http://www.w3.org/TR/CSS21/selector.html#first-formatted-line

The CSS2 specification[14] states that only certain CSS properties are to be supported for this pseudo-class.

Let's look at a code fragment that shows how this pseudo-element works:

```
<p>Hello, World!</p>
```

The selector p:first-letter matches the letter H. It's as if there were an extra element in the markup:

```
<p><p:first-letter>H</p:first-letter>ello, World!</p>
```

The above markup isn't valid HTML—it's just a visualization of the pseudo-element concept.

If the first child node of an element is another block element, this pseudo-element will propagate to the child node. Here's an example:

```
<div>
  <p>Hello, World!</p>
</div>
```

Both selectors—div:first-letter and p:first-letter—will match the letter H. The equivalent pseudo-markup is:

```
<div>
  <p>
    <div:first-letter>
      <p:first-letter>H</p:first-letter>
    </div:first-letter>ello, World!
  </p>
</div>
```

Compatibility

Internet Explorer			Firefox			Safari			Opera
5.5	6.0	7.0	1.0	1.5	2.0	1.3	2.0	3.0	9.2
Buggy	Buggy	Buggy	Buggy	Buggy	Buggy	Full	Full	Full	Buggy

---

[14]   http://www.w3.org/TR/CSS21/selector.html#first-letter

Internet Explorer versions up to and including 7, and Firefox versions up to and including 2 ignore the `letter-spacing` property when it's applied to this pseudo-element.

The behavior mentioned above, where if the first child node of an element is another block element, this pseudo-element is propagated to the child node, is not supported by Internet Explorer up to and including version 7, Firefox up to and including version 2, and Opera 9.2. However, Safari, up to and including version 3, does support this behavior correctly.

In Internet Explorer versions up to and including 7:

- Quotation marks are treated as punctuation, but all other characters are treated as letters.

- The list-item marker is included within this pseudo-element.

- The `float` property is not applied correctly—only a value of `left` is supported, and once it's set, it can't be overwritten with a value of `none` later in the style sheet.

- When this pseudo-element is applied to a positioned element that has a layout (p. 158), and whose first character is an inline descendant, the first line box isn't displayed.

- Bizarre specificity and inheritance problems affect this pseudo-element.[15]

Internet Explorer versions up to and including 7, Firefox versions up to and including 2, and Opera 9 will not include punctuation immediately following the first character in this pseudo-element.

In Opera 9.2, whitespace is counted as a letter if it's preceded only by punctuation.

In Internet Explorer 6, this pseudo-element fails if it's not immediately followed by whitespace. This means that whitespace must appear between the pseudo-element and the declaration block, as well as between the pseudo-element and the comma, if the pseudo-element isn't the last selector in a group of selectors.

---

[15] You can find some examples of this behavior at http://www.satzansatz.de/cssd/pseudocss.html.

Internet Explorer versions up to and including 6 will crash in certain situations involving this pseudo-element and underlined links. This problem's documented on the Quirksmode web site.[17]

:first-line

```
:first-line {
declaration block
}
```

SPEC			
CSS1			
BROWSER SUPPORT			
IE5.5+	FF1+	Saf1.3+	Op9.2+
BUGGY	PARTIAL	FULL	PARTIAL

This pseudo-element represents the first formatted line of text in a block-level element, an inline block, a table caption, or a table cell. As with the `:first-letter` pseudo-element, the first line may actually occur inside a block-level child element.

Example

The following selector will match the first line of a p element:

```
p:first-line {
  ⋮ declarations
}
```

The amount of text that's represented by `:first-line` depends on how the text is rendered—it's affected by factors like font size and line width. If the user changes the text size or the width of the browser window, more or fewer characters could become part of the pseudo-element.

Here's an example rule set and HTML block:

```
p:first-line {
   text-transform: uppercase;
}
```

```
<p>This is a paragraph of text containing several lines of text.
How this text is broken up into lines by a user agent depends on
how the text is rendered, font properties, size of browser window,
and size of viewing device.</p>
```

---

[17] http://tinyurl.com/2eecpg

The selector `p:first-line` will match the first line of text rendered by the user agent. We can see how a user agent might insert the pseudo-element into the HTML block like this:

```
<p><p:first-line>This is a paragraph of text</p:first-line>
containing several lines of text.
How this text is broken up into
lines by a user agent depends on
how the text is rendered, font
properties, size of browser
window, and size of viewing
device.</p>
```

The above markup isn't valid HTML; it's just a visualization of the pseudo-element concept.

If the first child node of an element is another block element, this pseudo-element will propagate to the child node. Here's another example:

```
<div>
  <p>This is a paragraph of text containing several lines of text.
  How this text is broken up into lines by a user agent depends on
  how the text is rendered, font properties, size of browser
  window, and size of viewing device.</p>
</div>
```

Both the `div:first-line` and `p:first-line` selectors will be able to be matched in this case. The equivalent pseudo-markup is:

```
<div>
  <p>
    <div:first-line>
      <p:first-line>This is a paragraph of text</p:first-line>
    </div:first-line>
    containing several lines of text.
    How this text is broken up into
    lines by a user agent depends on
    how the text is rendered, font
    properties, size of browser
    window, and size of viewing
    device.</p>
</div>
```

Compatibility

Internet Explorer			Firefox			Safari			Opera
5.5	6.0	7.0	1.0	1.5	2.0	1.3	2.0	3.0	9.2
Buggy	Buggy	Buggy	Partial	Partial	Partial	Full	Full	Full	Partial

The behavior mentioned above, where if the first child node of an element is another block element, this pseudo-element is propagated to the child node, is not supported by Internet Explorer up to and including version 7, Firefox up to and including version 2, and Opera 9.2. However, Safari, up to and including version 3, does support this behavior correctly.

In Internet Explorer 6, this pseudo-element fails if it's not immediately followed by whitespace. This means that whitespace must appear between the pseudo-element and the declaration block, as well as between the pseudo-element and the comma, if the pseudo-element isn't the last selector in a group of selectors.

In Internet Explorer versions up to and including 7:

■ This pseudo-element doesn't work when it's used on a positioned element that has a layout (p. 158).

■ This pseudo-element acts like a block element—it spans the entire width of the containing block instead of displaying inline (p. 166).

■ The list-item marker is included within this pseudo-element.

■ Bizarre specificity and inheritance problems affect this pseudo-element.[18]

---

[18] You can find some examples of this behavior at http://www.satzansatz.de/cssd/pseudocss.html.

:before

```
:before {
declaration block
}
```

	SPEC
	CSS2
BROWSER SUPPORT	

IE7	FF1+	Saf1.3+	Op9.2+
NONE	PARTIAL	FULL	BUGGY

This pseudo-element represents generated content (p. 347) rendered before another element, and is used in conjunction with the `content` property (p. 348). Additional properties can be specified to style the pseudo-element. Note that the generated content is only rendered—it doesn't become part of the document tree.

Example

In this example, the text "You are here:" is rendered before the document element with the `id` value of `"breadcrumbs"`, and given a right margin value of `0.5em`:

```
#breadcrumbs:before {
    content: "You are here:";
    margin-right: 0.5em;
}
```

Compatibility

Internet Explorer			Firefox			Safari			Opera
5.5	6.0	7.0	1.0	1.5	2.0	1.3	2.0	3.0	9.2
None	None	None	Partial	Partial	Partial	Full	Full	Full	Buggy

In Firefox versions up to and including 2, this pseudo-element is not fully stylable, most notably when it comes to applying positioning properties. Firefox appears to have implemented the original CSS2 specification.

In Firefox 1.5 and 2, this pseudo-element doesn't work for `fieldset` elements.

In Opera 9.2, whitespace is always displayed within this pseudo-element as if it's preformatted text—like whitespace in an HTML <pre> tag.

Other Relevant Stuff

content (p. 348)

inserts content before or after an element

{} :after

```
:after {
declaration block
}
```

	SPEC		
	CSS2		
BROWSER SUPPORT			
IE7	FF1+	Saf1.3+	Op9.2+
NONE	PARTIAL	FULL	BUGGY

This pseudo-element represents generated content (p. 347) that's rendered after another element. This pseudo-element is used in conjunction with the content property (p. 348), and additional properties can be specified to style it. Note that the generated content is only rendered—it doesn't become part of the document tree.

Example

This example will render the text "cm" in the color #cccccc, after a span element with a class value of "centimeters":

```
span.centimeters:after {
    content: "cm";
    color: #cccccc;
}
```

Compatibility

Internet Explorer			Firefox			Safari			Opera
5.5	6.0	7.0	1.0	1.5	2.0	1.3	2.0	3.0	9.2
None	None	None	Partial	Partial	Partial	Full	Full	Full	Buggy

In Firefox versions up to and including 2, this pseudo-element is not fully stylable, most notably when it comes to applying positioning properties. Firefox appears to have implemented the original CSS2 specification.

In Firefox 1.5 and 2, this pseudo-element doesn't work for fieldset elements.

In Opera 9.2, whitespace is always displayed within this pseudo-element as if it's preformatted text—like whitespace in an HTML <pre> tag.

Other Relevant Stuff

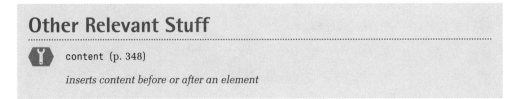

content (p. 348)

inserts content before or after an element

::selection

```
::selection {
declaration block
}
```

	SPEC	
	CSS3	
	BROWSER SUPPORT	
IE7	FF2	Saf1.3+	Op9.2
NONE	NONE	PARTIAL	NONE

This CSS3 pseudo-element represents a part of the document that's been highlighted by the user, including text in editable text fields. Only a small subset of CSS properties can be used in rules that apply to this pseudo-element; user agents must allow the `background` and `color` properties to be used, and can optionally allow the use of the `cursor` and `outline` properties.

Example

A selector like `textarea::selection` will match any user-selected text within a `textarea` element.

Compatibility

Internet Explorer			Firefox			Safari			Opera
5.5	6.0	7.0	1.0	1.5	2.0	1.3	2.0	3.0	9.2
None	None	None	None	None	None	Partial	Partial	Partial	None

Safari versions up to and including 3 don't support this pseudo-element in the case of `input` and `textarea` elements.

Chapter 5

The Cascade, Specificity, and Inheritance

Other than being the C in the acronym CSS, the fact that style sheets are described as "cascading" is an important, if complex, part of the way styles are applied to the elements in a document. It's called the CSS cascade (p. 118), because style declarations cascade down to elements from many origins.

The cascade combines the importance, origin, specificity (p. 126), and source order of the applicable style declarations to determine exactly—and without conflict—which declaration should be applied to any given element.

Inheritance (p. 133) is the means by which, in the absence of any specific declarations applied by the CSS cascade, a property value of an element is obtained from its parent element.

The Cascade

The CSS cascade uses selector pattern matching to apply to elements style declarations that have cascaded down through the document from various sources. But when two or more declarations apply to the same element, and set the same property, how does the browser determine which declaration to apply?

By combining importance, origin, specificity (p. 126), and the source order of the style concerned, the CSS cascade assigns a weight to each declaration. This weight is used to determine exactly, and without conflict, which style declarations should be applied to a specific element: the declaration with the highest weight takes precedence.

The Process of Resolution

The process of resolution employed by the CSS cascade for each property involves these four steps:

1. For a given property, find all declarations that apply to a specific element.
2. Sort the declarations according to their levels of importance, and origins.
3. Sort declarations with the same level of importance and origin by selector specificity.
4. Finally, if declarations have the same level of importance, origin, and specificity, sort them by the order in which they're specified; the last declaration wins.

In step one, a user agent finds all the valid declarations for the specific property to be applied to the element in question; to do so, it looks at all the sources that specify CSS styles for the given media type. Declarations can come from three sources: the user agent, the author, and user style sheets.

User agent style sheets are the default sets of declarations applied by the user agent. For example, according to the CSS specification,[1] the default value for the `text-decoration` (p. 332) property is `none`, but typically, user agents set this property to `underline` for a elements. In some user agents, the default settings can be changed;

---

[1] http://www.w3.org/TR/CSS21/text.html#decoration

for example, a user might be able to change the default background color, which may change the user agent style sheet.

A user agent may also allow a user to create a customized set of styles to use by default, or for specific documents. This custom style sheet is called a **user style sheet**. For instance, both Opera and Safari offer a facility that allows the user to select and use a separate style sheet file.

Author style sheets are those that are linked to the document via a `link` element, specified using a `style` element within the document's `head` element, or specified within an element `style` attribute (inline styles).

The user agent must search through all the user agent, author, and user style sheets until it has all the style declarations that are available for the property, and applicable to the element in question. The applicability of a declaration is determined by **selector pattern matching** (p. 59); a declaration is applied to an element if the declaration's selector matches the element. If there's more than one applicable declaration that sets a specific property on an element, the cascade proceeds to step two.

In step two, declarations that set the same property for the same element are sorted by their levels of importance, and their origins. A declaration can have either of two levels of importance: declarations that are appended with the `!important` statement are called **important declarations**; declarations that aren't are called **normal declarations**. You can read more about `!important` in !important Declarations (p. 124).

Declarations are sorted in the following order (from lowest to highest priority):

1. user agent declarations
2. normal declarations in user style sheets
3. normal declarations in author style sheets
4. important declarations in author style sheets
5. important declarations in user style sheets

The declaration with the highest priority is applied to the element. If two or more declarations that set the same property for the same element also have the same priority (that is, the same combination of importance level and origin), the cascade proceeds to step three.

In step three, declarations are sorted on the basis of the specificity of their selectors. The specificity of a selector is represented by four comma-separated values, and is calculated by counting the occurrences of different elements in the selector. For example, inline styles have the highest specificity, while element type selectors have the lowest specificity. A complete explanation of the specificity calculation requires more space than is available here; read more about it in Specificity (p. 126).

The declaration that has the selector with the highest specificity is applied to the element. However, if two or more declarations that set the same property for the same element also have the same levels of priority and specificity, the CSS cascade proceeds to step four.

Step four is the simplest step and makes the final determination about which declaration to apply to the element without ambiguity. The declaration that's specified last is the one that's applied to the element—a process that's often expressed as the latter declaration overwriting the former. A declaration can be overwritten by another within the same declaration block, within the same style sheet, or in another style sheet.

Declarations in external style sheets are specified in the order in which they're linked to the document. This is true for style sheets linked via the `link` element as well as those linked via the `@import` statement. Declarations within the style sheet containing the `@import` statements will overwrite all of the declarations in the linked style sheets.

Pay careful attention to the order of `link` and `style` elements within the document's `head`. Declarations in a `style` element will overwrite those in a style sheet linked via a `link` element if the `style` element is specified after the `link` element. However, it's a common mistake to assume that declarations in a `style` element automatically overwrite those in an external style sheet: if a `link` element is specified after a `style` element, the declarations in the linked style sheet will in fact overwrite those in the `style` element.

The conclusion of this whole process is that the CSS property for the element is set. However, you may be wondering about all the properties the CSS cascade doesn't set. For example, what happens when there's no applicable declaration to set the color property for an element? How does it get a foreground color? In the absence of such a declaration, some properties are inherited from the parent of the element.[2]

The alternative to relying on the inheritance mechanism is to use the property value inherit. Doing so ensures that the inherited value is included in the CSS cascade calculations, but be careful when you use inherit, as browser support for this property value is limited in Internet Explorer.[3] If a property isn't set via the CSS cascade, and it's not inherited, it's up to the user agent to supply a default value for the property.

The Cascade in Action

Let's explore the cascade's effect on a particular element. Consider this HTML fragment:

```
<!DOCTYPE HTML PUBLIC "-//W3C//DTD HTML 4.01//EN"
    "http://www.w3.org/TR/html4/strict.dtd">
<html>
  <head>
    <style type="text/css">
      body {
        color: #000;
        background-color: #fff;
      }
      #wrap {
        font-size: 2em;
        color: #333;
      }
      div {
        font-size: 1em;
      }
      em {
        color: #666;
      }
      p.item {
        color: #fff;
        background-color: #ccc;
```

---

[2] You can read more about inheritance in Inheritance (p. 133).
[3] Read more about inherit in The CSS Property Value inherit (p. 135).

```
         border-style: dashed;
      }
      p {
         border: 1px solid black;
         padding: 0.5em;
      }
    </style>
  </head>
  <body>
    <div id="wrap">
      <p class="item">
         This is the <em>cascade</em> in
         <a href="#">action</a>
      </p>
    </div>
  </body>
</html>
```

For the sake of brevity, all the styles affecting this document are specified in a `style` element in the document's `head` so they all have the same levels of importance and origin. Looking at the styles above, what do you expect the border style, font size, and foreground color to be for the `p` element?

Have a look at Figure 5.1 and see if you were correct.

Figure 5.1: The cascade in action

As you can see, the `border-style` is dashed, the `font-size` is 2em and the `color` is white. So where did these properties come from?

There are two CSS rules that apply to the `p` element:

```
p.item {
   color: #fff;
   background-color: #ccc;
   border-style: dashed;
}
p {
```

```
  border: 1px solid black;
  padding: 0.5em;
}
```

You can see there's no conflict for the color property; there's only one applicable declaration, so the `color` is set to `#fff`, or white. We do have a conflict for the `background-style` property, however, because there are two applicable declarations: `dashed` and `solid`. The next step, then, is to compare the specificity of the selectors. The selector `p.item`, has a higher specificity (0,0,1,1) than that of the selector p (0,0,0,1), so the property is set to `dashed`.

But where does the `font-size` value come from? There are no explicit declarations that set the `font-size` for the p element, but `font-size` is one of the properties that's inherited from an element's parent. The `div` element is the parent to our p element, and the CSS cascade has set its `font-size` to `2em` in response to the rule with the selector `#wrap`:

```
#wrap {
  font-size: 2em;
  color: #333;
}
```

Thus, our p element inherits the `font-size` value of `2em`. If our p element didn't have an applicable, explicit `color` declaration, it would have inherited the value `#333` from its parent, too.

The `em` element has a foreground color of `#666` because an applicable declaration is present in the code, as shown in the rule below:

```
em {
  color: #666;
}
```

Because the `em` element is a child of our p element, it would have inherited the foreground color `#fff` had the declaration not been present.

You may also be wondering why the anchor element is a different color and underlined, since we haven't applied any styling to it, and `color` is normally inherited from the parent element. In most user agent style sheets, anchor elements are styled blue and underlined, and the cascade applies user agent style sheet styles first. We could of course redefine the anchor's CSS properties ourselves; as we already know, declarations in an author style sheet will overwrite the same declarations in a user agent style sheet.

As you can see, the cascade works very well, and once you understand where the styles are coming from, you can control them much more easily.

💡 CSS Inspectors

Many useful tools are available for analyzing the document and identifying exactly where the styles on the page are coming from; they'll also help you comprehend this subject. One such tool for the Firefox browser is an extension called Firebug.[4] Similar extensions are available for Safari,[5] Opera,[6] and Internet Explorer.[7]

!important Declarations

During the importance and origin calculation in step two of the cascade resolution process, the !important statement can be used to add weight to a declaration. A declaration appended with the ! operator followed immediately by the keyword important, is said to be an **important declaration**, rather than a normal declaration. An important declaration in an author style sheet has more weight than a normal declaration in an author style sheet, but an important declaration in a user style sheet will trump them both.

In CSS1, important declarations in an author style sheet had greater weight than important declarations in a user style sheet. In order to improve the accessibility of documents that use CSS for presentation, CSS2 reversed the ranking and gave important declarations in user style sheets the highest weight. This facility allows users with special needs to specify desired settings like a larger font size, and to be confident that those settings will be applied.

---

[4] http://getfirebug.com/
[5] http://webkit.org/blog/?p=41
[6] http://dev.opera.com/tools/
[7] http://www.microsoft.com/downloads/details.aspx?familyid=e59c3964-672d-4511-bb3e-2d5e1db91038

Here's an example of an important declaration—in this case, a `font-size` declaration:

```
p {
  font-size: 1em !important;
}
```

If important declarations have the same origin, the normal rules of specificity and order specified apply. If `!important` is used on a declaration with a shorthand property, it's equivalent to adding `!important` to all of the individual subproperties.

Placement of `!important`

Make sure the `!important` statement is placed at the end of the declaration, just before the semicolon, and after the value. It will be invalid if it's located anywhere else. Note also that when a shorthand property is used, the statement must still appear at the end of the list of values for that property, not against each individual value. Here's an example:

```
.example {
  margin: 10px 12px 9px 8px !important;
}
```

The above rule would make all the margin values (top, right, bottom, and left margins) for elements within a class of `"example"` `!important`.

Internet Explorer Support

In Internet Explorer 6 and earlier, if an important declaration appears before a normal declaration for the same property within the same declaration block, the normal declaration will overwrite the important declaration.

Internet Explorer 6 and 7 give importance to a declaration when an illegal identifier is used in place of the keyword `important`, instead of ignoring the declaration as they should.

`!important` and Maintenance

Introducing even one uncommented important declaration into an author style sheet has a huge negative impact on the style sheet's maintainability, so it should be used with care. The only way to overwrite an important declaration is by using even more important declarations—an approach that soon becomes unmanageable. A style sheet that's littered with important declarations often signals that an author hasn't thought clearly enough about the structure of the CSS.

Specificity

Specificity is a mechanism within the CSS cascade that aids conflict resolution. The concept of specificity states that when two or more declarations that apply to the same element, and set the same property, have the same importance and origin (p. 118), the declaration with the most specific selector will take precedence.

Consider this example:

```
p {
    color: black;
    background-color: white;
}
div.warning p {
    color: red;
}
div#caution p {
    color: yellow;
}
body#home div p {
    color: white;
}
```

The above example style sheet contains four style rules that have a selector that matches p elements. Because one of those rules has an element type selector p, it's guaranteed that two or more rules will apply to the same p element, and because they all contain a color property declaration, the user agent needs a way to determine which of the declarations should be applied. What will the final color value be for the p element?

The simple answer is that the more specific selector's declaration will take precedence. The user agent calculates each selector's specificity so that a comparison can be made, and resolves the deadlock by choosing the declaration whose selector has the highest specificity.

Calculating Specificity

Here's a simplified description of the process by which the specificity of the selectors of two or more declarations is compared:

1. If one declaration is from a `style` attribute, rather than a rule with a selector (an inline style), it has the highest specificity. If none of the declarations are inline, proceed to step two.
2. Count the ID selectors (p. 65). The declaration with the highest count has the highest specificity. If two or more have the same number of ID selectors, or they all have zero ID selectors, proceed to step three.
3. Count the class selectors (p. 63) (for example, `.test`), attribute selectors (p. 67) (for example, `[type="submit"]`), and pseudo-classes (p. 80) (for example, `:hover`). The declaration with the highest total has the highest specificity. If two or more have the same total, or they all have totals of zero, proceed to step four.
4. Count the element type selectors (p. 62) (for example `div`) and pseudo-elements (p. 106) (for example, `:first-letter`). The declaration with the highest total has the highest specificity.

If two or more selectors have the same specificity, then, according to the rules of the CSS cascade, the latter specified rule takes precedence.

If you want to be technical, the W3C recommendation (6.4.3)[8] describes the method for calculating a selector's specificity. The result of this calculation takes the form of four comma-separated values, `a,b,c,d`,[9] where the values in column "a" are the most important and those in column "d" are least important. A selector's specificity is calculated as follows:

- To calculate `a`, count 1 if the declaration is from a `style` attribute rather than a rule with a selector (an inline style), 0 otherwise.
- To calculate `b`, count the number of ID attributes in the selector.
- To calculate `c`, count the number of other attributes and pseudo-classes in the selector.

---

[8]   http://www.w3.org/TR/CSS21/cascade.html#specificity
[9]   This is different from the CSS1 specification, in which specificity took the form of a number score, as explained at http://www.w3.org/TR/CSS1#cascading-order.

▦ To calculate d, count the number of element names and pseudo-elements in the selector.

The result of counting these elements is not a score, but a matrix of values that can be compared column by column. As an example, consider the following rule which contains an element type selector from the previous example:

```
p {
  color: black;
  background-color: white;
}
```

If we try to work out the specificity of the above selector on the basis of the specificity formula, we arrive at a result that looks like 0,0,0,1, as it has one element name.

As we said before, this is not a number but four comma-separated values, where the values in column a (inline styles) are the most important, and those in column d (element names and pseudo-elements) are the least important. When comparing selectors to determine which has the highest specificity, look from left to right, and compare the highest value in each column. So a value in column b will override values in columns c and d, no matter what they might be. As such, specificity of 0,1,0,0 would be greater than one of 0,0,10,10.

Specificity Step by Step

Let's try and break down each part of the calculation procedure so that it's more understandable.

The first step is to calculate the value for column a, which we've done in Table 5.1. If the style rule is specified within the element's HTML `style` attribute, a should equal 1; otherwise, it should equal 0. In fact, this is the only case where there is a value in column a.

Table 5.1: Inline Style: Column a = 1

Inline Style	IDs	Classes, Attributes, and Pseudo-classes	Element Types and Pseudo-elements
1	0	0	0

As you can see, an inline style rule will always have a specificity of 1,0,0,0—the highest level of specificity. Here's an example of such a style rule:

```
<p style="color:red;">Red Text</p>
```

This is one of the reasons why inline styles should be avoided. As inline style rules always have the highest specificity, the only way to overwrite them within the CSS cascade is to use the !important statement (p. 124) on the relevant declarations—an approach that creates a maintenance nightmare.

For rules other than inline styles, we need to calculate columns b, c, and d. Let's run through a full calculation for the following rule:

```
body#home div#warning p.message {
   color: red;
}
```

The above rule has a selector, body#home div#warning p.message, and a single declaration, color: red;. Since this isn't an inline style, we start off with a 0 in the first column, as Table 5.2 shows.

Table 5.2: Column a = 0

Inline Style	IDs	Classes, Attributes, and Pseudo-classes	Element Types and Pseudo-elements
0	?	?	?

To calculate the value for column b, we count the number of ID selectors in the selector. In our selector, body#home div#warning p, there are two—#home and #warning—thus, column b is equal to 2, as is depicted in Table 5.3.

Table 5.3: Column b = 2

Inline Style	IDs	Classes, Attributes, and Pseudo-classes	Element Types and Pseudo-elements
0	2	?	?

Next, we calculate the value for column c, counting the number of class selectors, attribute selectors, and pseudo-classes in the selector.

Attribute Selectors for IDs

Note that [id="foo"] is not equivalent to #foo—you can see there's a significant difference in their levels of specificity.

In our example selector, body#home div#warning p.message, there's one class selector, .message, so, as you can see in Table 5.4, c is equal to 1.

Table 5.4: Column c = 1

Inline Style	IDs	Classes, Attributes, and Pseudo-classes	Element Types and Pseudo-elements
0	2	1	?

Finally, for column d, we count the number of element type selectors and pseudo-elements in the selector. In our example selector, body#home div#warning p.message, there are three: body, div, and p. There are no pseudo-elements to be counted, so we put a 3 in the last column, as Table 5.5 shows.

Table 5.5: Column d = 3

Inline Style	IDs	Classes, Attributes, and Pseudo-classes	Element Types and Pseudo-elements
0	2	1	3

We now have our result. The specificity for the selector body#home div#warning p.message can be expressed as: 0,2,1,3.

All right, let's consider a crazy situation where more than half a dozen color declarations for the same p element have the same levels of importance and origins. Which color would the browser apply to the element?

Here's our crazy style sheet:

```
p.message {
  color: green;
}
#home #warning p.message {
  color: yellow;
}
#warning p.message {
  color: white;
}
body#home div#warning p.message {
  color: blue;
}
p {
  color: teal;
}
* body#home>div#warning p.message {
  color: red;
}
#warning p {
  color: black;
}
```

We should be able to use the specificity calculation method to work out which of the declarations would be applied. But, wait a minute! What are the levels of specificity of the universal selector (p. 60), *, and the child combinator (p. 76), >?

The answer is that they don't have any specificity at all; they're simply ignored in all calculations. This is true for all combinators, which you can treat as though they had a specificity of zero, as they will make no difference to your calculation. After all, five out of the seven selectors above use the descendant combinator (p. 74) and you weren't worried about those!

See if you can work out the specificity of all the selectors above for yourself before looking at the answer in Table 5.6.

Table 5.6: Selector Specificity Results

Selector	Inline Style	IDs	Classes, Attributes, and Pseudo-classes	Element Types and Pseudo-elements
body#home div#warning p.message	0	2	1	3
* body#home>div#warning p.message	0	2	1	3
#home #warning p.message	0	2	1	1
#warning p.message	0	1	1	1
#warning p	0	1	0	1
p.message	0	0	1	1
p	0	0	0	1

The results have been ordered according to specificity—the highest are at the top, and the lowest are at the bottom. As you can see, the top two selectors have exactly the same specificity, despite the extra universal selector and combinator in one of them. In this case, they tie for specificity and the one that appears last in the style sheet will be the winner. If you look at the original style sheet source above, the red color will be applied to the p element.

You can see from Table 5.6 that the selector p.message has a lower specificity than the selector #warning p. This is a common cause of head scratching among those new to CSS, who often think that a class selector will be specific enough to match an element in all cases.

Inheritance

Inheritance is the process by which properties are passed from parent to child elements even though those properties have not been explicitly defined by other means. Certain properties are inherited automatically, and as the name implies, a child element will take on the characteristics of its parent with regards to these properties.

Inheritance and the Cascade

Inheritance is a mechanism that's separate from the cascade: inheritance applies to the DOM (Document Object Model) tree, while the cascade deals with the style sheet rules. However, CSS properties set on an element via the cascade can be inherited by that element's child elements.

For example, if a `div` element has a `font-size` of `20px` then, assuming that no other `font-size` declarations have been explicitly defined, any children will also inherit that `font-size` value.

Why is this a good thing? Consider the following code:

```
div {
    font-size: 20px;
}
```

```
<div>
  <p>
    This <em>sentence</em> will have a 20px
    <a href="#">font-size</a>.
  </p>
</div>
```

If inheritance wasn't at work in the above code, we'd have to specify a `font-size` declaration for each element in turn, to make sure that all the content in the sentence was rendered at `20px`:

```
p {
    font-size: 20px;
}
```

```
em {
  font-size: 20px;
}
a {
  font-size: 20px;
}
```

With inheritance working in our favor, we merely have to set the `font-size` on the parent; all the children will inherit the `font-size` automatically. This is why you only need to set the `font-size` on the body element to have the whole page rendered at that font size—unless of course it has been explicitly defined elsewhere.

Quirks Mode Inheritance Bugs

Note that modern browsers operating in quirks mode behave a little buggily in that they don't inherit certain properties into tables. This quirks mode behavior emulates the buggy behavior of much older browsers. Usually, these properties have to be specifically applied to the table element, although a better approach would be to avoid the issue altogether by using a doctype that causes the browser to use standards mode rendering. To learn more about doctypes and rendering modes, see Standards Mode, Quirks Mode, and Doctype Sniffing (p. 17).

`font-size` Inheritance

In the above example, we used a `font-size` of 20px on the parent `div` element. That value was inherited by the `div`'s child elements, but can you imagine what would happen if we set the `font-size` property of the `div` element to a percentage size:

```
div {
  font-size: 130%;
}
```

At first glance, you may be thinking that the `p` element inside the `div` will inherit a `font-size` of 130%, and will therefore be 130% bigger than its parent. You don't need to worry, though, because this is taken care of for you: the `p` element will inherit only the actual computed font size of the parent—not the 130% scaling factor—and will therefore be the same size as the parent. This is not the same as if we had specified the following:

```
div, p, a {
  font-size: 130%;
}
```

In the above code, the p element would be 130% bigger than its parent div, and the nested anchor element would be 130% bigger still than the p element. Take care when you're setting percentage and em font sizes on nested elements, or this sort of compounding will occur.

As we already mentioned (before we were sidetracked!), only some properties are inherited from the parent automatically. The reason for this is quite obvious if you think about it. If, for instance, borders were inherited from the parent, the result would look very messy! Not only would the parent element have a border, but so would every child element; the result would be disastrous.

The foreground color is inherited by default, but backgrounds aren't. Again, the reason for this is obvious: in most cases, you'd want the foreground color to be inherited by child elements, but if the parent element had a background image, you wouldn't want the child elements to have the same image, as their background images probably conflict with their parent's background image.

A lot of people think that the background-color property is also inherited. In fact this is not the case. The default value for background-color is transparent. This accomplishes what's usually desired anyway, because the parent's background color will be visible through the child element's transparent background.

On the other hand, you may want to force the background to be inherited. If so, you may be able to use the inherit property value (p. 135). The inherit property value has other uses too; it allows you to increase the weight of an inherited property by adding it to the author style sheet.

The CSS Property Value `inherit`

Even though certain characteristics are inherited automatically in CSS, there may be situations in which you want to increase the weight of the inherited property. Specifying a value of inherit for any CSS property that's applied to an element will cause the element to gain its parent's computed value for the property in question. By specifying in the author style sheet that a property should inherit its value, you can increase its weight.

Internet Explorer Support for `inherit`

Internet Explorer 7 and earlier versions don't support the value `inherit` for any properties other than `direction` (p. 343) and `visibility` (p. 273).

Normally, in the absence of any applicable declaration, the `color` property is inherited. However, in the case of anchor elements, the `color` property is commonly set to blue in the user agent style sheet. If you wanted to reinforce the importance of the inherited value, you could use the value `inherit` in an author or user style sheet, overwriting the user agent style sheet declaration. In the following example, we set the foreground color of the `p` element to `#000`, or black, and specify that any child anchor elements should inherit the value of the foreground color from their parent element:

```
p {
  color: #000;
}
p a:link {
  color: inherit;
}
```

When you're using shorthand notation such as `background`, you can't mix `inherit` with other values. For example, the following `background` declaration is wrong:

```
p {
  background: #fff inherit left top;
}
```

In this case, you might be hoping that this element will inherit the parent's `background-image` property. Unfortunately, you'd be out of luck. `inherit` must be the only value in the declaration, because there's simply no way of identifying the subproperty to which the value `inherit` refers—after all, it's not unique within the sequence. In the example above, `inherit` becomes ambiguous: it could refer to the `background-image` property, or to the `background-attachment` property, and the user agent has no way of knowing which one it applies to. To have an element inherit a specific property, you need to use the full notation instead of shorthand. In this case, we need to specify the `background-image` property:

```
p {
  background-image: inherit;
}
```

To find if a property is inherited by default, refer to the specific property reference page.

Summary

The word "cascading" in the name Cascading Style Sheets refers to the way that styles cascade from various style sheet sources to the elements in the document tree. The CSS cascade (p. 118) is the process of resolution that determines the final value of a property when multiple applicable declarations exist for that property.

The process can be summarized as:

1. Find all declarations that apply to a specific element.
2. Sort the declarations according to their importance and origins.
3. Sort declarations with the same levels of importance and origin by selector specificity.
4. Sort declarations with the same levels of importance, origin, and specificity by their source order.

To calculate the priority of importance and origin, the cascade uses this list (in order from lowest to highest priority):

1. user agent declarations
2. normal declarations in user style sheets
3. normal declarations in author style sheets
4. important declarations in author style sheets
5. important declarations in user style sheets

To give importance to a declaration, append `!important` (p. 124) to it. The use of `!important` in author style sheets isn't recommended, however, because it can make maintenance difficult.

Specificity (p. 126) is calculated by counting the components of the declarations' selectors. Inline styles have the highest degree of specificity; element type selectors have the lowest.

If a property isn't set via the CSS cascade, it may be inherited (p. 133) automatically from a parent element. Not all properties are inherited in this way.

The property value `inherit` can be used to increase the weight of the inherited property in the cascade; however, lack of support from Internet Explorer limits its usefulness.

Chapter

CSS Layout and Formatting

While CSS1 didn't have much to offer for the graphical layout of documents, CSS2 has introduced several new properties for layout, and CSS3 will probably add even more. Although CSS still doesn't provide total control over the page layout, it's far more powerful than the old-school technique of using layout tables and presentational markup.

A web browser typically reads and renders HTML documents. This happens in two phases: the **parsing phase** and the **rendering phase**.

During the parsing phase, the browser reads the markup in the document, breaks it down into components, and builds a document object model (DOM) tree.[1]

Consider this example HTML document:

---

[1] It's called a tree, because a graphical representation of the DOM looks much like an upside-down tree.

```
<!DOCTYPE html PUBLIC "-//W3C//DTD HTML 4.01//EN"
    "http://www.w3.org/TR/html4/strict.dtd">
<html>
  <head>
    <title>Widgets</title>
  </head>
  <body>
    <h1>Widgets</h1>
    <p>Welcome to Widgets, the number one company
    in the world for selling widgets!</p>
  </body>
</html>
```

The above HTML document can be visualized as the DOM tree in Figure 6.1 (in which the text nodes have been omitted for clarity).

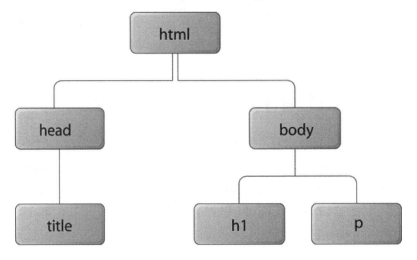

Figure 6.1: The DOM tree

Each object in the DOM tree is called a **node**. There are several types of nodes, including element nodes and text nodes. At the top of the tree is a document node, which contains an element node called the **root node**; this is always the html element in HTML and XHTML documents, and it branches into two child element nodes—head and body—which then branch into other children.

A **child node** is structurally subordinate to its **parent node**. In HTML terms, this means that the child's tags are nested inside the tags of the parent. For example, we can see in Figure 6.1 that the h1 element is a child node of the body element and the body element is the parent node of the h1 element. A node can be called a

descendant node if it's a child, grandchild, and so on, of another node. A node can be called an **ancestor node** if it's a parent, grandparent, and so on, of another node. For example, the h1 element is a descendant node of the html element, and the html element is an ancestor node of the h1 element. Nodes that have the same parent are called **siblings**. The h1 and p elements are sibling nodes.

When the DOM tree has been constructed, and any CSS style sheets have been loaded and parsed, the browser starts the rendering phase. Each node in the DOM tree will be rendered as zero or more boxes.

Just as there are block-level elements and inline elements in HTML, there are block boxes and inline boxes in CSS. In fact, there are several other box types, but they can be seen as subtypes of the block and inline boxes.

A CSS box is always rectangular.[2] It has four sides with a 90° angle between each of them.

From a somewhat simplified perspective, we can say that it's the user agent style sheet (p. 118) which specifies that block-level HTML elements generate block boxes, while inline-level HTML elements generate inline boxes. We can, of course, use the display property to change the type of the box generated for any element.

CSS does not, however, affect the markup in any way. The separation into block-level and inline elements in HTML is specified in the HTML document type definition, and cannot be changed. For example, setting the display property to block for a span element doesn't allow us to nest an h1 element inside it, because the HTML document type definition forbids it.

The Viewport, the Page Box, and the Canvas

In a continuous output medium, such as a computer monitor, a browser displays a web document in a **viewport**—a rectangular window through which we can view a part of the document. In a paged medium, such as printed paper, each page can

---

[2] This may change in future versions of CSS, but then we will have to call them something other than "boxes."

be seen as a viewport whose dimensions are the same as the **page box** (the printable part of the page, excluding any page margins).

The browser renders the document on a **canvas**, which, consequently, is at least as large as the document itself. If the viewport is larger than the document, the canvas fills the viewport.

Any background color or image that's specified for the root element—the `html` element for HTML and XHTML documents—will be rendered as the background for the whole canvas, rather than for the root element alone.[3] In other words, the background specified for the root element will cover the entire content area of the browser window, even if the document doesn't contain enough content to fill the whole window.

The CSS Box Model

Your understanding of the box model concept, and how it relates to the way in which an element's final dimensions are determined, will be essential to your understanding of how an element is positioned on a web page. The box model applies to block-level elements. A companion concept, the inline layout model, defines how inline elements are positioned, and is covered in Inline Formatting (p. 166).

Calculating Box Dimensions

In CSS2.1, block-level elements can only be rectangular. We calculate the overall dimensions of a block-level element by taking into account the height and width of the content area, as well as any margins, padding, and borders that are applied to the element.

We can define the content width of an element by declaring its `width` (p. 194) and `height` (p. 188) properties. If no declarations are applied, the default value for the `width` and `height` properties is `auto`.

---

[3] This is not the case in Internet Explorer 5.5 and prior versions, where if a background is specified for the `body` element, it will cover the whole canvas and obscure any background that's specified for the `html` element.

For static (non-positioned) elements, and relatively positioned (p. 176) elements where the `width` property has the value `auto`, the **computed width** will be the width of the containing block minus any horizontal margins, borders, padding, and scrollbars. That is, it will be whatever's left over when horizontal margins, borders, padding, and scrollbars (if any) have been deducted from the width of the containing block.

The **containing block** is the reference rectangle whose position and dimensions are used for relative calculations of descendant elements' positions and dimensions. Although elements are positioned with respect to their containing block, they're not confined by it, and they may overflow. In most cases, generated boxes act as containing blocks for descendant boxes. The full details of containing blocks are covered in Containing Block (p. 147).

For floated (p. 180) or absolutely positioned (p. 178) elements (including elements for which `position` is set to `fixed` (p. 178)), a `width` of `auto` will make the generated box shrink to the intrinsic dimensions of its contents.

Floated Elements and Width

Previously, in CSS2, floated elements without a declared `width` value would not shrink to wrap their content; instead, they'd expand to the full width of their parent element. This behavior was changed in CSS2.1 to allow the shrink-wrapping to take place. However, in Internet Explorer 6 and earlier versions, a floated element with no declared `width` value will shrink to wrap its content as per the specifications unless a child element has a layout (p. 158), in which case the floated parent will expand to fill the available content width of the parent.[4]

It should also be noted that when a float (without a declared width) contains a right-floated child element, it will also expand to fill the parent's available content width in IE browsers up to and including version 7 (Firefox up to and including version 2.0 also exhibits this bug but, the problem appears to have been fixed as of Firefox 3.0 Alpha 6).

Therefore, it's always safer to specify an explicit value for the width of a floated element where possible, and thereby to avoid the buggy behavior described above. However, as long as you're aware of the problems mentioned above, you'll likely

---

[4] A quick fix for this bug is to float the offending child element as well (where the situation allows for it).

find that widthless floats can be useful in certain situations, such as fluid-width horizontal menus.

No matter how the content area is positioned, its `height` value will be equal to the content height if no values have been declared for `height`, or for `min-height` and `max-height`.

Therefore, to ascertain the total space required to place an element on the page, add the content area's dimensions to any padding, borders, and margins that have been declared. Of course, an element may have no padding, border, or margins, in which case its dimensions will be dictated solely by its content.

If an element contains only floated or absolutely positioned elements, it will have no content at all, and its height will be zero. We'll discuss this more in Floating and Clearing (p. 180).

Implementing the Box Model

The box model is best demonstrated with a short example. The calculation we'll use to ascertain the total space required to accommodate an element on the page (ignoring margin collapse for the time being—see below for more on this) will be as follows:

```
Total width = left margin + left border + left padding + width +
              right padding + right border + right margin

Total height = top margin + top border + top padding + height +
               bottom padding + bottom border + bottom margin
```

Here's our example CSS—a rule set that contains declarations for all the box properties of an element that has the `class` `"box"`:

```
.box {
  width: 300px;
  height: 200px;
  padding: 10px;
  border: 1px solid #000;
  margin: 15px;
}
```

The total size of the element above will be calculated as follows:

```
Total width  = 15 + 1 + 10 + 300 + 10 + 1 + 15 = 352px
Total height = 15 + 1 + 10 + 200 + 10 + 1 + 15 = 252px
```

The above calculation is depicted in Figure 6.2, which is taken from the element layout display from Firebug,[5] the JavaScript and CSS development add-on for Firefox.

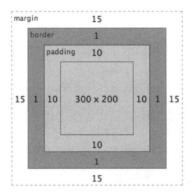

Figure 6.2: The CSS box model in action

In Figure 6.2, we can clearly see the content area in the center, the padding around the content area, the border area, and the margin area. The outer edge of the content area is called the **content edge** or **inner edge**; the outer edge of the padding area is called the **padding edge**; the outer edge of the border area is called the **border edge**; and the outer edge of the margin area is called—you guessed it—the **margin edge** or **outer edge**.

You can see from this short example that, for this element to fit on the page, we'll need a space that's at least 352px wide and 252px high. If the space available is any smaller than this, the element will be misplaced, or will overflow its containing block. Note that Internet Explorer 6 and earlier versions will most likely stretch the containing block to accommodate this extra height, and could severely disrupt the layout. Other browsers will let the element overflow its boundaries, but will ignore the content.

[5] http://getfirebug.com/

Watch Out for Collapsing Margins

Although margins are included in the above calculations for the total space required to place the element, note that vertically adjacent margins on static (non-positioned) elements would collapse into the bigger margin of the elements that are adjacent above and below. This means that the actual space required to place an element would not necessarily extend from the margin edges of elements existing on the page: only the biggest margin will apply, and the smaller margins will appear to overlap the bigger margins. See Collapsing Margins (p. 148) for the full details of this quite complicated subject.

Practical Considerations of the Box Model

An important point to note is that an element that has its `width` set to 100% (that is, 100% of the content width of its parent element) shouldn't have any margins, padding, or borders applied, as this would make it far too big for the space that it sits in. This is often overlooked by authors and can severely disrupt a page's layout, as content will either overflow or push elements wider than they should be.

The solution, in most cases, is to avoid adding a value for the property `width` (other than `auto`), and to apply the margins, padding, and borders only. The `width` property of a static element will default to `auto`, and even with padding, borders, and margins added, it will still assume the full available content width.

Of course, this approach may not be feasible in some instances, such as cases where the element is not a static element, and requires the definition of a specific width value (as in the case of a floated element that doesn't automatically expand to fill its parent). In these cases, you have two options.

If the available space is of a fixed width, you can simply add the value of each component together to ensure that it matches the available width. For example, if the available space is 500px wide, and you require an element to have 20px padding, simply set the `width` to 460px and the `padding` to 20px for that element (20 + 460 + 20 = 500). This solution assumes that the length values specified for the element's box properties use the same unit of measurement, since you won't be able to add together a mixture of units (200px + 10%, for example, makes no sense in this context).

When the available content space has an unknown width—as in the case of a fluid layout—this method can't be used, as percentages and pixels can't be added together. In this case, the solution is to declare a `width` of `100%` for the element concerned, and to apply the padding, border, and margin values to a nested element instead. That nested element has no `width` declaration, and can display the required padding, borders, and margins without encroaching on the parent element.

Now that you have a clear understanding of the CSS box model, you should also make yourself familiar with what's commonly called the Internet Explorer 5 box model (p. 156).

Containing Block

CSS rendering comprises the tasks of laying out and rendering numerous boxes. Element boxes are positioned within a formatting context, which, by default, is provided by the box generated by a parent element.

When we specify the positions or dimensions of element boxes, we're doing so relative to what's known as the **containing block**, which is a very important concept in CSS layout.

The containing block for the root element is called the **initial containing block**, and has the same dimensions as the viewport (p. 141) for continuous media (such as the screen) and the page area for paged media (such as print).

The containing block for any other element box is determined by the value of the `position` property for that element.

If the value of the `position` property is `static` (the default) or `relative`, the containing block is formed by the edge of the content box of the nearest ancestor element whose `display` property value is one of:

- `block`
- `inline-block`
- `list-item`
- `run-in` (only in a block formatting context; see Formatting Concepts (p. 163))

CSS Layout and Formatting

- `table`
- `table-cell`

If the value of the `position` property is `absolute`, the containing block is the nearest positioned ancestor—in other words, the nearest ancestor whose `position` property has one of the values `absolute`, `fixed`, or `relative`. The containing block is formed by the padding edge of that ancestor.

If the value of the `position` property is `fixed`, the containing block is the viewport (for continuous media) or the page box (for paged media).

Note that although positions and dimensions are given with respect to the containing block, a descendant box isn't constrained by its containing block; it may overflow.

Content Edge and Padding Edge

The content edge of a box is defined by the outer limits of the content area—it doesn't include any padding that may exist outside the content.

The padding edge of a box is defined by the outer limits of the padding area—it doesn't include any borders that may exist outside the padding. If a box has no padding, the padding edge is equivalent to the content edge.

Refer to The CSS Box Model (p. 142) for a graphic illustration of these concepts.

Collapsing Margins

Let's explore exactly what the consequences of collapsing margins are, and how they will affect elements on the page.

The W3C specification[6] defines collapsing margins as follows:

"In this specification, the expression collapsing margins means that adjoining margins (no non-empty content, padding, or border areas, or clearance separate them) of two or more boxes (which may be next to one another or nested) combine to form a single margin."

---

[6] http://www.w3.org/TR/CSS21/box.html#collapsing-margins

In simple terms, this definition indicates that when the vertical margins of two elements are touching, only the margin of the element with the largest margin value will be honored, while the margin of the element with the smaller margin value will be collapsed to zero.[7] In the case where one element has a negative margin, the margin values are added together to determine the final value. If both are negative, the greater negative value is used. This definition applies to adjacent elements and nested elements.

There are other situations where elements do not have their margins collapsed:

- floated elements
- absolutely positioned elements
- inline-block elements
- elements with `overflow` set to anything other than `visible` (They do not collapse margins with their children.)
- cleared elements (They do not collapse their top margins with their parent block's bottom margin.)
- the root element

This is a difficult concept to grasp, so let's dive into some examples.

Collapsing Margins Between Adjacent Elements

Margins collapse between adjacent elements. In simple terms, this means that for adjacent vertical block-level elements in the normal document flow, only the margin of the element with the largest margin value will be honored, while the margin of the element with the smaller margin value will be collapsed to zero. If, for example, one element has a 25px bottom margin and the element immediately underneath it has a 20px top margin, only the 25px bottom margin will be enforced, and the elements will remain at a distance of 25px from each other. They will not be 45px (25+20) apart, as might be expected.

This behavior is best demonstrated with a short example. Consider the following code:

---

[7] In CSS2.1, horizontal margins do not collapse.

```
h1 {
  margin: 0 0 25px 0;
  background: #cfc;
}
p {
  margin: 20px 0 0 0;
  background: #cf9;
}
```

Heading Content

25px gap

Paragraph content

Figure 6.3: Collapsing margins in action

As you'll see from Figure 6.3, the gap between the elements is only 25px, and the smaller margin has collapsed to zero. If in the above example the elements had equal margins (say, 20 pixels each), the distance between them would be only 20px.[8]

There is one situation that will cause a slight deviation from the behavior of collapsing margins: should one of the elements have a negative top or bottom margin, the positive and negative margins will be added together to reach the final, true margin. Here's an example style sheet that demonstrates the concept:

```
h1 {
  margin: 0 0 25px 0;
  background: #cfc;
}
p {
  margin: -20px 0 0 0;
  background: #cf9;
}
```

The bottom margin of the h1 element is a positive number (25px), and the top margin of the p element is a negative number (-20px). In this situation, the two numbers are added together to calculate the final margin: 25px + (-20px) = 5px.

If the result of this calculation is a negative number, this value will have the effect of one element overlapping the other. You could say that the negative margin pulls

---

[8] This will also hold true for the margins between nested children and their parents.

the element in the opposite direction to that of a positive margin. See margin (p. 209) for more details about negative margins.

Collapsing Margins Between Parent and Child Elements

So far, we've only addressed the collapsing effect on adjacent elements, but the same process holds true for parents and children whose margins touch. By "touch," we mean the places at which no padding, borders, or content exist between the adjacent margins. In the following example, a parent element has a child element on which a top margin is set:

```
h1 {
  margin: 0;
  background: #cff;
}
div {
  margin: 40px 0 25px 0;
  background: #cfc;
}
p {
  margin: 20px 0 0 0;
  background: #cf9;
}
```

In the style sheet above, you can see that a top margin value is declared for the p element, and in the code excerpt below, you can see that the p element is a child of the div element:

```
<h1>Heading Content</h1>
<div>
  <p>Paragraph content</p>
</div>
```

The result of this code is illustrated in Figure 6.4.

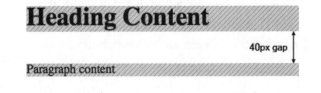

Figure 6.4: Collapsing margins on a child paragraph

You may have expected that the paragraph would be located 60px from the heading, since the div element has a margin-top of 40px and there is a further 20px margin-top on the p element. You may also have expected that 20px of the background color of the div element would show above the paragraph. This does not happen because, as you can see in Figure 6.4, the margins collapse together to form one margin. Only the largest margin applies (as in the case of adjoining blocks), as we've already seen.

In fact we would get the same result if our div element had no top margin and the p element had a 40px margin-top. The 40px margin-top on the p element effectively becomes the top margin of the div element, and pushes the div down the page by 40px, leaving the p element nesting snugly at the top. No background would be visible on the div element above the paragraph.

In order for the top margins of both elements to be displayed, and for the background of the div element to be revealed above the p element, there would need to be a border or padding that would stop the margins collapsing. If we simply add a top border to the div element, we can achieve the effect we were originally looking for:

```
h1 {
  margin: 0;
  background: #cff;
}
div {
  margin: 40px 0 25px 0;
  background: #cfc;
  border-top: 1px solid #000;
}
p {
  margin: 20px 0 0 0;
  background: #cf9;
}
```

In Figure 6.5, we can see that the div element is still 40px away from the heading, but the paragraph has been pushed a further 20px down the page, thus revealing 20px of the background of the div element (through the presence of the border).

Figure 6.5: Adding a border to the parent

If we didn't want a visible top border showing in the design, a `1px` top padding on the `div` element would have achieved the same effect. Note that the border or padding should be applied to the parent `div` because a border on the paragraph would not stop the margins from collapsing, since the paragraph's margin is outside of the border.

Internet Explorer and Layout

As of this writing, Internet Explorer versions 7 and below will not collapse margins where the element has a layout. If the `div` in our example simply had a width set (one of the triggers that causes an element to gain a layout), we'd get the result shown in Figure 6.5, without the need to add padding or borders.

This is non-standard behavior for IE, and is perhaps one of the reasons why beginners are a little confused by the concept of collapsing margins when they first come across it. Most of the time, the elements will have a value (other than `auto`) for the `width` property (or one of the other properties that causes an element to gain a layout), and will not exhibit the collapsing margin behavior in IE.

The example above deals with a single parent and single child that have touching margins, but the same approach would apply if there were several children (that is, nested elements) that all had adjacent vertical margins: it would still mean that all the margins would collapse into one single margin. Although the examples above mentioned top margins, the same effect is true for bottom margins, as can be seen below.

In the following contrived example, we've nested four `div` elements, all of which have a `10px` margin applied. Each `div` has a different background color, so the effects of the margin collapse will be clearly visible:

```css
.box {
  margin: 10px;
}
.a {
  background: #777;
}
.b {
  background: #999;
}
.c {
  background: #bbb;
}
.d {
  background: #ddd;
}
.e {
  background: #fff;
}
```

```html
<div class="box a">
  <div class="box b">
    <div class="box c">
      <div class="box d">
        <div class="box e">
          The vertical margins collapse but the horizontal
          margins don't. The vertical margins also collapse
          in IE because the elements don't have a layout.
        </div>
      </div>
    </div>
  </div>
</div>
```

The result of the above CSS is shown in Figure 6.6.

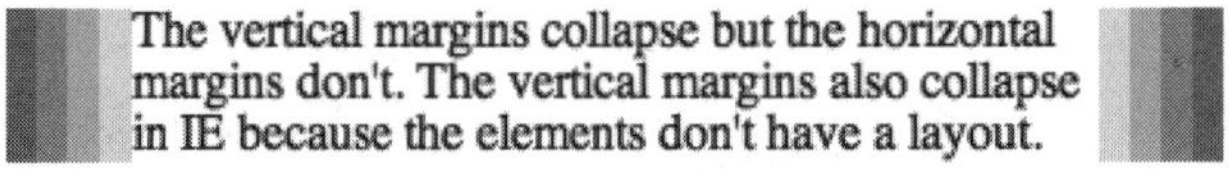

The vertical margins collapse but the horizontal margins don't. The vertical margins also collapse in IE because the elements don't have a layout.

Figure 6.6: Vertical margins after collapse

As you can see in this example, the effect of our CSS is quite dramatic: all the vertical margins have collapsed to form a single, 10px margin. Unlike the horizontal margin example, where all the margins were visible, the vertical margins show no such colors at all, thanks to the background-color that has been applied to each element.

The whole block will be positioned 10px from other in-flow elements on the page, but each nested block will collapse its margins into a single margin.

As discussed earlier, the simplest way to stop the margin collapse from occurring is to add padding or borders to each element. If we wanted 10px margins on each element we could simply use a 9px margin and 1px of padding to get the result we wanted:

```
.box {
  margin: 9px;
  padding: 1px;
}
```

The result of that small change will "un-collapse" the vertical margins, as you can see in Figure 6.7.

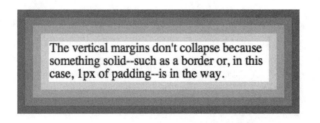

Figure 6.7: Margins haven't collapsed

Again, it's important to consider the effects that layout in Internet Explorer would have in the above demonstrations. Should the elements in the first example (Figure 6.6) have a layout in IE, the result would be exactly as shown in Figure 6.7. It's also worth noting that in browsers other than IE, the same effect would occur if the overflow property was added with a value other than visible.

Wrapping It Up

Although the margin collapse behavior is at first a little unintuitive, it does make life easier in the case of multiple nested elements, where the behavior is often desirable. As shown above, easy methods are available to help you stop the collapse if required.

The Internet Explorer 5 Box Model

Relevance of the Internet Explorer 5 Box Model

This topic is included mainly for a historical reference, as Internet Explorer 5.5 and earlier versions have less than 1% market share today. However, Internet Explorer 6 and 7, and Internet Explorer 5 for Mac, all use this box model when they're operating in quirks mode (p. 17), so the topic still has some relevance today.

In the CSS box model (p. 142), as defined by the CSS2.1 specifications, an element ascertains its total dimensions by adding together the content area dimensions plus any margin, padding, or borders that may have been declared. Conversely, if we use the Internet Explorer 5 box model (the IE5 box model for short),[9] padding and borders will shrink the content area's dimensions instead of increasing the element's total dimensions.

To demonstrate, the following rule sets several properties that affect the dimensions of .box elements:

```
.box {
  width: 200px;
  height: 150px;
  padding: 10px;
  border: 1px solid #000;
  margin: 15px;
}
```

The total size of the element, using the IE5 box model, will be calculated as follows:

```
Total width = 200 + 15 + 15 = 230px (width + margins)
Total height = 150 + 15 + 15 = 180px (height + margins)
```

It follows that the available content area is reduced, because padding and borders have to be subtracted from the dimensions that were declared. The available content size, using the IE5 box model, would be calculated as follows:

---

[9]   Although we're calling it the IE5 box model, it's also known as the broken box model.

```
Available content width = 200 - 10 - 10 - 1 - 1 = 178px
Available content height = 150 - 10 - 10 - 1 - 1 = 128px
```

Compare this with the dimensions for the correct box model in Table 6.1, and you can see that this method of calculation will make a considerable difference to the element's size.

Table 6.1: Box Model Dimensions

	Standard Box Model	IE5 Box Model
Available content width	200px	178px
Available content height	150px	128px
Total width required	252px	230px
Total height required	202px	180px

The size difference can be seen clearly in Figure 6.8.

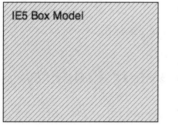
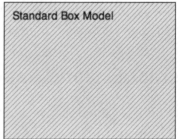

Figure 6.8: The size difference between box models

The fundamental differences between these two box models means it's important that you understand and are aware of both models when you're creating code. Internet Explorer for Windows 5 (including 5.5) uses the IE5 box model at all times, but Internet Explorer 6 and 7, and Internet Explorer 5 for Mac, use it only when in quirks mode.

You may well be wondering why two box models exist. To answer this question, we need to travel back in time to the creation of Internet Explorer 5 for Windows, when Microsoft decided that the box model would contain borders and padding within the stated dimensions, rather than increasing them. This approach wasn't as silly as it may seem at first glance: in cases in which you have an element with a width of 100%, the IE5 box model allows you to add padding and borders safely. Compare this to the correct CSS box model, in which you cannot add any padding or borders to an element with a width of 100% without breaking the layout.

Although the IE5 box model appears superior in this example, the correct box model is more useful in nearly all other cases. No other browser implemented the IE5 box model, and Microsoft eventually complied with the CSS standards and corrected its box model implementation in Internet Explorer 6 (when in standards mode). Before that, though, there was a long period in which CSS authors were forced to deal with two competing box model implementations—a situation that explains why so many CSS hacks (p. 391) were created.

As the IE5 box model had some merit, it has been proposed that CSS3 will provide authors with the choice of specifying which model to use via a `box-sizing` property.[10] Firefox, Opera, and Safari have all implemented versions of this property, which you can read more about in -moz-box-sizing (p. 375).

The Internet Explorer `hasLayout` Property

In a perfect world, we shouldn't need to know anything about the `hasLayout` property—after all, it's an internal component of the Windows Internet Explorer rendering engine. Its effect, however, is far reaching, and has major consequences for the appearance and behavior of elements, affecting how an element bounds its content and reacts with its neighbors.

This topic is solely concerned with Internet Explorer for Windows.

---

[10]   http://www.w3.org/TR/css3-ui/#box-sizing

What Is the `hasLayout` Property?

In Internet Explorer, an element is either responsible for sizing and arranging its own contents, or relies on a parent element to size and arrange its contents.

In order to accommodate these two different concepts, the rendering engine makes use of a property called `hasLayout` that can have the values `true` or `false` for the element concerned. We say an element gains a layout or has a layout when the `hasLayout` property has the value `true`.[11]

When an element has a layout, it is responsible for sizing and positioning itself and possibly any descendant elements.[12] In simple terms, this means that the element takes more care of itself and its contents, instead of relying on an ancestor element to do all the work. Therefore, some elements will have a layout by default, though the majority do not.

Elements that are responsible for arranging their own contents will have a layout by default, and include the following (this list is not exhaustive):

- `body` and `html` (in standards mode)
- `table`, `tr`, `th`, `td`
- `img`
- `hr`
- `input`, `button`, `file`, `select`, `textarea`, `fieldset`
- `marquee`
- `frameset`, `frame`, `iframe`
- `objects`, `applets`, `embed`

The main reasons Microsoft gives for the fact that not all elements have a layout by default are "performance and simplicity." If all elements had a layout by default, a detrimental effect on performance and memory usage would result.

---

[11] Once an element has a layout, the `hasLayout` property can be queried by the rendering engine or through scripting.

[12] If a descendant element also has a layout it is responsible for sizing itself and any descendants, but it is positioned by the ancestor element's layout.

So why should any of us even care about the `hasLayout` property? Because many Internet Explorer display inconsistencies which can be attributed to this property.

In most cases, the issues caused by elements that lack a layout are easy to spot: the content is often misplaced or completely missing. For example, when an element, such as a `div`, that doesn't have a layout by default, contains floated or absolutely positioned content, it will often exhibit strange and buggy behavior. The types of strange behavior that can arise are varied, and include such behaviors as missing or misplaced content, or elements that fail to redraw fully while a window is moved or scrolled.[13]

If you notice that a piece of your content appears and disappears, and sections of the page only get half-drawn, these are good indications that an element requires a layout. When the key element gains a layout, the problem miraculously goes away. In fact, 99% of the Internet Explorer CSS bugs you encounter on a daily basis can be fixed using a `hasLayout` fix in the correct place. A `hasLayout` fix involves nothing more than declaring a CSS property that causes an element to gain a layout, when it wouldn't ordinarily have a layout by default.

The simplest way for an element to gain a layout is for it to have a dimensional CSS property applied—for example, a `width` or `height`. However, in situations where you don't wish to apply a specific `width` or `height` to the element, there are several other CSS properties that, when you apply them to the element, will cause that element to gain a layout.

Those other properties are:

- `display: inline-block`
- `height:` (any value except `auto`)
- `float:` (`left` or `right`)
- `position: absolute`
- `width:` (any value except `auto`)
- `writing-mode: tb-rl`

---

[13] A detailed description of some examples of these behaviors can be found at the Position Is Everything web site at http://positioniseverything.net/explorer.html.

▓ `zoom`: (any value except `normal`)[15]

Internet Explorer 7 has some additional properties that cause an element to gain a layout (this is not an exhaustive list):

▓ `min-height`: (any value)

▓ `max-height`: (any value except `none`)

▓ `min-width`: (any value)

▓ `max-width`: (any value except `none`)

▓ `overflow`: (any value except `visible`)

▓ `overflow-x`: (any value except `visible`)

▓ `overflow-y`: (any value except `visible`)[16]

▓ `position`: `fixed`

Declaring any of these CSS properties will cause the element to gain a layout—assuming, of course, that the property is valid for the element concerned. For example, we can't apply a height to inline elements unless the document is being run in quirks mode (p. 17).

It's not a good idea to give all elements a layout—not just because of the performance and memory issues already mentioned, but because a number of other unwanted CSS side effects will occur. For example:

▓ Children of absolutely positioned or floated elements will not shrink to wrap their content when the child has a layout.

▓ Static content positioned next to a float will not wrap around the float, but will instead form a rectangular block to the side of the float.

More examples of unwanted behavior are documented on the MSDN web site.[17]

---

[15] `zoom` and `writing-mode` are proprietary Internet Explorer CSS properties, and will not pass CSS validation.
[16] `overflow-x` and `overflow-y` are proposed property names for CSS3, but have been proprietary CSS properties in Internet Explorer since version 5.
[17] http://msdn2.microsoft.com/en-us/library/bb250481.aspx

Debugging `hasLayout` Issues

If you notice that your web page is behaving strangely in Internet Explorer, try setting a CSS property for an element in order to cause it to gain a layout, and see if the problem vanishes.

Some skill is involved in identifying the correct element to which the property should be applied. With experience, it can become easy to identify the culprit—it'll usually be a parent container for which no explicit `width` is set, or whose width is defined by margins alone. If this parent element contains floated or absolute elements, it's likely to be the one causing the problem; the problems are likely to exist because it's not taking proper care of its child elements.

A useful approach to debugging layout issues is to set the proprietary CSS property `zoom` (p. 380) to 1 for elements within the document, one at time, in order to isolate the element that's causing the problem. If you set the property on an element, and the issue is resolved, you know you're on the right track. The `zoom` property is useful because, as well as being a property that triggers an element to gain a layout, in most cases, setting it will not alter the look of the page in any other way (apart from possibly fixing the bug that you're experiencing). A process of elimination can be used to narrow the problem down quite quickly.

Once you have found the element that's causing the problem, you can apply the necessary fix. The preferred approach is to set one or more dimensional CSS properties on the element. However, if dimensions can't be applied normally, a workaround must be employed.

For Internet Explorer 7, the best approach is to set the `min-height` property to 0; this technique is harmless, since 0 is the initial value for the property anyway. There's no need to hide the property from other browsers—which is definitely not the case with our next suggestion!

The standard approach for triggering an element to gain a layout in Internet Explorer 6 and earlier versions is to set the `height` property to 1%, as long as the `overflow` property is *not* set to anything except `visible`. This approach exploits a bug in these browser versions whereby if the `overflow` property is set to the default value of `visible`, the height of a containing box will expand to fit its contents regardless of the height property's value. However, most other browsers will respect the height value of 1%, which is usually not what you want them to do, so this declaration will need to be hidden from all other browsers.

In previous years, the technique of setting `height` to 1%, and hiding the declaration from all browsers except Internet Explorer 6 and earlier versions, was known as the Holly hack.[18] These days, the recommended method for specifying CSS declarations for Internet Explorer only is through the use of conditional comments (p. 394).

The good news is that Internet Explorer 7 is a lot more robust than previous versions, and many (though not all, unfortunately) of the issues concerning layout have disappeared—you'll need far fewer fixes than you might have in previous versions of the browser. For more information about the layout issue, see "On Having Layout" at the Satzansatz web site.[19]

Formatting Concepts

This section describes how boxes are laid out in the normal document flow. It applies to elements whose `float` property has the value `none`, and whose `position` property has the value `static` or `relative`, although in the latter case, additional factors described in Relative Positioning (p. 176) must be taken into consideration.

As we already saw in CSS Layout and Formatting (p. 139), just as there are block-level elements and inline elements in HTML, CSS boxes are also either block or inline (although there are subtypes of each), as determined by the element's `display` property (p. 264) value.

The values `block`, `list-item`, and `table` will cause an element to generate a block box and participate in a block formatting context.[20]

Other values, such as `inline` and `inline-table`, cause elements to generate inline boxes, which participate in an inline formatting context.

---

[18] http://www.communitymx.com/content/article.cfm?page=2&cid=C37E0
[19] http://www.satzansatz.de/cssd/onhavinglayout.html
[20] List item (p. 168) and table (p. 168) formatting are described separately, since they're special cases.

The value `run-in` is special, because it can make the generated box's formatting either block or inline. A run-in box that doesn't contain a block box, and is followed by a sibling block box in the normal document flow, becomes the first inline box of the sibling block box (unless the sibling is or contains a run-in). Otherwise, the run-in box becomes a block box. Run-in boxes are mainly intended for run-in headings. See display (p. 264) for more information about `run-in` and browser support.

The value `inline-block` generates a block box that's laid out as an inline box. On the inside, the box is a block box, but on the outside, it's an inline box. Similarly, the value `inline-table` generates a table that's laid out as an inline box.

The value `none` is a special case, because an element with this display value will not generate any sort of box at all. This means that no descendant element will be able to generate a box. It's important to note that applying the value `none` isn't the same as using an invisible box; if you use `none`, no box will be generated at all.

Elements whose `position` properties have the value `absolute` (p. 178) or `fixed` (p. 178) are laid out in a very different fashion, as are floated or cleared (p. 180) elements.

An absolutely positioned or floated element will, however, establish a new containing block and formatting context for its static children.

Block Formatting

In a block formatting context, boxes are laid out vertically, starting at the top. Block-level elements—elements with a display property value of `block`, `list-item`, `table`, and (in certain circumstances) `run-in`—participate in block formatting contexts.

A block-level element with a `display` property value other than `table` will generate a **principal box** block. A principal box will contain either block boxes or inline boxes as children, never both. If the element contains a mix of block-level and inline children, anonymous block boxes will be generated where necessary, so that the principal box will only contain block boxes. Consider the following example:

```
<div>
  <p>A paragraph</p>
  Some text in an anonymous box
  <p>Another paragraph</p>
</div>
```

The HTML snippet above will, by default, generate a principal box for the `div`
element and the two `p` elements, plus an anonymous block box for the text that
appears between the paragraphs, as seen in Figure 6.9.[21]

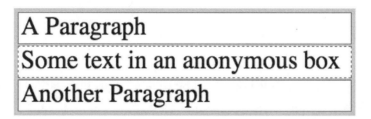

Figure 6.9: An anonymous block box

An anonymous block box inherits its properties from the enclosing non-anonymous
box—the div box in this example. Any non-inherited properties are set to their
initial (default) values.

The principal box becomes the containing block (p. 147) for non-positioned
descendant boxes, and it's also the box that's affected for any value of `position`
other than `static`, and for any value of `float` other than `none`.

In a block formatting context the vertical distance between two sibling boxes is
determined by their respective margin properties; vertical margins between adjacent
block boxes collapse if there are no borders or padding in the way. For more
information, see Collapsing Margins (p. 148).

In a left-to-right environment, the left outer edge of each block box touches the left
edge of the containing block. In a right-to-left environment, the right edges touch.
This happens even if there are floated elements in the way, except if the block box

---

[21] Note that mixing block and inline content like this is semantically questionable, and it's not
     something we recommend. This example is provided just to illustrate how CSS handles the
     situation.

establishes a new block formatting context. In that case, the block box becomes narrower to accommodate the floated elements.

Inline Formatting

Just as anonymous block boxes are sometimes created in a block formatting context, anonymous inline boxes can be created when necessary. Here's an example of the automatic creation of anonymous inline boxes:

```
<p>In 1912, <em>Titanic</em> sank on her maiden voyage.</p>
```

Since there's a child element—the em element, which generates an inline box of its own—two anonymous inline boxes will be generated to contain the text nodes that are immediate children of the p element, as shown in Figure 6.10.

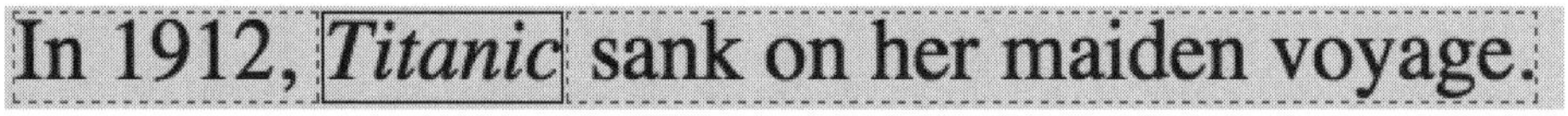

In 1912, *Titanic* sank on her maiden voyage.

Figure 6.10: Anonymous inline boxes

An anonymous inline box inherits its properties from its parent block box—the p element box in this example. Any non-inherited properties are set to their initial values.

In an inline formatting context, boxes are laid out horizontally, starting at the top of the containing block. Horizontal margins, padding, and borders can exist between the boxes, but vertical margins are ignored for inline boxes. Dimensions (width and height) can't be specified for inline boxes.[22]

The inline boxes that form a single line are enclosed by a rectangle that's called a **line box**. Boxes within a line box are aligned vertically according to their vertical-align properties. A line box is always tall enough to accommodate all its inline boxes.

---

[22]   This advice applies to non-replaced inline boxes. We can specify dimensions for replaced inline boxes, such as images. See Replaced Elements (p. 175) for more information.

When several inline boxes can't fit into a single line box, they're distributed over two or more stacked line boxes.

When a single inline box can't fit into a line box, it's split into two or more boxes that are distributed over as many line boxes as necessary. Margins, borders, and padding aren't applied where such splits occur.[23] Consider the following example markup and CSS:

```
<p>Text in a <em>narrow column</em> can break.</p>
```

```
em {
  margin: 0 1em;
  padding: 0 1em;
  border: 1px solid #000;
}
```

If margins, padding, and borders are set on that em element, the result may not be what the author intended if the element's box is split into two line boxes as a result of line wrapping—Figure 6.11 shows the potential result.

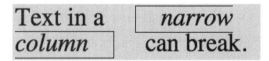

Figure 6.11: A split inline box

As you can see, the margin and padding are applied to the left of the word "narrow" and to the right of the word "column." The borders are applied on three sides of each of the two inline boxes.

If the total width of the inline boxes is less than the width of the line box, the `direction` and `text-align` properties control how the boxes are distributed inside the line box.

CSS Layout and Formatting

---

[23] CSS3 may provide more control in such cases.

The left and right edges of a line box normally touch the edges of its containing block. When there are floats in the way, however, the line boxes adjacent to the floats are shortened—see Floating and Clearing (p. 180) for more information.

Although line boxes are stacked with no space between them, we can affect the height of a line box with the `line-height` property. If the computed value of the `line-height` property is greater than the vertical distance occupied by the inline boxes in a line box, the line box is vertically centered within the specified line height. Half the difference is added at the top of the line box and half at the bottom. This behavior corresponds to the typographical concept of half-leading, where strips of lead (hence the name) or brass were inserted between the lines of type to increase the line spacing.

List Formatting

An element with a `display` property value of `list-item` generates a principal box just as any other block box. It will also generate an additional box for the list marker. This box is generated outside the principal box and can't be styled independently in CSS2.1.

There are three properties (p. 285) that apply only to elements with a `display` property value of `list-item`, but properties like `margin-left` and `padding-left` (in a left-to-right reading environment) also affect the way in which list items are rendered.

In addition to the available list item properties, generated content (p. 347) can also be useful for more advanced list numbering.

Table Formatting

Tables are the most complex elements in HTML, and table formatting is among the most complex parts of CSS.

CSS defines a number of objects that are involved in table formatting, as Figure 6.12 reveals.

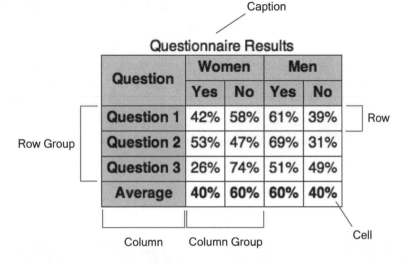

Figure 6.12: Table formatting objects

A table may contain a caption, row groups, and column groups. A row group contains rows, while a column group contains columns. Rows and columns contain cells. Tables are rendered as layers in a specified order from the bottom up: table, column groups, columns, row groups, rows, and cells.

The table model in HTML is row-centric. Although you can specify columns and column groups in markup, cells are structurally contained within rows. Columns and column groups are more esoteric items that are derived from the set of cells in all rows of the table.

A table can be included in a formatting context as either a block-level or inline-level box. It can have padding (p. 211), borders (p. 220), and margins (p. 200).

A table element generates an anonymous box that encompasses the table box and the caption box (if they're present). The caption box is rendered outside the table box, but is inextricably tied to it. When a table is repositioned, it's the outer anonymous box that's moved to enable the caption to follow the table.

Captions inherit inheritable properties from the table. A caption is formatted as a block box, but it doesn't behave like general block boxes in all respects. If a run-in element precedes the table, it will not run into a caption box.

The placement of the caption can be controlled via the `caption-side` property. The valid values in CSS2.1 are `top` and `bottom`, which should be fairly self-explanatory.

The internal elements of tables—row groups, column groups, rows, columns, and cells—generate regular boxes that can have borders. Cells can also have padding, but internal table objects don't have margins.

Ten of the valid values for the `display` property denote table-related formatting styles. These values, and the HTML element types with which they're associated by default, are shown in Table 6.2.

Table 6.2: Table `display` Property Values

Element Type	Property Value	HTML Element
Table	table	table
	inline-table	n/a
Caption	table-caption	caption
Row group	table-header-group	thead
	table-footer-group	tfoot
	table-row-group	tbody
Row	table-row	tr
Column group	table-column-group	colgroup
Column	table-column	col
Cell	table-cell	td
		th

These display values can also be specified for other element types than those that belong to the HTML table model; however, Internet Explorer versions up to and including 7 don't support these values.

When table-related `display` values are used for non-table elements, anonymous table-related elements may have to be generated in order to render the elements correctly. Here, we've listed situations in which anonymous table-related elements may be created:

- Cells must have a row as their parent. A row object will be generated as the parent of one or more consecutive cells that don't have a row as their parent.

- Rows must have a row group or a table as their parent. Columns must have a column group or a table as their parent. Row groups and column groups must have a table as their parent. A table object will be generated as the parent of one or more consecutive objects of those types that don't have the required parent.

- If a child of a table object is not a caption, row group, column group, row, or column, a row object will be generated as the parent of that child, and any consecutive siblings that require a row as their parent.

- If a child of a row group object isn't a row, a row object will be generated as the parent of that child and any consecutive siblings that require a row as their parent.

- If a child of a row object is not a cell, a cell object will be generated as the parent of that child and any consecutive siblings that are not cells.

Properties that Apply to Column and Column-group Elements

Only a few properties can be applied to elements with a `display` property value of `table-column` or `table-column-group`:

- the `border` properties, but only in the collapsing borders model (see below)
- the `background` properties, where cells and rows have transparent backgrounds
- the `width` property
- the `visibility` property value `collapse`—any other visibility values are ignored for columns and column groups

Table Width Algorithms

Unlike other block boxes, a table with zero horizontal margins and a width property that's set to auto doesn't size to fill its containing block. Instead, the table size will be determined by its contents. A table can be horizontally centered by setting margin-left and margin-right to auto, though.

There are two very different algorithms for determining the widths of table columns: the fixed table layout algorithm and the automatic table layout algorithm. These are specified with the table-layout property (which takes values of fixed, for fixed layouts, and auto, for automatic layouts); its initial value is auto. If the table's width is specified as auto, the automatic table layout algorithm is normally used. In the case of block-level tables (when display is set to table), user agents are allowed to use the fixed table layout algorithm anyway, but they aren't required to.

With the fixed table layout algorithm, the widths of columns and of the table are not governed by the contents of the table's cells. Instead, the width of each column is determined as follows:

- Column objects whose width is not auto set the width for that column.
- A cell in the first row, whose width is not auto, sets the width of the column it belongs to. If the cell spans more than one column, the width is divided over the columns.
- Any remaining columns equally divide the remaining horizontal space, minus any borders or cell spacing.

The width of the table is the greater of the value of the table's width property, and the sum of the column widths (plus borders or cell spacing). If the table is wider than the columns, the extra space will be distributed over the columns.

Don't Omit Cells!

Since the cells in the first row of the table are used to determine the column widths, you shouldn't omit any cells from the first row if you use the fixed table layout algorithm. The behavior in such case is undefined by the CSS2.1 specification.

The automatic table layout algorithm usually requires more than one pass. The CSS2.1 specification suggests an algorithm for determining column widths,[24] but user agents are not required to use it.

The suggested algorithm for determining column widths examines every cell in the entire table, computing the minimum and maximum widths required for rendering each cell. These values are then used to determine how wide each column should be, which in turn may decide the width of the table itself.

Performance and Automatic Table Layouts

Since every single cell must be inspected, the automatic table layout algorithm can become very time-consuming when it's calculated for a table with a large number of rows and/or columns.

Table Height Algorithms

If the table's `height` property has a value other than `auto`, and the specified height differs from the sum of the row heights plus borders or cell spacing, the behavior is undefined.

Percentage values for the `height` property are undefined for rows, row groups, and cells.

The `vertical-align` property of each cell determines its alignment within the row. Only the values `baseline`, `top`, `bottom`, and `middle` are allowed. For any other value, `baseline` will be used.

Borders On Table Objects

There are two different models in CSS2 for rendering borders around internal table objects: the separated borders model and the collapsing borders model. We can choose the model we prefer by using the `border-collapse` property, and setting the value to `separate` (the initial value) or `collapse`.

---

[24] http://www.w3.org/TR/CSS21/tables.html#auto-table-layout

In the separated borders model only cells (and the table itself) can have borders; rows, row groups, columns, and column groups cannot. Borders are drawn individually around the cells and the cells are separated by the vertical and horizontal distances specified by the `border-spacing` property. In the space between cell borders, the backgrounds of rows, row groups, columns, and column groups are invisible. Only the table background is visible in the inter-cell spacing. Figure 6.13 shows an example of a table that's rendered using the separated borders model.

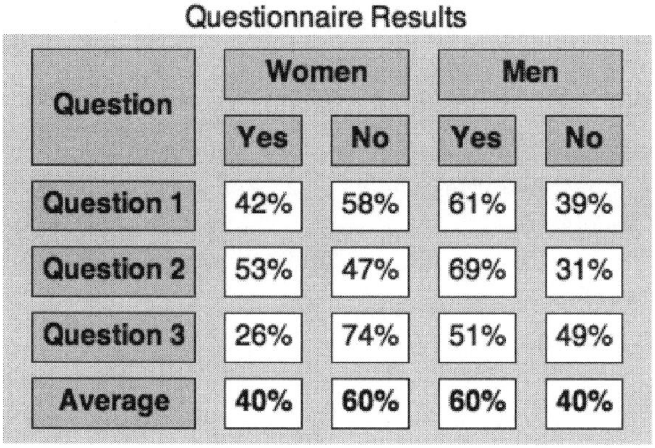

Questionnaire Results

Question	Women		Men	
	Yes	No	Yes	No
Question 1	42%	58%	61%	39%
Question 2	53%	47%	69%	31%
Question 3	26%	74%	51%	49%
Average	40%	60%	60%	40%

Figure 6.13: Rendering a table with separated borders

Here's the relevant CSS for the table:

```
table {
  border-collapse: separate;
  border-spacing: 1em 0.5em;
  background-color: #ddd;
}
```

Another property that applies in the separated borders model is the `empty-cells` property. It controls whether cells that lack visible content have borders and backgrounds (if the value is `show`, the initial value) or not (if the value is `hide`). Carriage returns, line feeds, tabs, and blanks are not considered to be visible content, although a non-breaking space is.

In the collapsing borders model, the cells aren't separated from one another and their borders—along with borders of rows, row groups, columns, column groups and the table itself—collapse (or overlap) in a rather complicated way. An example of a table to which the collapsing borders model is applied is shown in Figure 6.14.

Questionnaire Results

Question	Women		Men	
	Yes	No	Yes	No
Question 1	42%	58%	61%	39%
Question 2	53%	47%	69%	31%
Question 3	26%	74%	51%	49%
Average	40%	60%	60%	40%

Figure 6.14: Rendering a table with collapsed borders

With this model, quite a few borders may be specified in such a way that they would be rendered in the same place. The CSS2.1 specification provides an algorithm for border conflict resolution—that is, which border will win, or be rendered, in these situations. Very broadly speaking, the most eye-catching border will be rendered, unless at least one of the borders has `border-style` set to `hidden`, in which case no border will be rendered.

If none of the borders are hidden, wide borders win over narrow borders. If two or more borders have the same width, the `border-style` property decides which one will be rendered. The styles are preferred in the following order: `double`, `solid`, `dashed`, `dotted`, `ridge`, `outset`, `groove`, and `inset`. Borders with `border-style` set to `none` have the lowest priority, and will never win over other border styles—even if they have a large width value.

If there is still no winner, the algorithm looks at the objects for which the borders are set. The preferred order is: cell, row, row group, column, column group, and table.

The `border-spacing` and `empty-cells` properties are ignored when the collapsing borders model is used.

Replaced Elements

A **replaced element** is any element whose appearance and dimensions are defined by an external resource. Examples include images (`<img>` tags), plugins (`<object>`

tags), and form elements (`<button>`, `<textarea>`, `<input>`, and `<select>` tags). All other elements types can be referred to as **non-replaced elements**.

Replaced elements can have **intrinsic dimensions**—width and height values that are defined by the element itself, rather than by its surroundings in the document. For example, if an `image` element has a `width` set to `auto`, the width of the linked image file will be used. Intrinsic dimensions also define an intrinsic ratio that's used to determine the computed dimensions of the element should only one dimension be specified. For example, if only the `width` is specified for an image element—at, say, `100px`—and the actual image is 200 pixels wide and 100 pixels high, the `height` of the element will be scaled by the same amount, to `50px`.

Replaced elements can also have visual formatting requirements imposed by the element, outside of the control of CSS; for example, the user interface controls rendered for form elements.

In an inline formatting context, you can also think of a replaced element as being one that acts as a single, big character for the purposes of wrapping and layout. A width and height can be specified for replaced inline elements, in which case the height of the line box in which the element is positioned is made tall enough to accommodate the replaced element, including any specified box properties.

Positioning

In CSS2, each box has a position in three dimensions. Three positioning schemes are used for the horizontal and vertical positioning (along the x and y axes) of boxes—the normal flow (p. 163) (which includes relative positioning (p. 176)), floating (p. 180), and absolute positioning (p. 178) (which includes fixed positioning (p. 178)). The box's stack level (p. 179) determines its position on the z axis.

Relative Positioning

An element whose `position` property has the value `relative` is first laid out just like a static element. The rendered box is then shifted vertically (according to the `top` or `bottom` property) and/or horizontally (according to the `left` or `right` property).

> ### Only the Box Is Shifted
>
> As far as the flow is concerned, the element is still in its original position. If the relative shift is significant, it will leave a "hole" in the flow, in which case the rendered box may overlap other content.

The properties `top`, `right`, `bottom`, and `left` can be used to specify by how much the rendered box will be shifted. A positive value means the box will be shifted away from that position, towards the opposite side. For instance, a `left` value of `20px` shifts the box 20 pixels to the right of its original position. Applying a negative value to the opposite side will achieve the same effect: a `right` value of `-20px` will accomplish the same result as a `left` value of `20px`. The initial value for these properties is `auto`, which makes the computed value 0 (zero)—that is, no shift occurs.

Evidently, it's pointless to specify both `left` and `right` for the same element, because the position will be over-constrained. If the content direction is left to right, the `left` value is used, and `right` will be ignored. In a right-to-left direction, the `right` value "wins." If both `top` and `bottom` are specified, `top` will be used and `bottom` will be ignored.

Since it's only the rendered box that moves when we relatively position an element, this positioning scheme isn't useful for laying out columns of content. Relative positioning is commonly used when we need to shift a box a few pixels or so, although it can also be useful, in combination with negative margins on floated elements, for some more complex designs.

> ### Control Your Containing Blocks
>
> One side effect of relative positioning is quite handy: a relatively positioned element is "positioned," which means it becomes the containing block for any absolutely positioned descendants. This gives us an easy-to-use tool for controlling the position of our containing blocks: just set `position` to `relative` without moving the box at all.

Absolute Positioning

An element whose `position` property has the value `absolute` is said to be absolutely positioned, and is completely removed from the document flow: it doesn't affect subsequent elements at all. It's positioned with respect to its containing block (p. 147), and it establishes a new containing block for normal flow children, and for descendants whose `position` property is set to `absolute`.

The `top`, `right`, `bottom`, `left`, `width`, and `height` properties determine the position and dimensions of an absolutely positioned element.

Both the position and the dimensions can be expressed using all four of the positional properties (`top`, `right`, `bottom`, `left`).[25] Alternatively, you can specify the position of one corner of the box using `top` or `bottom` in combination with `left` or `right`, and you can specify the dimensions using `width` and (optionally) `height`.

An absolutely positioned element will overlap other content unless we make room for it in some way; for instance, by setting margins or padding on other elements. When several absolutely positioned elements occupy the same location, they'll be stacked according to a stacking context (p. 179).

Absolute positioning also makes it possible to place an element partly or entirely outside the viewport (p. 141). This technique, which is known as the off-left technique, is sometimes used intentionally to hide content from visual user agents while keeping it visible for those using assistive technologies such as screen readers.[26]

Fixed Positioning

Fixed positioning is a subcategory of absolute positioning. An element whose `position` property is set to `fixed` always has the viewport (p. 141) as its containing block. For continuous media, such as a computer screen, a fixed element won't

---

[25] This capability isn't supported by Internet Explorer versions up to and including 6.
[26] Setting `display` to none isn't recommended, since some screen readers won't announce such elements.

move when the document is scrolled. For paged media, a fixed element will be repeated on every page.

Internet Explorer Compatibility

Fixed positioning isn't supported by Internet Explorer 6 or prior versions.

Stacking Contexts

Although we tend to regard a web page as a two-dimensional entity, boxes are positioned in three dimensions. The third dimension is the z axis, which is perpendicular to the screen.

Positioned elements can overlap, since they can be rendered at the same position. Each box has an associated stack level, which is its position along the z axis, and belongs to a stacking context. A box with a higher stack level is rendered "in front of" a box with a lower stack level; in other words, it's rendered closer to a user facing the viewport (p. 141). A stack level can also be negative.

We can specify the stack level via the `z-index` property. The value `auto` means the box will have the same stack level as its parent, and implies that the box doesn't establish a new stacking context. A value that's provided as an integer specifies an explicit stack level, and causes the box to establish a new local stacking context. The box itself has the stack level 0 in this new context.

A stacking context consists of seven different layers (from bottom to top):

1. the background and borders of the element that establishes the stacking context
2. the stacking contexts of descendants with negative stack levels
3. block-level descendants in the normal flow
4. floated descendants and their contents
5. inline-level descendants in the normal flow
6. positioned descendants whose `z-index` is `auto` or 0
7. the stacking contexts of descendants with positive stack levels

A stacking context is also generated by any positioned element (including relatively positioned elements) whose computed z-index value is anything other than auto.

Boxes within a stacking context can't occur between two boxes that belong to another stacking context.

Floating and Clearing

A floated element is one whose float property has a value other than none. The element can be shifted to the left (using the value left) or to the right (using the value right); non-floated content will flow along the side opposite the specified float direction.[27]

The floated box is shifted to the left or right until its margin edge touches the padding edge of the containing block, or the margin edge of another floated element. If the floated element is within a line box, the top of the floated box is aligned with the top of the line box. If there isn't enough horizontal room left for non-floated content to flow alongside the floated box on the current line, it's shifted down until it fits, or there are no more floated elements.

Defining the Margin Edge

The **margin edge** of a box surrounds the margin of the box. If the box has no margins, the margin edge is the same as the border edge. See The CSS Box Model (p. 142) for more information.

A floated box is taken out of the flow, so it doesn't affect the block-level boxes around it. Line boxes located next to a floated box, however, are shortened to make room for the float. A containing block will not expand to accommodate a floating child box, unless the containing block is also floating, or has its overflow property set to something other than visible.[28]

---

[27] Contrary to what some may think (or wish for), float does not support the value center.
[28] In Internet Explorer 6 and prior versions, the overflow property does not cause the containing block to expand as described here.

Figure 6.15 shows a schematic view of the following HTML fragment, in which the image is floated to the left:

```
<p>
  <img src="image.png" alt="">
   text text … text text
</p>
<p>text text … text text</p>
```

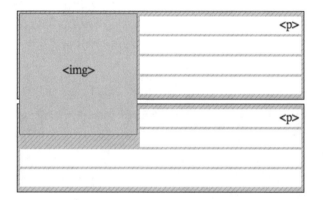

Figure 6.15: A floated element

A floated box can have margins like any normal box, but those margins will never collapse with the margins of adjacent boxes.

Negative margins on floated boxes behave slightly differently from negative margins on non-floated boxes. If the negative margin is on the same side as the float direction (for example, a negative left margin on a box that's floated to the left), or the top or bottom of the box, the effect is to pull the box further in that direction. This enables the floated box to move outside the boundaries of its containing block, which means that this technique can be used to create an overlapping effect. Care must be taken, though, because the final appearance of elements floated in this way may differ between user agents.

If the negative margin is applied to the side that's opposite the float direction (for example, a negative right margin is applied on a box that's floated to the left), it moves the margin further inside the element itself (without changing the element's width), which causes floated elements adjacent to the element to overlap its content.

This approach can be used to create layout effects such as the multi-column layout documented on A List Apart.[29]

Clearing Floated Elements

To force an element to start below any floated elements, we can use the `clear` property with a value of `left`, `right`, or `both`. An element whose `clear` property is set to `left` will start below all left-floated boxes in the same block formatting context, while a `clear` value of `right` will clear all right-floated boxes. If `clear` is set to `both`, the element will start below any floated box in that context. Figure 6.16 shows the example above, but this time, the second paragraph has a `clear` value of `left`.

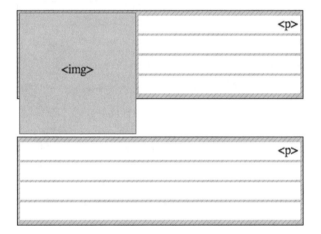

Figure 6.16: A cleared element

To achieve this clearing, we add space above the cleared element's top margin until it's clear of the affected floated boxes. As a result, we can't use the top margin on the cleared element if we want a specific amount of space between it and the floated box. Space is added above the cleared element's top margin until it's free of the float, but that's all. If we want to create space beneath the floated box, we must set the bottom margin of the floated element, or set top padding on the cleared element.

---

[29] http://www.alistapart.com/articles/negativemargins/

Internet Explorer for Windows will automatically clear all floated children of an element that has a layout, though this implementation disagrees with the CSS specification.

See The Internet Explorer hasLayout Property (p. 158) for more information about IE and layout.

Floating Versus Absolute Positioning for Multi-column Layouts

Floated boxes were intended to be used primarily for floating images so that text would flow around them. Nowadays, `float` is commonly used for the purpose of page layout; for example, floating the columns in a multi-column layout.

If the source order is the same as the presentational order, we can float each column to the left. In a narrow viewport, where there isn't enough room for all columns to appear side by side, one or more columns on the right-hand side will drop below the others. Although this result may not be aesthetically pleasing, it has the advantage of avoiding a horizontal scroll bar.

Another advantage of floating columns is that it's easy to achieve a full-width footer below the columns, regardless of which column is the longest. Using the `clear` property, we can make the footer drop below all floated columns.

Absolute positioning can also be used to lay out a page with columns, as it allows you to specify the exact position of the columns.

So what are the pros and cons of using floats instead of absolute positioning?

Firstly, a complicated float-based layout can be difficult and fragile in Internet Explorer. IE versions up to and including 6 have numerous float-related bugs.[30]

Floating an element will only shift it to the left or to the right—you can't move an element up or down with the `float` property. Consequently, a float-based layout can become very tricky if you want to preserve a certain source order in your markup.

---

[30] See http://positioniseverything.net for well-documented workarounds.

There are ways to do this using a combination of negative margins and relative positioning,[32] but if you use them, you'll likely run into many nasty IE bugs.

Using absolute positioning incurs fewer browser compatibility problems, although IE and older versions of Opera (prior to version 9) use the wrong containing block in some cases. As long as you (and the browser) know your containing blocks, you can shift parts of the content around without being bound by the source order to the same extent that you are when working with floats.

Absolute positioning has its own complications, though. The main problem with this type of layout is that an absolutely positioned element is removed from the document flow, and doesn't affect subsequent elements at all. A multi-column, absolutely positioned layout, in which any column can be the longest, makes it virtually impossible to display a footer at the bottom of the rendered document.

You can use the following checklist as a rough guide when deciding which type of layout to use for a multi-column document in which any column can be the longest:

- If the source order is important, and it's different from the presentational order, *and* you don't need a footer on the document, use absolute positioning.
- If you need a footer, use floats. Source order can be maintained with the help of negative margins and relative positioning, if necessary, albeit with a lot of extra work for IE—especially if the page width is variable.

A third option is to use the table-related values for the `display` property, but, unfortunately, lack of support by Internet Explorer hinders the use of those values for any general-audience site at this time.

The Relationship Between `display`, `position`, and `float`

The three properties `display`, `float`, and `position` interact in certain ways.

---

[32]   For an example, see the A List Apart article at
http://www.alistapart.com/articles/multicolumnlayouts

If an element's `display` property is set to `none`, no box is generated. In this case, `float` and `position` are ignored.

If an element's `position` property is set to `absolute` or `fixed`, it's absolutely positioned. In this case, `float` is ignored (the computed value is `none`).

For absolutely positioned elements, floated elements (elements whose `float` property is set to `left` or `right`), and the root element, the computed value for `display` is set according to Table 6.3.

Otherwise, the computed value for `display` is the same as the specified value.

Table 6.3: Computed Display Values

Specified Value	Computed Value
`inline, inline-block, run-in, table-caption, table-cell, table-column, table-column-group, table-footer-group, table-header-group, table-row,` or `table-row-group`	`block`
`inline-table,`	`table`
other	as specified

Summary

In this section, we covered the way in which elements are described according to the CSS box model. In the CSS box model, padding and borders are added to the element's width, whereas in the IE5 box model, padding and borders reduce the available content area.

CSS boxes can be block-level or inline. The two types are laid out very differently. Box layout occurs in formatting contexts, relative to a containing block. The `display` property controls which type of box is generated for an element.

Boxes are laid out in the normal flow if they're static or relatively positioned. Floated or absolutely positioned boxes are taken out of the normal flow and laid out according to special rules.

Table rendering is quite complex, and hampered by a lack of browser support. There are two table layout algorithms (fixed and automatic) and two border models (separated and collapsing).

Relatively positioned boxes are shifted from their normal position in the flow. Only the rendered box is shifted—the element still occupies the original position as far as the flow is concerned.

Absolutely positioned boxes are removed entirely from the flow. Boxes with fixed positioning don't scroll with the document for continuous media; they're repeated on every page for paged media.

The `z-index` property controls the stacking of overlapping positioned boxes.

Floated boxes are shifted to the left or right and non-floated content flows along their sides. The `clear` property can be used to force an element to clear all or some floated boxes within the same block formatting context.

Chapter 7

Box Properties

Box properties allow the author to control the presentation of generated boxes for document elements, including dimensions, margins, padding, and borders. You can also see The CSS Box Model (p. 142) for more information.

Dimensions

These properties allow us to control the height and width of element boxes. You can also read The CSS Box Model (p. 142) for more information about the calculation of box dimensions.

height

`height: { length | percentage | auto | inherit } ;`

SPEC		
inherited	initial	version
NO	auto	CSS1
BROWSER SUPPORT			
IE7+	FF1+	Saf1.3+	Op9.2+
FULL	FULL	FULL	FULL

This property sets the content height of a block or a replaced element (p. 175). This height does not include padding, borders, or margins—see The CSS Box Model (p. 142).

If the contents of a block require more vertical space than is afforded by the height you assign, their behavior is defined by the `overflow` (p. 280) property.

Example

This style rule assigns a fixed height of 100 pixels to paragraphs within the element with ID `"example"`:

```
#example p {
    height: 100px;
}
```

Value

The property takes a CSS length (px, pt, em, etc.), a percentage, or the keyword `auto`. Negative length values are illegal.

Percentage values refer to the height of the element's containing block (p. 147). If the height of the containing block isn't specified explicitly (that is, it depends on content height), and this element isn't absolutely positioned, the percentage value is treated as `auto`. A percentage value is also treated as `auto` for table cells, table rows, and row groups.

The special `auto` value allows the browser to calculate the content height automatically, based on other factors. For absolutely positioned elements, for example, the content height may be calculated on the basis of the `top` (p. 275) and `bottom` (p. 277) property values, or the top and bottom margins, borders, and padding applied to the element. If no hard constraints are imposed by other properties, the element is allowed to assume its "natural" content height, on the basis of the height of the content it contains.

Compatibility

Internet Explorer			Firefox			Safari			Opera
5.5	6.0	7.0	1.0	1.5	2.0	1.3	2.0	3.0	9.2
Buggy	Buggy	Full	Full	Full	Full	Full	Full	Full	Full

Internet Explorer for Windows versions up to and including 5.5 (and up to and including version 7 in quirks mode) incorrectly include padding, borders, and margins in the content height calculation. This is known as the box model bug, or the IE5 box model—see The CSS Box Model (p. 142).

Internet Explorer for Windows versions up to and including 6 (and up to and including version 7 in quirks mode) incorrectly treat height as min-height, extending the content height of a block if its content can't fit within the specified height. The result is that other elements in the flow will be moved around to account for this extra height, which can result in a broken layout or, at the least, a different layout from the one that was expected.

The correct behavior would simply allow the content to overflow without affecting the height at all, as the default setting for overflow is visible. This would mean that the overflowing content would be ignored for the purposes of the layout, and might therefore overlap other elements on the page.

In standards mode, Internet Explorer version 7 treats height correctly and in accordance with the CSS specifications.

Internet Explorer for Windows versions up to and including 6 don't support the specification of both the position and the dimensions of an absolutely positioned element using top, right, bottom, and left together. They will use the last vertical and horizontal position specified, and need the dimensions to be specified using width and height.

Internet Explorer for Windows versions up to and including 7 don't support the value inherit.

min-height

min-height: { *length* | *percentage* | inherit } ;

SPEC		
inherited	initial	version
NO	0	CSS2
BROWSER SUPPORT			
------	------	------	------
IE7+	FF1+	Saf2+	Op9.2+
FULL	FULL	FULL	FULL

This property sets the minimum content height of a block or a replaced element (p. 175). This minimum height doesn't include padding, borders, or margins—see The CSS Box Model (p. 142).

An element to which min-height is applied will never be smaller than the minimum height specified, but will be allowed to grow normally if the content exceeds the minimum height set.

Example

This style rule assigns a minimum height of 100 pixels to paragraphs within the element with ID "example":

```
#example p {
  min-height: 100px;
}
```

min-height is usually used to ensure that an element has at least a minimum height even if no content is present; it's also commonly used in conjunction with max-height to produce a height range for the element concerned.

Combining min-height and height

Note that min-height and height shouldn't be applied to the same element using the same unit, as this will cause one to override the other. If, for example, the height is set as 150px, and the min-height is set as 60px, the actual height of the element is 150px, and the min-height declaration becomes redundant:

```
#example {
  min-height: 60px;
  height: 150px;
}
```

In the above example, the height of the element will be fixed at 150px. However, it's acceptable to set min-height and height when the values are different units:

```
#example {
  min-height: 3em;
  height: 138px;
}
```

Here, the `min-height` declaration is based on `em`, which means that at some stage (due to text resizing) the em height may be larger than the `138px` `height` we've set. In cases such as this, the element will be allowed to expand further than the `138px` `height`, thus accommodating the resizing of the em-based text.

If the contents of a block require more vertical space than the limits that have been set, that behavior is defined by the `overflow` (p. 280) property.

Value

The property takes a CSS length (px, pt, em, etc.) or a percentage. Negative length values are illegal.

Percentage values refer to the height of the containing block. If the height of the containing block is not specified explicitly (that is, it depends on content height), and this element is not absolutely positioned, the percentage value is treated as zero.

Compatibility

Internet Explorer			Firefox			Safari			Opera
5.5	6.0	7.0	1.0	1.5	2.0	1.3	2.0	3.0	9.2
None	None	Full	Full	Full	Full	Partial	Full	Full	Full

Although the support table above indicates that Internet Explorer 6 provides no support for `min-height`, note that in quirks mode only it will support `min-height` on `td`, `th`, and `tr` elements in fixed-layout tables—see table-layout (p. 292). This behavior is contrary to the CSS2.1 specifications, and is corrected in standards mode, which provides no support for this property.

Internet Explorer versions up to and including 6 treat the `height` property in much the same way as `min-height`, and will always expand a container to encompass the content unless `overflow` has been set to something other than `visible`.

Internet Explorer for Windows versions up to and including 7 don't support the value `inherit`.

Safari's support for this property, when applied to positioned elements, is limited to versions 2.0.2 or above.

 # max-height

max-height: { *length* | *percentage* | none | inherit } ;

SPEC		
inherited	initial	version
NO	none	CSS2
BROWSER SUPPORT			
IE7+	FF1+	Saf2+	Op9.2+
FULL	FULL	FULL	FULL

This property sets the maximum content height of a block or a replaced element (p. 175). This maximum height does not include padding, borders, or margins—see The CSS Box Model (p. 142).

Example

This style rule assigns a maximum height of 100 pixels to paragraphs within the element with ID "example":

```
#example p {
  max-height: 100px;
}
```

An element that has max-height applied will never be taller than the value specified, even if the height property is set to something larger. There is an exception to this rule, however: if min-height is specified with a value that's greater than that of max-height, the container's height will be the largest value, which, in this case, means that the min-height value will in fact be the one that's applied.

max-height is usually used in conjunction with min-height to produce a height range for the element concerned.

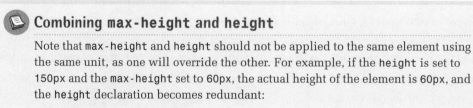

Combining max-height and height

Note that max-height and height should not be applied to the same element using the same unit, as one will override the other. For example, if the height is set to 150px and the max-height set to 60px, the actual height of the element is 60px, and the height declaration becomes redundant:

```
#example {
  max-height: 60px;
  height: 150px;
}
```

In the above example, the height of the element will be fixed at 60px.

However, it is acceptable (although it may not be entirely useful) to set `max-height` and `height` when the values are different units:

```
#example {
   max-height: 10em;
   height: 138px;
}
```

The height in the above example will be whichever is the smaller of the values.

Since the `max-height` declaration is based on `em` units, at some stage (due to text resizing) the em height may be smaller than the 138px `height` we've set. In cases such as these, the element will be allowed to shrink from the 138px `height`, thus keeping track with the em-based text. See the entry on `min-height` (p. 190) for the reverse of this scenario.

If the contents of a block require more vertical space than is afforded by the limits that have been set, their behavior is defined by the `overflow` (p. 280) property.

Value

The property takes a CSS length (px, pt, em, and so on), a percentage, or the keyword `none`. Negative length values are illegal.

Percentage values refer to the height of the containing block. If the height of the containing block is not specified explicitly (that is, it depends on content height), and this element is not absolutely positioned, the percentage value is treated as `none`.

Compatibility

Internet Explorer			Firefox			Safari			Opera
5.5	6.0	7.0	1.0	1.5	2.0	1.3	2.0	3.0	9.2
None	None	Full	Full	Full	Full	Partial	Full	Full	Full

Safari's support for this property, when applied to positioned elements, is limited to versions 2.0.2 or above.

Internet Explorer for Windows versions up to and including 7 don't support the value `inherit`.

width

```
width: { length | percentage | auto | inherit } ;
```

SPEC		
inherited	initial	version
NO	auto	CSS1
BROWSER SUPPORT		
IE7+	FF1+	Saf1.3+	Op9.2+
FULL	FULL	FULL	FULL

This property sets the content width of a block or a replaced element (p. 175). This width does not include padding, borders, or margins—see The CSS Box Model (p. 142).

If the contents of a block require more horizontal space than the width you assign, their behavior is defined by the `overflow` (p. 280) property.

Example

This style rule assigns a fixed width of 100 pixels to paragraphs within the element with ID `"example"`:

```
#example p {
  width: 100px;
}
```

Value

The property takes a CSS length (px, pt, em, and so on), a percentage, or the keyword `auto`. Negative length values are illegal.

Percentage values refer to the width of the element's containing block (p. 147). If the containing block's width depends on this element's width, the resulting layout is undefined in CSS2.1.

The special `auto` value allows the browser to calculate the content width automatically on the basis of other factors.

For absolutely positioned elements, for example, the content width may be calculated on the basis of the `left` (p. 278) and `right` (p. 276) property values, or on the left and right margins, borders, and padding applied to the element. Note that Internet Explorer versions up to and including 6 don't correctly apply the properties `left` and `right` when they're used at the same time. See the section on `position` for more details.

If no hard constraints are imposed by other properties, the element is allowed to assume its natural content width, based on the width of the horizontal space available. For static or (relatively positioned) elements, this means that an element whose width is set to auto will expand to fill the parent without our needing to set a specific width such as width: 100%. This is useful when padding and borders need to be set on the same element as it avoids any box model problems—see the box model (p. 142).

Compatibility

Internet Explorer			Firefox			Safari			Opera
5.5	6.0	7.0	1.0	1.5	2.0	1.3	2.0	3.0	9.2
Buggy	Buggy	Full	Full	Full	Full	Full	Full	Full	Full

Internet Explorer for Windows versions up to and including 5.5 (and up to and including version 7 in quirks mode) incorrectly include padding, borders, and margins in the content width. This is known as the box model bug (see the box model (p. 142)).

Internet Explorer for Windows versions up to and including 6 (and up to and including version 7 in quirks mode) in some respects incorrectly treat width as though it were min-width, by extending the content width of a block if its content cannot fit within the specified space. Such a scenario would arise if an image was bigger than the available content area, or if unbroken text content couldn't wrap, and pushed the boundaries of an element wide enough to fit. This bug may push other elements on the page out of place, or cause floated elements to drop down. The correct behavior would let the content overflow without affecting the width of the element, and would leave other elements unaffected.

However, this stretching of the width will only occur in the types of cases mentioned above—it won't be caused by the addition of content that will automatically wrap within the element, such as normal text. In simple terms, the parent element will only stretch when the element it holds has a specific width that's greater than that of the parent.

Internet Explorer for Windows versions up to and including 6 don't support the specification of both the position and the dimensions of an absolutely positioned element using `top`, `right`, `bottom`, and `left` together. They will use the last vertical and horizontal position specified, and need the dimensions to be specified using `width` and `height`.

Internet Explorer for Windows versions up to and including 7 don't support the value `inherit`.

min-width

```
min-width: { length | percentage | inherit } ;
```

SPEC		
inherited	initial	version
NO	0	CSS2
BROWSER SUPPORT			
IE7+	FF1+	Saf2+	Op9.2+
FULL	FULL	FULL	FULL

This property sets the minimum content width of a block or a replaced element (p. 175). This minimum width does not include padding, borders, or margins—see The CSS Box Model (p. 142).

An element to which `min-width` is applied will never be narrower than the minimum width specified, but it will be allowed to grow normally if its content exceeds the minimum width set.

Example

This style rule assigns a minimum width of 100 pixels to paragraphs within the element with ID `"example"`:

```
#example p {
    min-width: 100px;
}
```

`min-width` is often used in conjunction with `max-width` to produce a width range for the element concerned.

Combining min-width and width

It should be noted that `min-width` and `width` values should not be applied to the same element if they use the same unit, as one will override the other. For example, if the `width` is set to 150px and the `min-width` is set to 60px, the actual width of the element is 150px, and the `min-width` declaration becomes redundant:

```
#example {
    min-width: 60px;
    width: 150px;
}
```

In the above example, the width of the element will be fixed at 150px.

However, it's acceptable to set both `min-width` and `width` when their values are given in different units:

```
#example {
    min-width: 3em;
    width: 138px;
}
```

As the `min-width` is based on `em` units, at some stage, due to text resizing (for example), the `em` width may be larger than the 138px `width` we've set. In cases such as this, the element will be allowed to expand further than the 138px `width`, thus accommodating the resizing of the `em`-based text.

If the contents of a block require more horizontal space than is afforded by the limits that have been set, the behavior is defined by the `overflow` (p. 280) property.

Value

The property takes a CSS length (px, pt, em, and so on), or a percentage. Negative length values are illegal.

Percentage values refer to the width of the element's containing block. If the containing block's width is negative, the used value is zero.

Compatibility

Internet Explorer			Firefox			Safari			Opera
5.5	6.0	7.0	1.0	1.5	2.0	1.3	2.0	3.0	9.2
None	None	Full	Full	Full	Full	Partial	Full	Full	Full

Safari's support for this property, when applied to positioned elements, is limited to versions 2.0.2 or above.

Internet Explorer for Windows versions up to and including 7 don't support the value `inherit`.

max-width

```
max-width:
{ length | percentage | none | inherit }
;
```

SPEC		
inherited	initial	version
NO	none	CSS2
BROWSER SUPPORT			

IE7+	FF1+	Saf2+	Op9.2+
FULL	FULL	FULL	FULL

This property sets the maximum content width of a block or a replaced element (p. 175). This maximum width does not include padding, borders, or margins—see The CSS Box Model (p. 142).

An element to which a max-width is applied will never be wider than the value specified even if the width property is set to be wider. There is an exception to this rule, however: if min-width is specified with a value greater than that of max-width, the container's width will be the largest value, which in this case means that the min-width value will be the one that's applied.

max-width is often used in conjunction with min-width to produce a width range for the element concerned.

Example

This style rule assigns a maximum width of 400 pixels and a minimum width of 100 pixels to paragraphs within the element with ID "example":

```
#example p {
  max-width: 400px;
  min-width: 100px;
}
```

Combining max-width and width

Note that max-width and width shouldn't be applied to the same element using the same unit, as one will override the other. If, for example, the width is set to 150px and the max-width is set to 60px, the actual width of the element will be 60px, and the width declaration will become redundant.

The following style rule shows how conflicts are resolved where an element has been given both a width and a max-width using the same unit (pixels in this case):

```
.example {
  max-width: 60px;
  width: 150px;
}
```

In the above example, the width of the element will be fixed at `60px`.

However, it's acceptable to set `max-width` and `width` when the values are different units (although it may not be entirely useful, there are a few cases where it can be used to good effect).

This style rule assigns a `max-width` of `160px` to images with the class `"example"`, and also assigns a `width` of `50%`:

```
img.example {
  width: 50%;
  max-width: 160px;
  height: auto;
}
```

The final width of the image in the above example will be the smallest value.

If you want an image to scale when the page width is small, so that the image doesn't break out of its column, you could use the above example to ensure that the image's size decreases once the available space is less than 160 pixels.

If the available space is greater than 160 pixels, the image will expand until it's 160 pixels wide—but no further. This ensures that the image stays at a sensible size—or its correct aspect ratio—when space allows.

The `min-width` property can be used for the reverse of this scenario.

If the contents of a block require more horizontal space than is allowed by the limits that have been set, the behavior is defined by the `overflow` (p. 280) property.

Value

The property takes a CSS length (px, pt, em, and so on), a percentage, or the keyword `none`. Negative length values are illegal.

Percentage values refer to the width of the containing block (p. 147). If the containing block's width is negative, the used value is `none`.

Compatibility

Internet Explorer			Firefox			Safari			Opera
5.5	6.0	7.0	1.0	1.5	2.0	1.3	2.0	3.0	9.2
None	None	Full	Full	Full	Full	Partial	Full	Full	Full

Safari's support for this property, when applied to positioned elements, is limited to versions 2.0.2 or above.

Internet Explorer for Windows versions up to and including 7 don't support the value inherit.

Margins

These properties allow the author to control a box's margin—the area outside its border. You can also read The CSS Box Model (p. 142) for more information about margins.

margin-top

```
margin-top: { length | percentage | auto |
inherit } ;
```

SPEC		
inherited	initial	version
NO	0	CSS1
BROWSER SUPPORT			
IE5.5+	FF1+	Saf1.3+	Op9.2+
BUGGY	FULL	FULL	FULL

This property defines the vertical distance from the top border edge of an element to the edge of its containing block, or the element that's vertically adjacent above it. Its effect is also dependent on other factors, such as the presence of collapsing margins on vertically adjacent elements.

Example

This style rule assigns a margin of 20 pixels to the tops of paragraphs within the element with ID "example":

```
#example p {
  margin-top: 20px;
}
```

If the element above the element in question is floated, or absolutely positioned, the top margin will pass through the floated element, because floats and absolute elements are removed from the flow. The margin will only be affected by static elements (or elements for which position is set to relative, and which have no coordinates) in the normal flow of the document—this includes the containing block itself.

Refer to the sections on the CSS box model (p. 142), collapsing margins (p. 148), containing blocks (p. 147), and floating and clearing (p. 180) to understand exactly how margins work for all elements. The section on inline formatting (p. 166) also explains how margins affect inline elements.

Value

The property takes a CSS length (px, pt, em, and so on), the keyword `auto`, or a percentage of the width of the element's containing block (p. 147). Note that even for the top and bottom margins the percentage value will refer to the *width* of the containing block. If the containing block's width depends on the element to which percentage margins are applied, the resulting layout is undefined in CSS2.1.

Negative values are allowed for margins (although implementation-specific limits may apply), and have the effect of pulling the element in the direction of the margin specified. This may cause the element to overlap other elements, which may, of course, be the desired effect. In cases where overlap occurs, we can determine the elements' stacking levels by applying `z-index` values to them. In the case of non-positioned or floated elements, a z-index only takes effect when a `position` is set to `relative` for the elements, as a `z-index` can be applied only to positioned elements.

Negative margins on floats are handled differently and the details are covered in Floating and Clearing (p. 180).

When you use the value `auto`, you're allowing the browser to calculate the margins for you automatically. In most cases, the calculated value will default either to zero or to the distance required to reach the parent element's edge. In the case of a block element that has a specified width, left and right margins to which a value of `auto` is applied will be set to be equal. This will effectively center the element in the available space.

If margins are over-constrained—that is, the total of their specified dimensions is greater than the available content space—the browser will reset one of the margins to `auto` to overcome the problem.

Vertical margins will have no effect on non-replaced (p. 175) inline elements.

Compatibility

Internet Explorer			Firefox			Safari			Opera
5.5	6.0	7.0	1.0	1.5	2.0	1.3	2.0	3.0	9.2
Buggy	Buggy	Buggy	Full	Full	Full	Full	Full	Full	Full

Internet Explorer version 6 in some instances incorrectly bases vertical margin percentage values on the width of the body element, rather than the containing block.

Internet Explorer for Windows versions up to and including 7 differ in their handling of margin collapse from the CSS2.1 specifications. See Collapsing Margins (p. 148) for a detailed analysis.

Internet Explorer for Windows versions up to and including 7 don't support the value inherit.

margin-right

```
margin-right: { length | percentage | auto |
inherit } ;
```

SPEC		
inherited	initial	version
NO	0	CSS1
BROWSER SUPPORT		
IE5.5+	FF1+ Saf1.3+	Op9.2+
BUGGY	FULL FULL	FULL

This property defines the horizontal distance from the right border edge of the element concerned to the edge of its containing block, or the element that's horizontally adjacent to it.

If the element to the side is floated, or absolutely positioned, the margin will pass through it, because floats and absolute elements are removed from the flow. The margin will only be affected by static elements (or elements for which position is set to relative, and which have no coordinates) in the normal flow of the document—this includes the containing block itself.

Example

This style rule assigns a margin of 20 pixels to the right of paragraphs within the element with ID "example":

```
#example p {
  margin-right: 20px;
}
```

Refer to the sections on the CSS box model (p. 142), collapsing margins (p. 148), containing blocks (p. 147), and floating and clearing (p. 180) to understand exactly how margins work for all elements. The section on inline formatting (p. 166) also explains how margins affect inline elements.

Value

The property takes a CSS length (px, pt, em, and so on), the keyword `auto`, or a percentage of the width of the element's containing block (p. 147). Note that even for the top and bottom margins the percentage value will refer to the *width* of the containing block. If the containing block's width depends on the element to which percentage margins are applied, the resulting layout is undefined in CSS2.1.

Negative values are allowed for margins (although implementation-specific limits may apply), and have the effect of pulling the element in the direction of the margin specified. This may cause the element to overlap other elements, which may, of course, be the desired effect. In cases where overlap occurs, we can determine the elements' stacking levels by applying `z-index` values to them. In the case of non-positioned or floated elements, a z-index only takes effect when a `position` is set to `relative` for the elements, as a `z-index` can be applied only to positioned elements.

Negative margins on floats are handled differently and the details are covered in Floating and Clearing (p. 180).

When you use the value `auto`, you're allowing the browser to calculate the margins for you automatically. In most cases, the calculated value will default either to zero or to the distance required to reach the parent element's edge. In the case of a block element that has a specified width, left and right margins to which a value of `auto` is applied will be set to be equal. This will effectively center the element in the available space.

If margins are over-constrained—that is, the total of their specified dimensions is greater than the available content space—the browser will reset one of the margins to `auto` to overcome the problem.

Compatibility

Internet Explorer			Firefox			Safari			Opera
5.5	6.0	7.0	1.0	1.5	2.0	1.3	2.0	3.0	9.2
Buggy	Buggy	Buggy	Full	Full	Full	Full	Full	Full	Full

Internet Explorer version 5.5 (and version 6 in quirks mode) does not support the centering of a block element that has a specified width by setting its left and right margins to auto.

In Internet Explorer versions up to and including 6, the left or right margins are doubled on floated elements that touch their parents' side edges. The margin value is doubled on the side that touches the parent. A simple fix for this problem is to set display to inline for the floated element.

If the value of the horizontal negative margins are greater or equal to the sum of the width, padding, and borders of the element, the width of the element effectively becomes zero. Some older browsers (for example, Mozilla 1.6 and earlier versions) will appear to ignore the position of the element, much as they would an absolute element. This causes issues where following elements may not correctly clear the element in question. However, most modern browsers don't experience this issue.

Internet Explorer for Windows versions up to and including 7 don't support the value inherit.

margin-bottom

```
margin-bottom: { length | percentage | auto |
inherit } ;
```

SPEC		
inherited	initial	version
NO	0	CSS1
BROWSER SUPPORT		
IE5.5+	FF1+	Saf1.3+	Op9.2+
BUGGY	FULL	FULL	FULL

This property defines the vertical distance from the bottom border edge of the element concerned to the edge of its containing block, or the element that's vertically adjacent underneath. Its effect is also dependent on other factors, such as the presence of collapsing margins on vertically adjacent elements.

Example

This style rule assigns a margin of 20 pixels to the bottom of paragraphs within the element with ID "example":

```
#example p {
  margin-bottom: 20px;
}
```

Note that, unlike margin-top, an element's bottom margin will repel a floated element that's beneath it, because floats take their vertical positions from their current positions in the normal flow.

Refer to the sections on the CSS box model (p. 142), collapsing margins (p. 148), containing blocks (p. 147), and floating and clearing (p. 180) to understand exactly how margins work for all elements. The section on inline formatting (p. 166) also explains how margins affect inline elements.

Value

The property takes a CSS length (px, pt, em, and so on), the keyword auto, or a percentage of the width of the element's containing block (p. 147). Note that even for the top and bottom margins the percentage value will refer to the *width* of the containing block. If the containing block's width depends on the element to which percentage margins are applied, the resulting layout is undefined in CSS2.1.

Negative values are allowed for margins (although implementation-specific limits may apply), and have the effect of pulling the element in the direction of the margin specified. This may cause the element to overlap other elements, which may, of course, be the desired effect. In cases where overlap occurs, we can determine the elements' stacking levels by applying z-index values to them. In the case of non-positioned or floated elements, a z-index only takes effect when a `position` is set to `relative` for the elements, as a `z-index` can be applied only to positioned elements.

Negative margins on floats are handled differently and the details are covered in Floating and Clearing (p. 180).

When you use the value `auto`, you're allowing the browser to calculate the margins for you automatically. In most cases, the calculated value will default either to zero or to the distance required to reach the parent element's edge. In the case of a block element that has a specified width, left and right margins to which a value of `auto` is applied will be set to be equal. This will effectively center the element in the available space.

If margins are over-constrained—that is, the total of their specified dimensions is greater than the available content space—the browser will reset one of the margins to `auto` to overcome the problem.

Vertical margins will have no effect on non-replaced (p. 175) inline elements.

Compatibility

Internet Explorer			Firefox			Safari			Opera
5.5	6.0	7.0	1.0	1.5	2.0	1.3	2.0	3.0	9.2
Buggy	Buggy	Buggy	Full	Full	Full	Full	Full	Full	Full

Internet Explorer version 6 in some instances incorrectly bases vertical margin percentage values on the width of the `body` element, rather than the containing block.

Internet Explorer for Windows versions up to and including 7 differ in their handling of margin collapse from the CSS2.1 specifications. See Collapsing Margins (p. 148) for a detailed analysis.

Internet Explorer for Windows versions up to and including 7 don't support the value `inherit`.

margin-left

```
margin-left: { length | percentage | auto |
inherit } ;
```

SPEC		
inherited	initial	version
NO	0	CSS1
BROWSER SUPPORT		
IE5.5+	FF1+	Saf1.3+	Op9.2+
BUGGY	FULL	FULL	FULL

This property defines the horizontal distance from the left border edge of the element concerned to the edge of its containing block, or the element that's horizontally adjacent to it.

If the element to the side is floated, or absolutely positioned, the margin will pass through it, because floats and absolute elements are removed from the flow. The margin will only be affected by static elements (or elements for which position is set to relative, and which have no coordinates) in the normal flow of the document—this includes the containing block itself.

Example

This style rule assigns a margin of 20 pixels to the left of paragraphs within the element with ID "example":

```
#example p {
    margin-left: 20px;
}
```

Refer to the sections on the CSS box model (p. 142), collapsing margins (p. 148), containing blocks (p. 147), and floating and clearing (p. 180) to understand exactly how margins work for all elements. The section on inline formatting (p. 166) also explains how margins affect inline elements.

Value

The property takes a CSS length (px, pt, em, and so on), the keyword auto, or a percentage of the width of the element's containing block (p. 147). Note that even for the top and bottom margins the percentage value will refer to the *width* of the containing block. If the containing block's width depends on the element to which percentage margins are applied, the resulting layout is undefined in CSS2.1.

Negative values are allowed for margins (although implementation-specific limits may apply), and have the effect of pulling the element in the direction of the margin specified. This may cause the element to overlap other elements, which may, of course, be the desired effect. In cases where overlap occurs, we can determine the elements' stacking levels by applying z-index values to them. In the case of non-positioned or floated elements, a z-index only takes effect when a `position` is set to `relative` for the elements, as a `z-index` can be applied only to positioned elements.

Negative margins on floats are handled differently and the details are covered in Floating and Clearing (p. 180).

When you use the value `auto`, you're allowing the browser to calculate the margins for you automatically. In most cases, the calculated value will default either to zero or to the distance required to reach the parent element's edge. In the case of a block element that has a specified width, left and right margins to which a value of `auto` is applied will be set to be equal. This will effectively center the element in the available space.

If margins are over-constrained—that is, the total of their specified dimensions is greater than the available content space—the browser will reset one of the margins to `auto` to overcome the problem.

Compatibility

Internet Explorer			Firefox			Safari			Opera
5.5	6.0	7.0	1.0	1.5	2.0	1.3	2.0	3.0	9.2
Buggy	Buggy	Buggy	Full	Full	Full	Full	Full	Full	Full

Internet Explorer version 5.5 (and version 6 in quirks mode) does not support the centering of a block element that has a specified width by setting its left and right margins to `auto`.

In Internet Explorer versions up to and including 6, the left or right margins are doubled on floated elements that touch their parents' side edges. The margin value is doubled on the side that touches the parent. A simple fix for this problem is to set `display` to `inline` for the floated element.

If the value of the horizontal negative margins are greater or equal to the sum of the width, padding, and borders of the element, the width of the element effectively becomes zero. Some older browsers (for example, Mozilla 1.6 and earlier versions) will appear to ignore the position of the element, much as they would an absolute element. This causes issues where following elements may not correctly clear the element in question. However, most modern browsers don't experience this issue.

Internet Explorer for Windows versions up to and including 7 don't support the value inherit.

margin

```
margin: { { length | percentage | auto } ¹ ᵗᵒ ⁴ ᵛᵃˡᵘᵉˢ
| inherit } ;
```

	SPEC		
inherited	initial		version
NO	0		CSS1
BROWSER SUPPORT			
IE5.5+	FF1+	Saf1.3+	Op9.2+
BUGGY	FULL	FULL	FULL

In the normal flow of a document, margins are generally used to control the horizontal and vertical whitespace around elements. You can think of a margin as having the effect of pushing the element away from other elements on the page.

Refer to the sections on the CSS box model (p. 142), collapsing margins (p. 148), containing blocks (p. 147), and floating and clearing (p. 180) to understand exactly how margins work for all elements. The section on inline formatting (p. 166) also explains how margins affect inline elements.

Also see The CSS Box Model (p. 142) for an overview of how margins are handled in relation to an element's borders, padding, and width.

Example

This style rule assigns a margin of ten pixels to all four sides of paragraphs within the element with ID "example":

```
#example p {
  margin: 10px;
}
```

Value

The shorthand property margin allows all four sides of an element's margins to be set using either one, two, three or four specified values. Refer to the mnemonic (TRouBLe) in Shorthand Properties (p. 39) as an easy way to remember the shorthand order of margins.

The property takes a CSS length (px, pt, em, and so on), the keyword auto, or a percentage of the width of the element's containing block (p. 147). Note that even for the top and bottom margins the percentage value will refer to the *width* of the containing block. If the containing block's width depends on the element to which percentage margins are applied, the resulting layout is undefined in CSS2.1.

Negative values are allowed for margins (although implementation-specific limits may apply), and have the effect of pulling the element in the direction of the margin specified. This may cause the element to overlap other elements, which may, of course, be the desired effect. In cases where overlap occurs, we can determine the elements' stacking levels by applying `z-index` values to them. In the case of non-positioned or floated elements, a z-index only takes effect when a `position` is set to `relative` for the elements, as a `z-index` can be applied only to positioned elements.

Negative margins on floats are handled differently and the details are covered in Floating and Clearing (p. 180).

When you use the value `auto`, you're allowing the browser to calculate the margins for you automatically. In most cases, the calculated value will default either to zero or to the distance required to reach the parent element's edge. In the case of a block element that has a specified width, left and right margins to which a value of `auto` is applied will be set to be equal. This will effectively center the element in the available space.

If margins are over-constrained—that is, the total of their specified dimensions is greater than the available content space—the browser will reset one of the margins to `auto` to overcome the problem.

Compatibility

Internet Explorer			Firefox			Safari			Opera
5.5	6.0	7.0	1.0	1.5	2.0	1.3	2.0	3.0	9.2
Buggy	Buggy	Buggy	Full	Full	Full	Full	Full	Full	Full

Internet Explorer version 6 in some instances incorrectly bases vertical margin percentage values on the width of the `body` element, rather than the containing block.

Internet Explorer version 5.5 (and version 6 in quirks mode) does not support the centering of a block element that has a specified width by setting its left and right margins to `auto`.

In Internet Explorer versions up to and including 6, the left or right margins are doubled on floated elements that touch their parents' side edges. The margin value is doubled on the side that touches the parent. A simple fix for this problem is to set `display` to `inline` for the floated element.

Internet Explorer for Windows versions up to and including 7 differ in their handling of margin collapse from the CSS2.1 specifications. See Collapsing Margins (p. 148) for a detailed analysis.

If the value of the horizontal negative margins are greater or equal to the sum of the width, padding, and borders of the element, the width of the element effectively becomes zero. Some older browsers (for example, Mozilla 1.6 and earlier versions) will appear to ignore the position of the element, much as they would an absolute element. This causes issues where following elements may not correctly clear the element in question. However, most modern browsers don't experience this issue.

Internet Explorer for Windows versions up to and including 7 don't support the value `inherit`.

Padding

These properties allow the author to control a box's padding—the area between its content and its border. You can also read The CSS Box Model (p. 142) for more information about padding.

padding-top

`padding-top: { length | percentage | inherit } ;`

SPEC		
inherited	initial	version
NO	0	CSS1, 2.1
BROWSER SUPPORT		
IE6+ FF1+ Saf1.3+ Op9.2+		
FULL FULL FULL FULL		

The property `padding-top` sets the padding on the top side of an element using the value specified.

Padding is the area that's sandwiched between an element's borders and its content. Any background image or background color that's applied to the element will extend across the padding area. Refer to The CSS Box Model (p. 142) for an in-depth discussion of how padding is accommodated within the CSS box model.

Example

This style rule assigns a 2em padding to the top side of paragraphs within the element with ID `"example"`:

```
#example p {
  padding-top: 2em;
}
```

When vertical padding (`padding-top` and `padding-bottom`) is used on an inline, non-replaced element, it can cause the overlapping of elements above and below that element in cases where the padding causes the element in question to exceed the line height. See Inline Formatting (p. 166) for more information.

Value

The property takes a CSS length (px, pt, em, and so on) or a percentage of the width of the element's containing block (p. 147). Note that even for top and bottom padding the percentage value will refer to the *width* of the containing block. Negative length values are not allowed.

In CSS2.1, if the containing block's width depends on an element with percentage padding, the resulting layout is undefined.

Compatibility

Internet Explorer			Firefox			Safari			Opera
5.5	6.0	7.0	1.0	1.5	2.0	1.3	2.0	3.0	9.2
Buggy	Full	Full	Full	Full	Full	Full	Full	Full	Full

Internet Explorer versions up to and including 5.5 (and IE6 and IE7 when in quirks mode) incorrectly apply `padding` inside the stated `width`, thus reducing the space available for content—see The Internet Explorer 5 Box Model (p. 156).

Internet Explorer up to and including version 6 will often need a `position:relative;` declaration added to inline elements in order to show the full amount of vertical padding.

Internet Explorer for Windows versions up to and including 7 don't support the value `inherit`.

padding-right

`padding-right: { length | percentage | inherit } ;`

SPEC		
inherited	initial	version
NO	0	CSS1, 2.1
BROWSER SUPPORT		
IE6+	FF1+	Saf1.3+	Op9.2+
FULL	BUGGY	FULL	FULL

The `padding-right` property sets the padding to the right side of an element using the value specified.

Padding is the area that's sandwiched between an element's borders and its content. Any background image or background color that's applied to the element will extend across the padding area. Refer to The CSS Box Model (p. 142) for an in-depth discussion of how padding is accommodated within the CSS box model.

Example

This style rule assigns a 2em padding value to the right side of paragraphs within the element with ID "example":

```
#example p {
  padding-right: 2em;
}
```

When horizontal padding (`padding-left` and `padding-right`) is used on inline, non-replaced elements, it has a different effect than it has on block-level elements. The `padding-left` value is applied at the start of the inline element, while `padding-right` is applied at the end of the inline element. If the element is split over two or more line boxes, the right padding wraps to the next line with the element. It doesn't apply padding to the start and end of each single line, as is the case with block-level elements. See Inline Formatting (p. 166) for more information.

Value

The property takes a CSS length (px, pt, em, and so on) or a percentage of the width of the element's containing block (p. 147). Note that even for top and bottom padding the percentage value will refer to the *width* of the containing block. Negative length values are not allowed.

In CSS2.1, if the containing block's width depends on an element with percentage padding, the resulting layout is undefined.

Compatibility

Internet Explorer			Firefox			Safari			Opera
5.5	6.0	7.0	1.0	1.5	2.0	1.3	2.0	3.0	9.2
Buggy	Full	Full	Buggy	Buggy	Buggy	Full	Full	Full	Full

Internet Explorer versions up to and including 5.5 (and IE6 and IE7 when in quirks mode) incorrectly apply `padding` inside the stated `width`, thus reducing the space available for content—see The Internet Explorer 5 Box Model (p. 156).

Firefox versions up to and including 2.0.0.7 incorrectly apply `padding-right` on inline elements when the element wraps to a new line. The preceding line and the current line both appear to have padding applied (see Bugzilla[2]).

Internet Explorer for Windows versions up to and including 7 don't support the value `inherit`.

---

[2] http://bugzilla.mozilla.org/show_bug.cgi?id=122795

padding-bottom

padding-bottom: { *length* | *percentage* | inherit } ;

SPEC		
inherited	initial	version
NO	0	CSS1, 2.1
BROWSER SUPPORT			
IE6+	FF1+	Saf1.3+	Op9.2+
FULL	FULL	FULL	FULL

The `padding-bottom` property sets the padding to the bottom side of an element using the value specified.

Padding is the area that's sandwiched between an element's borders and its content. Any background image or background color that's applied to the element will extend across the padding area. Refer to The CSS Box Model (p. 142) for an in-depth discussion of how padding is accommodated within the CSS box model.

Example

This style rule assigns a 2em padding to the bottom side of paragraphs within the element with ID "example":

```
#example p {
    padding-bottom: 2em;
}
```

When vertical padding (`padding-top` and `padding-bottom`) is used on an inline, non-replaced element, it can cause the overlapping of elements above and below that element in cases where the padding causes the element in question to exceed the line height. See Inline Formatting (p. 166) for more information.

Value

The property takes a CSS length (px, pt, em, and so on) or a percentage of the width of the element's containing block (p. 147). Note that even for top and bottom padding the percentage value will refer to the *width* of the containing block. Negative length values are not allowed.

In CSS2.1, if the containing block's width depends on an element with percentage padding, the resulting layout is undefined.

Compatibility

Internet Explorer			Firefox			Safari			Opera
5.5	6.0	7.0	1.0	1.5	2.0	1.3	2.0	3.0	9.2
Buggy	Full	Full	Full	Full	Full	Full	Full	Full	Full

Internet Explorer versions up to and including 5.5 (and IE6 and IE7 when in quirks mode) incorrectly apply `padding` inside the stated `width`, thus reducing the space available for content—see The Internet Explorer 5 Box Model (p. 156).

Internet Explorer up to and including version 6 will often need a `position:relative;` declaration added to inline elements in order to show the full amount of vertical padding.

Internet Explorer for Windows versions up to and including 7 don't support the value `inherit`.

padding-left

`padding-left: { length | percentage | inherit } ;`

SPEC		
inherited	initial	version
NO	0	CSS1, 2.1
BROWSER SUPPORT		
IE6+	FF1+	Saf1.3+	Op9.2+
FULL	FULL	FULL	FULL

The property `padding-left` sets the padding to the left side of an element using the value specified.

Padding is the area that's sandwiched between an element's borders and its content. Any background image or background color that's applied to the element will extend across the padding area. Refer to The CSS Box Model (p. 142) for an in-depth discussion of how padding is accommodated within the CSS box model.

Example

This style rule assigns a 2em padding to the left side of paragraphs within the element with ID "example":

```
#example p {
    padding-left: 2em;
}
```

When horizontal padding (`padding-left` and `padding-right`) is used on inline, non-replaced elements, it has a different effect than it has on block-level elements. The `padding-left` value is applied at the start of the inline element, while `padding-right` is applied at the end of the inline element. If the element is split over two or more line boxes, the right padding wraps to the next line with the element. It doesn't apply padding to the start and end of each single line, as is the case with block-level elements. See Inline Formatting (p. 166) for more information.

Box Properties

Value

The property takes a CSS length (px, pt, em, and so on) or a percentage of the width of the element's containing block (p. 147). Note that even for top and bottom padding the percentage value will refer to the *width* of the containing block. Negative length values are not allowed.

In CSS2.1, if the containing block's width depends on an element with percentage padding, the resulting layout is undefined.

Compatibility

Internet Explorer			Firefox			Safari			Opera
5.5	6.0	7.0	1.0	1.5	2.0	1.3	2.0	3.0	9.2
Buggy	Full	Full	Full	Full	Full	Full	Full	Full	Full

Internet Explorer versions up to and including 5.5 (and IE6 and IE7 when in quirks mode) incorrectly apply `padding` inside the stated `width`, thus reducing the space available for content—see The Internet Explorer 5 Box Model (p. 156).

Internet Explorer for Windows versions up to and including 7 don't support the value `inherit`.

padding

```
padding: { { length | percentage } 1 to 4 values |
inherit } ;
```

SPEC		
inherited	initial	version
NO	0	CSS1, 2.1

BROWSER SUPPORT			
IE6+	FF1+	Saf1.3+	Op9.2+
FULL	FULL	FULL	FULL

The shorthand property padding sets the padding for all four sides of an element using the specified value or values. Each side can have its own value; refer to the mnemonic (TRouBLe) in Shorthand Properties (p. 39) for an easy way to remember the order in which each side is specified for the shorthand property.

Example

This style rule assigns a two-pixel padding value to the top side, a 4px padding value to the right side, a 6px padding value to the bottom side, and an 8px padding value to the left side of paragraphs within the element with ID "example":

```
#example p {
    padding: 2px 4px 6px 8px;
}
```

Padding is the area that's sandwiched between an element's borders and its content. Any background image or background color that's applied to the element will extend across the padding area. Refer to The CSS Box Model (p. 142) for an in-depth discussion of how padding is accommodated within the CSS box model.

When vertical padding (padding-top and padding-bottom) is used on an inline, non-replaced element, it can cause the overlapping of elements above and below that element in cases where the padding causes the element in question to exceed the line height. See Inline Formatting (p. 166) for more information.

When horizontal padding (padding-left and padding-right) is used on inline, non-replaced elements, it has a different effect than it has on block-level elements. The padding-left value is applied at the start of the inline element, while padding-right is applied at the end of the inline element. If the element is split over two or more line boxes, the right padding wraps to the next line with the element. It doesn't apply padding to the start and end of each single line, as is the case with block-level elements. See Inline Formatting (p. 166) for more information.

Value

The property takes a CSS length (px, pt, em, and so on) or a percentage of the width of the element's containing block (p. 147). Note that even for top and bottom padding the percentage value will refer to the *width* of the containing block. Negative length values are not allowed.

Consider the following example:

```css
.outer {
  width: 600px;
  height: 100px;
  background: blue;
}
.outer p {
  width: 300px;
  padding: 10% 0;
  background: red;
  height: 80%
}
```

```html
<div class="outer">
  <p>this is a test</p>
</div>
```

You may have expected the total height of the paragraph to add up to 100 pixels because 80% (height) + 10% (top padding) + 10% (bottom padding) = 100%. However, the paragraph will actually be 200 pixels high, as the percentage values used for the vertical padding are based on the 600px width of the parent element, resulting in values of 60px padding on the top and 60px padding on the bottom. The percentage value used for height is based on the parent elements height, resulting in a value of 80px, which results in a total height for the element of 200px (80 + 60 + 60).

In CSS2.1, if the containing block's width depends on an element with percentage padding, the resulting layout is undefined.

Compatibility

Internet Explorer			Firefox			Safari			Opera
5.5	6.0	7.0	1.0	1.5	2.0	1.3	2.0	3.0	9.2
Buggy	Full	Full	Full	Full	Full	Full	Full	Full	Full

Internet Explorer versions up to and including 5.5 (and IE6 and IE7 when in quirks mode) incorrectly apply `padding` inside the stated `width`, thus reducing the space available for content—see The Internet Explorer 5 Box Model (p. 156).

Internet Explorer up to and including version 6 will often need a `position:relative;` declaration added to inline elements in order to show the full amount of vertical padding.

Internet Explorer for Windows versions up to and including 7 don't support the value `inherit`.

Borders and Outlines

Border properties allow the author to control a box's border—the area between its padding and its margins. You can also read The CSS Box Model (p. 142) for more information about borders.

Outline properties allow the author to control a box's outline. The outline is usually drawn outside the border area but doesn't take up any space like borders do.

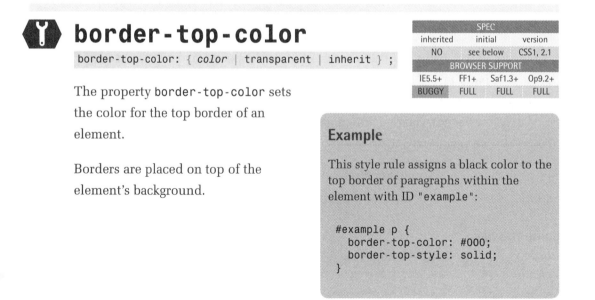

border-top-color

`border-top-color: { color | transparent | inherit } ;`

The property `border-top-color` sets the color for the top border of an element.

Borders are placed on top of the element's background.

SPEC		
inherited	initial	version
NO	see below	CSS1, 2.1
BROWSER SUPPORT			
IE5.5+	FF1+	Saf1.3+	Op9.2+
BUGGY	FULL	FULL	FULL

Example

This style rule assigns a black color to the top border of paragraphs within the element with ID `"example"`:

```
#example p {
  border-top-color: #000;
  border-top-style: solid;
}
```

Box Properties

Value

This property takes any valid CSS color value or color keyword (p. 33). The initial value for this property is the value of the `color` property for the element.

The value `transparent` allows the border to be transparent, but it will still occupy the space set by the `border-width` property and allow the background of the element to show through the transparent border.

Note that a border will only be visible as long as a `border-style` has been set. The default for `border-style` is `none`, which means that no border will display, and the `border-width` will be reset to zero.

Compatibility

Internet Explorer			Firefox			Safari			Opera
5.5	6.0	7.0	1.0	1.5	2.0	1.3	2.0	3.0	9.2
Buggy	Buggy	Buggy	Full	Full	Full	Full	Full	Full	Full

Internet Explorer for Windows versions up to and including 6 do not support `transparent` borders.

User agents are supposed to place borders on the element's background, but in Internet Explorer for Windows versions up to and including 7, the background only reaches the inside edge of the border when the element has a layout (p. 158). This means that for `dotted` or `dashed` borders, the background won't be visible through the spaces within the border. When the element doesn't have a layout, the background will extend under the borders.

The appearance of the borders may vary between user agents (within limits). The algorithms that define the relationship between the colors used to achieve an effect (for example, `groove`, `ridge`, `inset`, and `outset`) are not explicitly defined in the CSS specifications, so the colors may vary between user agents. In CSS2.1, the three-dimensional border styles (`groove`, `ridge`, `inset`, and `outset`) depend on the corresponding `border-color`, rather than on `color`.

Internet Explorer for Windows versions up to and including 7 don't support the value `inherit`.

border-top-style

```
border-top-style: { none | hidden | dotted | dashed
| solid | double | groove | ridge | inset | outset
| inherit } ;
```

SPEC		
inherited	initial	version
NO	none	CSS1, 2.1
BROWSER SUPPORT			
IE5.5+	FF1+	Saf1.3+	Op9.2+
BUGGY	FULL	FULL	FULL

The property `border-top-style` sets the style of the top border on an element. Borders are placed on top of the element's background.

Value

none   none means no border will show, and the computed `border-width` is zero.

hidden   hidden has the same meaning as none, except when it refers to table borders in cases where two cells share a border, and the table cells have collapsed borders (`border-collapse:collapse;`). The value hidden ensures that no border is drawn, since hidden takes precedence over all other border styles. If none had been used for one border in the cell, the border would still be drawn, as the adjacent cell's border would take precedence. See Table Formatting (p. 168) for more information.

dotted   dotted implements the border as a series of dots.

dashed   dashed implements the border as a series of dashes.

solid   solid implements the border as a solid line.

double   double implements the border as two solid lines. The sum of the two border widths and the space between them equals the value that has been set for `border-width`.

groove   groove is a three-dimensional effect that gives the impression that the border is carved into the canvas.

Example

This style rule assigns a solid border to the top edge of paragraphs within the element with ID "example":

```
#example p {
    border-top-style: solid;
}
```

ridge   ridge is a 3D effect that has the opposite effect of groove, in that the border appears to protrude from the canvas.

inset   inset is a 3D effect that gives the impression that the box is embedded into the canvas. When it's used on tables to which the separated borders model has been applied, the inset value appears to make the whole box look as though it were embedded into the canvas. When used with the collapsing border model, it's treated the same as the value ridge.

outset   outset is a 3D effect that has the opposite effect of inset in that the border gives the impression that the box protrudes from the canvas. When it's used on tables to which the separated borders model has been applied, the border makes the whole box look as though it were coming out of the canvas. When it's used with the collapsing border model, it behaves the same way as groove.

Previously, in CSS1, user agents were allowed to interpret all dotted, dashed, double, groove, ridge, inset, and outset styles as solid.

Compatibility

Internet Explorer			Firefox			Safari			Opera
5.5	6.0	7.0	1.0	1.5	2.0	1.3	2.0	3.0	9.2
Buggy	Buggy	Buggy	Full	Full	Full	Full	Full	Full	Full

User agents are supposed to place borders on the element's background, but in Internet Explorer for Windows versions up to and including 7, the background only reaches the inside edge of the border when the element has a layout (p. 158). This means that for dotted or dashed borders, the background won't be visible through the spaces within the border. When the element doesn't have a layout, the background will extend under the borders.

When dotted borders are specified as the border-style, and the border's width is only 1px, Internet Explorer for Windows versions up to and including 6 will display the borders as dashed instead of dotted. At a width of 2px and above, the dotted borders will display correctly. This glitch was fixed in Internet Explorer Version 7 for cases when all four sides are set to 1px. However, if one of the sides is set to 2px or more, the 1px dotted borders revert to dashed in IE7.

The appearance of the borders may vary between user agents (within limits). The algorithms that define the relationship between the colors used to achieve an effect (for example, groove, ridge, inset, and outset) are not explicitly defined in the CSS specifications, so the colors may vary between user agents. In CSS2.1, the three-dimensional border styles (groove, ridge, inset, and outset) depend on the corresponding border-color, rather than on color.

Internet Explorer for Windows versions up to and including 7:

- don't support the value hidden
- don't support the value inherit

border-top-width

```
border-top-width: { thin | medium | thick | length
| inherit } ;
```

SPEC		
inherited	initial	version
NO	medium	CSS1
BROWSER SUPPORT			
IE5.5+	FF1+	Saf1.3+	Op9.2+
BUGGY	FULL	FULL	FULL

The property border-top-width sets the width of the border to the top side of an element using the values specified.

Value

The property takes a CSS length (px, pt, em, and so on) or one of the allowed keywords; percentage values are not allowed.

Negative length values are illegal.

Example

This style rule assigns a 2px border width to the top of paragraphs within the element with ID "example":

```
#example p {
  border-top-width: 2px;
  border-top-style: solid;
}
```

The keyword width values of thin, medium, and thick aren't explicitly defined—their display will depend on the user agent—but have the following meaning: thin <= medium <= thick.

As an example, Internet Explorer versions (up to and including 7) size `thin`, `medium`, and `thick` borders at 2px, 4px, and 6px respectively, while Firefox 2.0 sizes them at 1px, 3px, and 5px.

Compatibility

Internet Explorer			Firefox			Safari			Opera
5.5	6.0	7.0	1.0	1.5	2.0	1.3	2.0	3.0	9.2
Buggy	Buggy	Buggy	Full	Full	Full	Full	Full	Full	Full

User agents are supposed to place borders on the element's background, but in Internet Explorer for Windows versions up to and including 7, the background only reaches the inside edge of the border when the element has a layout (p. 158). This means that for `dotted` or `dashed` borders, the background won't be visible through the spaces within the border. When the element doesn't have a layout, the background will extend under the borders.

When dotted borders are specified as the `border-style`, and the border's width is only 1px, Internet Explorer for Windows versions up to and including 6 will display the borders as `dashed` instead of `dotted`. At a width of 2px and above, the dotted borders will display correctly. This glitch was fixed in Internet Explorer Version 7 for cases when all four sides are set to 1px. However, if one of the sides is set to 2px or more, the 1px `dotted` borders revert to `dashed` in IE7.

Internet Explorer for Windows versions up to and including 7 don't support the value `inherit`.

border-top

```
border-top: { [border-width] [border-style]
[border-color] | inherit } ;
```

SPEC		
inherited	initial	version
NO	see below	CSS1
BROWSER SUPPORT			
IE5.5+	FF1+	Saf1.3+	Op9.2+
BUGGY	FULL	FULL	FULL

The border-top shorthand property sets border-top-width and/or border-top-style and/or border-top-color to the top side of an element simultaneously.

Borders are placed on top of the element's background.

Example

This style rule assigns a 2px red border to the top side of paragraphs within the element with ID "example":

```
#example p {
    border-top: 2px solid red;
}
```

Value

Refer to the following individual properties for specific information on allowed and initial values: border-width (p. 254), border-style (p. 251), and border-color (p. 249).

Negative length values are illegal.

As with most shorthand properties, you don't need to specify all the properties listed, but any omitted properties will revert to their default values. In the case of border-style, if you omit a value no border will show at all, because the default value is none. A border will only be visible as long as the border-style property has been set to something other than none or hidden, or has been restated explicitly after the initial shorthand declaration. Otherwise, no border will show and the border-width will be reset to zero. Therefore, it's good practice to specify a value for the border's style when you're using shorthand notation.

Compatibility

Internet Explorer			Firefox			Safari			Opera
5.5	6.0	7.0	1.0	1.5	2.0	1.3	2.0	3.0	9.2
Buggy	Buggy	Buggy	Full	Full	Full	Full	Full	Full	Full

User agents are supposed to place borders on the element's background, but in Internet Explorer for Windows versions up to and including 7, the background only reaches the inside edge of the border when the element has a layout (p. 158). This means that for `dotted` or `dashed` borders, the background won't be visible through the spaces within the border. When the element doesn't have a layout, the background will extend under the borders.

When dotted borders are specified as the `border-style`, and the border's width is only `1px`, Internet Explorer for Windows versions up to and including 6 will display the borders as `dashed` instead of `dotted`. At a width of `2px` and above, the dotted borders will display correctly. This glitch was fixed in Internet Explorer Version 7 for cases when all four sides are set to `1px`. However, if one of the sides is set to `2px` or more, the `1px` `dotted` borders revert to `dashed` in IE7.

Internet Explorer for Windows versions up to and including 6 do not support `transparent` borders.

Internet Explorer for Windows versions up to and including 7:

- don't support the value `hidden`
- don't support the value `inherit`

The appearance of the borders may vary between user agents (within limits). The algorithms that define the relationship between the colors used to achieve an effect (for example, `groove`, `ridge`, `inset`, and `outset`) are not explicitly defined in the CSS specifications, so the colors may vary between user agents. In CSS2.1, the three-dimensional border styles (`groove`, `ridge`, `inset`, and `outset`) depend on the corresponding `border-color`, rather than on `color`.

border-right-color

```
border-right-color: { color | transparent |
inherit } ;
```

SPEC		
inherited	initial	version
NO	see below	CSS1, 2.1
BROWSER SUPPORT			
IE5.5+	FF1+	Saf1.3+	Op9.2+
BUGGY	FULL	FULL	FULL

The property `border-right-color` sets the color for the right border of an element.

Borders are placed on top of the element's background.

Value

This property takes any valid CSS color value or color keyword (p. 33). The initial value for this property is the value of the `color` property for the element.

Example

This style rule assigns a blue color to the right border of paragraphs within the element with ID `"example"`:

```
#example p {
    border-right-color: blue;
    border-right-style: solid;
}
```

The value `transparent` allows the border to be transparent, but it will still occupy the space set by the `border-width` property and allow the background of the element to show through the transparent border.

Note that a border will only be visible as long as a `border-style` has been set. The default for `border-style` is `none`, which means that no border will display, and the `border-width` will be reset to zero.

Compatibility

Internet Explorer			Firefox			Safari			Opera
5.5	6.0	7.0	1.0	1.5	2.0	1.3	2.0	3.0	9.2
Buggy	Buggy	Buggy	Full	Full	Full	Full	Full	Full	Full

Internet Explorer for Windows versions up to and including 6 do not support `transparent` borders.

User agents are supposed to place borders on the element's background, but in Internet Explorer for Windows versions up to and including 7, the background only reaches the inside edge of the border when the element has a layout (p. 158). This means that for `dotted` or `dashed` borders, the background won't be visible through

the spaces within the border. When the element doesn't have a layout, the background will extend under the borders.

The appearance of the borders may vary between user agents (within limits). The algorithms that define the relationship between the colors used to achieve an effect (for example, groove, ridge, inset, and outset) are not explicitly defined in the CSS specifications, so the colors may vary between user agents. In CSS2.1, the three-dimensional border styles (groove, ridge, inset, and outset) depend on the corresponding border-color, rather than on color.

Internet Explorer for Windows versions up to and including 7 don't support the value inherit.

border-right-style

```
border-right-style: { none | hidden | dotted | dashed
| solid | double | groove | ridge | inset | outset
| inherit } ;
```

SPEC		
inherited	initial	version
NO	none	CSS1, 2.1
BROWSER SUPPORT		
IE5.5+	FF1+	Saf1.3+	Op9.2+
BUGGY	FULL	FULL	FULL

The property border-right-style sets the style of an element's right-hand border using the values specified.

Borders are placed on top of the element's background.

Value

none   none means no border will show, and the computed border-width is zero.

hidden   hidden has the same meaning as none, except when it refers to table borders in cases where two cells share a border, and the table cells have collapsed borders (border-collapse:collapse;). The value hidden ensures that no border is drawn, since hidden takes precedence over all other border styles. If none had been used for one border in the cell, the

Example

This style rule assigns a solid border to the right-hand edge of paragraphs within the element with ID "example":

```
#example p {
    border-right-style: solid;
}
```

border would still be drawn, as the adjacent cell's border would take precedence. See Table Formatting (p. 168) for more information.

dotted   `dotted` implements the border as a series of dots.

dashed   `dashed` implements the border as a series of dashes.

solid   `solid` implements the border as a solid line.

double   `double` implements the border as two solid lines. The sum of the two border widths and the space between them equals the value that has been set for `border-width`.

groove   `groove` is a three-dimensional effect that gives the impression that the border is carved into the canvas.

ridge   `ridge` is a 3D effect that has the opposite effect of `groove`, in that the border appears to protrude from the canvas.

inset   `inset` is a 3D effect that gives the impression that the box is embedded into the canvas. When it's used on tables to which the separated borders model has been applied, the `inset` value appears to make the whole box look as though it were embedded into the canvas. When used with the collapsing border model, it's treated the same as the value `ridge`.

outset   `outset` is a 3D effect that has the opposite effect of `inset` in that the border gives the impression that the box protrudes from the canvas. When it's used on tables to which the separated borders model has been applied, the border makes the whole box look as though it were coming out of the canvas. When it's used with the collapsing border model, it behaves the same way as `groove`.

Previously, in CSS1, user agents were allowed to interpret all `dotted`, `dashed`, `double`, `groove`, `ridge`, `inset`, and `outset` styles as `solid`.

Compatibility

Internet Explorer			Firefox			Safari			Opera
5.5	6.0	7.0	1.0	1.5	2.0	1.3	2.0	3.0	9.2
Buggy	Buggy	Buggy	Full	Full	Full	Full	Full	Full	Full

User agents are supposed to place borders on the element's background, but in Internet Explorer for Windows versions up to and including 7, the background only reaches the inside edge of the border when the element has a layout (p. 158). This means that for dotted or dashed borders, the background won't be visible through the spaces within the border. When the element doesn't have a layout, the background will extend under the borders.

When dotted borders are specified as the border-style, and the border's width is only 1px, Internet Explorer for Windows versions up to and including 6 will display the borders as dashed instead of dotted. At a width of 2px and above, the dotted borders will display correctly. This glitch was fixed in Internet Explorer Version 7 for cases when all four sides are set to 1px. However, if one of the sides is set to 2px or more, the 1px dotted borders revert to dashed in IE7.

The appearance of the borders may vary between user agents (within limits). The algorithms that define the relationship between the colors used to achieve an effect (for example, groove, ridge, inset, and outset) are not explicitly defined in the CSS specifications, so the colors may vary between user agents. In CSS2.1, the three-dimensional border styles (groove, ridge, inset, and outset) depend on the corresponding border-color, rather than on color.

Internet Explorer for Windows versions up to and including 7:

- don't support the value hidden
- don't support the value inherit

border-right-width

border-right-width: { thin | medium | thick | *length* | inherit } ;

SPEC		
inherited	initial	version
NO	medium	CSS1
BROWSER SUPPORT			
IE5.5+	FF1+	Saf1.3+	Op9.2+
BUGGY	FULL	FULL	FULL

The property border-right-width sets the width of the border on the right-hand side of an element using the values specified.

Value

The property takes a CSS length (px, pt, em, and so on) or one of the allowed keywords; percentage values are not allowed.

Negative length values are illegal.

Example

This style rule assigns a 2px border width to the right of paragraphs within the element with ID "example":

```
#example p {
    border-right-width: 2px;
    border-right-style: solid;
}
```

The keyword width values of thin, medium, and thick aren't explicitly defined—their display will depend on the user agent—but have the following meaning: thin <= medium <= thick.

As an example, Internet Explorer versions (up to and including 7) size thin, medium, and thick borders at 2px, 4px, and 6px respectively, while Firefox 2.0 sizes them at 1px, 3px, and 5px.

Compatibility

Internet Explorer			Firefox			Safari			Opera
5.5	6.0	7.0	1.0	1.5	2.0	1.3	2.0	3.0	9.2
Buggy	Buggy	Buggy	Full	Full	Full	Full	Full	Full	Full

User agents are supposed to place borders on the element's background, but in Internet Explorer for Windows versions up to and including 7, the background only reaches the inside edge of the border when the element has a layout (p. 158). This means that for dotted or dashed borders, the background won't be visible through

the spaces within the border. When the element doesn't have a layout, the background will extend under the borders.

When dotted borders are specified as the `border-style`, and the border's width is only 1px, Internet Explorer for Windows versions up to and including 6 will display the borders as `dashed` instead of `dotted`. At a width of 2px and above, the dotted borders will display correctly. This glitch was fixed in Internet Explorer Version 7 for cases when all four sides are set to 1px. However, if one of the sides is set to 2px or more, the 1px `dotted` borders revert to `dashed` in IE7.

Internet Explorer for Windows versions up to and including 7 don't support the value `inherit`.

border-right

```
border-right: { [border-width] [border-style]
[border-color] | inherit } ;
```

SPEC		
inherited	initial	version
NO	see below	CSS1
BROWSER SUPPORT		
IE5.5+	FF1+	Saf1.3+	Op9.2+
BUGGY	FULL	FULL	FULL

The `border-right` shorthand property sets the `border-right-width` and/or `border-right-style` and/or `border-right-color` to the right side of an element simultaneously.

Borders are placed on top of the element's background.

Value

Refer to the following individual properties for specific information on allowed and initial values: `border-width` (p. 254), `border-style` (p. 251), and `border-color` (p. 249).

Negative length values are illegal.

As with most shorthand properties, you don't need to specify all the properties listed, but any omitted properties will revert to their default values. In the case of

Example

This style rule assigns a 2px red border to the right-hand side of paragraphs within the element with ID "`example`":

```
#example p {
  border-right: 2px solid red;
}
```

`border-style`, if you omit a value no border will show at all, because the default value is `none`. A border will only be visible as long as the `border-style` property has been set to something other than `none` or `hidden`, or has been restated explicitly after the initial shorthand declaration. Otherwise, no border will show and the `border-width` will be reset to zero. Therefore, it's good practice to specify a value for the border's style when you're using shorthand notation.

Compatibility

Internet Explorer			Firefox			Safari			Opera
5.5	6.0	7.0	1.0	1.5	2.0	1.3	2.0	3.0	9.2
Buggy	Buggy	Buggy	Full	Full	Full	Full	Full	Full	Full

User agents are supposed to place borders on the element's background, but in Internet Explorer for Windows versions up to and including 7, the background only reaches the inside edge of the border when the element has a layout (p. 158). This means that for `dotted` or `dashed` borders, the background won't be visible through the spaces within the border. When the element doesn't have a layout, the background will extend under the borders.

When dotted borders are specified as the `border-style`, and the border's width is only 1px, Internet Explorer for Windows versions up to and including 6 will display the borders as `dashed` instead of `dotted`. At a width of 2px and above, the dotted borders will display correctly. This glitch was fixed in Internet Explorer Version 7 for cases when all four sides are set to 1px. However, if one of the sides is set to 2px or more, the 1px `dotted` borders revert to `dashed` in IE7.

Internet Explorer for Windows versions up to and including 6 do not support `transparent` borders.

Internet Explorer for Windows versions up to and including 7:

- don't support the value `hidden`
- don't support the value `inherit`

The appearance of the borders may vary between user agents (within limits). The algorithms that define the relationship between the colors used to achieve an effect (for example, `groove`, `ridge`, `inset`, and `outset`) are not explicitly defined in the

CSS specifications, so the colors may vary between user agents. In CSS2.1, the three-dimensional border styles (`groove`, `ridge`, `inset`, and `outset`) depend on the corresponding `border-color`, rather than on `color`.

 # border-bottom-color

```
border-bottom-color: { color | transparent |
inherit } ;
```

SPEC		
inherited	initial	version
NO	see below	CSS1, 2.1
BROWSER SUPPORT		
IE5.5+ FF1+ Saf1.3+ Op9.2+		
BUGGY FULL FULL FULL		

The property `border-bottom-color` sets the color for the bottom border of an element.

Borders are placed on top of the element's background.

Value

This property takes any valid CSS color value or color keyword (p. 33). The initial value for this property is the value of the `color` property for the element.

Example

This style rule assigns a black color to the bottom border of paragraphs within the element with ID `"example"`:

```
#example p {
    border-bottom-color: #000;
    border-bottom-style: solid;
}
```

The value `transparent` allows the border to be transparent, but it will still occupy the space set by the `border-width` property and allow the background of the element to show through the transparent border.

Note that a border will only be visible as long as a `border-style` has been set. The default for `border-style` is `none`, which means that no border will display, and the `border-width` will be reset to zero.

Compatibility

Internet Explorer			Firefox			Safari			Opera
5.5	6.0	7.0	1.0	1.5	2.0	1.3	2.0	3.0	9.2
Buggy	Buggy	Buggy	Full	Full	Full	Full	Full	Full	Full

Internet Explorer for Windows versions up to and including 6 do not support `transparent` borders.

Box Properties

User agents are supposed to place borders on the element's background, but in Internet Explorer for Windows versions up to and including 7, the background only reaches the inside edge of the border when the element has a layout (p. 158). This means that for `dotted` or `dashed` borders, the background won't be visible through the spaces within the border. When the element doesn't have a layout, the background will extend under the borders.

The appearance of the borders may vary between user agents (within limits). The algorithms that define the relationship between the colors used to achieve an effect (for example, `groove`, `ridge`, `inset`, and `outset`) are not explicitly defined in the CSS specifications, so the colors may vary between user agents. In CSS2.1, the three-dimensional border styles (`groove`, `ridge`, `inset`, and `outset`) depend on the corresponding `border-color`, rather than on `color`.

Internet Explorer for Windows versions up to and including 7 don't support the value `inherit`.

 # border-bottom-style

```
border-bottom-style: { none | hidden | dotted |
dashed | solid | double | groove | ridge | inset |
outset | inherit } ;
```

SPEC		
inherited	initial	version
NO	none	CSS1, 2.1
BROWSER SUPPORT		
IE5.5+	FF1+	Saf1.3+	Op9.2+
BUGGY	FULL	FULL	FULL

The property `border-bottom-style` sets the style of the bottom border on an element. Borders are placed on top of the element's background.

Value

none   none means no border will show, and the computed `border-width` is zero.

hidden   hidden has the same meaning as none, except when it refers to table borders in cases where two cells share a border, and the table cells have

Example

This style rule assigns a solid border to the bottom edge of paragraphs within the element with ID `"example"`:

```
#example p {
  border-bottom-style: solid;
}
```

collapsed borders (`border-collapse:collapse;`). The value `hidden` ensures that no border is drawn, since `hidden` takes precedence over all other border styles. If `none` had been used for one border in the cell, the border would still be drawn, as the adjacent cell's border would take precedence. See Table Formatting (p. 168) for more information.

dotted   `dotted` implements the border as a series of dots.

dashed   `dashed` implements the border as a series of dashes.

solid   `solid` implements the border as a solid line.

double   `double` implements the border as two solid lines. The sum of the two border widths and the space between them equals the value that has been set for `border-width`.

groove   `groove` is a three-dimensional effect that gives the impression that the border is carved into the canvas.

ridge   `ridge` is a 3D effect that has the opposite effect of `groove`, in that the border appears to protrude from the canvas.

inset   `inset` is a 3D effect that gives the impression that the box is embedded into the canvas. When it's used on tables to which the separated borders model has been applied, the `inset` value appears to make the whole box look as though it were embedded into the canvas. When used with the collapsing border model, it's treated the same as the value `ridge`.

outset   `outset` is a 3D effect that has the opposite effect of `inset` in that the border gives the impression that the box protrudes from the canvas. When it's used on tables to which the separated borders model has been applied, the border makes the whole box look as though it were coming out of the canvas. When it's used with the collapsing border model, it behaves the same way as `groove`.

Previously, in CSS1, user agents were allowed to interpret all dotted, dashed, double, groove, ridge, inset, and outset styles as solid.

Compatibility

Internet Explorer			Firefox			Safari			Opera
5.5	6.0	7.0	1.0	1.5	2.0	1.3	2.0	3.0	9.2
Buggy	Buggy	Buggy	Full	Full	Full	Full	Full	Full	Full

User agents are supposed to place borders on the element's background, but in Internet Explorer for Windows versions up to and including 7, the background only reaches the inside edge of the border when the element has a layout (p. 158). This means that for dotted or dashed borders, the background won't be visible through the spaces within the border. When the element doesn't have a layout, the background will extend under the borders.

When dotted borders are specified as the border-style, and the border's width is only 1px, Internet Explorer for Windows versions up to and including 6 will display the borders as dashed instead of dotted. At a width of 2px and above, the dotted borders will display correctly. This glitch was fixed in Internet Explorer Version 7 for cases when all four sides are set to 1px. However, if one of the sides is set to 2px or more, the 1px dotted borders revert to dashed in IE7.

The appearance of the borders may vary between user agents (within limits). The algorithms that define the relationship between the colors used to achieve an effect (for example, groove, ridge, inset, and outset) are not explicitly defined in the CSS specifications, so the colors may vary between user agents. In CSS2.1, the three-dimensional border styles (groove, ridge, inset, and outset) depend on the corresponding border-color, rather than on color.

Internet Explorer for Windows versions up to and including 7:

- don't support the value hidden
- don't support the value inherit

border-bottom-width

```
border-bottom-width: { thin | medium | thick | length
| inherit } ;
```

SPEC		
inherited	initial	version
NO	medium	CSS1
BROWSER SUPPORT		
IE5.5+ FF1+	Saf1.3+	Op9.2+
BUGGY FULL	FULL	FULL

The property border-bottom-width sets the width of the border to the bottom side of an element using the values specified.

Value

The property takes a CSS length (px, pt, em, and so on) or one of the allowed keywords; percentage values are not allowed.

Negative length values are illegal.

The keyword width values of thin, medium, and thick aren't explicitly defined—their display will depend on the user agent—but have the following meaning: thin <= medium <= thick.

As an example, Internet Explorer versions (up to and including 7) size thin, medium, and thick borders at 2px, 4px, and 6px respectively, while Firefox 2.0 sizes them at 1px, 3px, and 5px.

Example

This style rule assigns a 2px border width to the bottom of paragraphs within the element with ID "example":

```
#example p {
    border-bottom-width: 2px;
    border-bottom-style: solid;
}
```

Compatibility

Internet Explorer			Firefox			Safari			Opera
5.5	6.0	7.0	1.0	1.5	2.0	1.3	2.0	3.0	9.2
Buggy	Buggy	Buggy	Full	Full	Full	Full	Full	Full	Full

User agents are supposed to place borders on the element's background, but in Internet Explorer for Windows versions up to and including 7, the background only reaches the inside edge of the border when the element has a layout (p. 158). This means that for dotted or dashed borders, the background won't be visible through

Box Properties

the spaces within the border. When the element doesn't have a layout, the background will extend under the borders.

When dotted borders are specified as the `border-style`, and the border's width is only 1px, Internet Explorer for Windows versions up to and including 6 will display the borders as `dashed` instead of `dotted`. At a width of 2px and above, the dotted borders will display correctly. This glitch was fixed in Internet Explorer Version 7 for cases when all four sides are set to 1px. However, if one of the sides is set to 2px or more, the 1px `dotted` borders revert to `dashed` in IE7.

Internet Explorer for Windows versions up to and including 7 don't support the value `inherit`.

 # border-bottom

```
border-bottom: { [border-width] [border-style]
[border-color] | inherit } ;
```

SPEC		
inherited	initial	version
NO	see below	CSS1
BROWSER SUPPORT		
IE5.5+	FF1+	Saf1.3+	Op9.2+
BUGGY	FULL	FULL	FULL

The `border-bottom` shorthand property sets `border-bottom-width` and/or `border-bottom-style` and/or `border-bottom-color` to the bottom side of an element simultaneously.

Borders are placed on top of the element's background.

Example

This style rule assigns a 2px blue border to the bottom side of paragraphs within the element with ID "example":

```
#example p {
    border-bottom: 2px solid blue;
}
```

Value

Refer to the following individual properties for specific information on allowed and initial values: `border-width` (p. 254), `border-style` (p. 251), and `border-color` (p. 249).

Negative length values are illegal.

As with most shorthand properties, you don't need to specify all the properties listed, but any omitted properties will revert to their default values. In the case of `border-style`, if you omit a value no border will show at all, because the default value is none. A border will only be visible as long as the `border-style` property has been set to something other than none or hidden, or has been restated explicitly after the initial shorthand declaration. Otherwise, no border will show and the `border-width` will be reset to zero. Therefore, it's good practice to specify a value for the border's style when you're using shorthand notation.

Compatibility

Internet Explorer			Firefox			Safari			Opera
5.5	6.0	7.0	1.0	1.5	2.0	1.3	2.0	3.0	9.2
Buggy	Buggy	Buggy	Full	Full	Full	Full	Full	Full	Full

User agents are supposed to place borders on the element's background, but in Internet Explorer for Windows versions up to and including 7, the background only reaches the inside edge of the border when the element has a layout (p. 158). This means that for dotted or dashed borders, the background won't be visible through the spaces within the border. When the element doesn't have a layout, the background will extend under the borders.

When dotted borders are specified as the `border-style`, and the border's width is only 1px, Internet Explorer for Windows versions up to and including 6 will display the borders as dashed instead of dotted. At a width of 2px and above, the dotted borders will display correctly. This glitch was fixed in Internet Explorer Version 7 for cases when all four sides are set to 1px. However, if one of the sides is set to 2px or more, the 1px dotted borders revert to dashed in IE7.

Internet Explorer for Windows versions up to and including 6 do not support `transparent` borders.

Internet Explorer for Windows versions up to and including 7:

- don't support the value hidden
- don't support the value inherit

The appearance of the borders may vary between user agents (within limits). The algorithms that define the relationship between the colors used to achieve an effect (for example, groove, ridge, inset, and outset) are not explicitly defined in the

CSS specifications, so the colors may vary between user agents. In CSS2.1, the three-dimensional border styles (groove, ridge, inset, and outset) depend on the corresponding border-color, rather than on color.

 # border-left-color

```
border-left-color: { color | transparent |
inherit } ;
```

SPEC		
inherited	initial	version
NO	see below	CSS1, 2.1
BROWSER SUPPORT			
IE5.5+	FF1+	Saf1.3+	Op9.2+
BUGGY	FULL	FULL	FULL

The property border-left-color sets the color for the left border of an element.

Borders are placed on top of the element's background.

Value

This property takes any valid CSS color value or color keyword (p. 33). The initial value for this property is the value of the color property for the element.

Example

This style rule assigns a green color to the left-hand border of paragraphs within the element with ID "example":

```
#example p {
    border-left-color: green;
    border-left-style: solid;
}
```

The value transparent allows the border to be transparent, but it will still occupy the space set by the border-width property and allow the background of the element to show through the transparent border.

Note that a border will only be visible as long as a border-style has been set. The default for border-style is none, which means that no border will display, and the border-width will be reset to zero.

Compatibility

Internet Explorer			Firefox			Safari			Opera
5.5	6.0	7.0	1.0	1.5	2.0	1.3	2.0	3.0	9.2
Buggy	Buggy	Buggy	Full	Full	Full	Full	Full	Full	Full

Internet Explorer for Windows versions up to and including 6 do not support transparent borders.

User agents are supposed to place borders on the element's background, but in Internet Explorer for Windows versions up to and including 7, the background only reaches the inside edge of the border when the element has a layout (p. 158). This means that for `dotted` or `dashed` borders, the background won't be visible through the spaces within the border. When the element doesn't have a layout, the background will extend under the borders.

The appearance of the borders may vary between user agents (within limits). The algorithms that define the relationship between the colors used to achieve an effect (for example, `groove`, `ridge`, `inset`, and `outset`) are not explicitly defined in the CSS specifications, so the colors may vary between user agents. In CSS2.1, the three-dimensional border styles (`groove`, `ridge`, `inset`, and `outset`) depend on the corresponding `border-color`, rather than on `color`.

Internet Explorer for Windows versions up to and including 7 don't support the value `inherit`.

border-left-style

```
border-left-style: { none | hidden | dotted | dashed
| solid | double | groove | ridge | inset | outset
| inherit } ;
```

SPEC		
inherited	initial	version
NO	none	CSS1, 2.1
BROWSER SUPPORT		
IE5.5+	FF1+	Saf1.3+	Op9.2+
BUGGY	FULL	FULL	FULL

The property `border-left-style` sets the style of the left-hand border on an element using the values specified.

Borders are placed on top of the element's background.

Value

none   none means no border will show, and the computed `border-width` is zero.

hidden   hidden has the same meaning as none, except when it refers to table borders in cases where two cells share a border, and the table cells have

Example

This style rule assigns a solid border to the left-hand edge of paragraphs within the element with ID "example":

```
#example p {
   border-left-style: solid;
}
```

collapsed borders (`border-collapse:collapse;`). The value `hidden` ensures that no border is drawn, since `hidden` takes precedence over all other border styles. If `none` had been used for one border in the cell, the border would still be drawn, as the adjacent cell's border would take precedence. See Table Formatting (p. 168) for more information.

dotted   `dotted` implements the border as a series of dots.

dashed   `dashed` implements the border as a series of dashes.

solid   `solid` implements the border as a solid line.

double   `double` implements the border as two solid lines. The sum of the two border widths and the space between them equals the value that has been set for `border-width`.

groove   `groove` is a three-dimensional effect that gives the impression that the border is carved into the canvas.

ridge   `ridge` is a 3D effect that has the opposite effect of `groove`, in that the border appears to protrude from the canvas.

inset   `inset` is a 3D effect that gives the impression that the box is embedded into the canvas. When it's used on tables to which the separated borders model has been applied, the `inset` value appears to make the whole box look as though it were embedded into the canvas. When used with the collapsing border model, it's treated the same as the value `ridge`.

outset   `outset` is a 3D effect that has the opposite effect of `inset` in that the border gives the impression that the box protrudes from the canvas. When it's used on tables to which the separated borders model has been applied, the border makes the whole box look as though it were coming out of the canvas. When it's used with the collapsing border model, it behaves the same way as `groove`.

Previously, in CSS1, user agents were allowed to interpret all `dotted`, `dashed`, `double`, `groove`, `ridge`, `inset`, and `outset` styles as `solid`.

Compatibility

Internet Explorer			Firefox			Safari			Opera
5.5	6.0	7.0	1.0	1.5	2.0	1.3	2.0	3.0	9.2
Buggy	Buggy	Buggy	Full	Full	Full	Full	Full	Full	Full

User agents are supposed to place borders on the element's background, but in Internet Explorer for Windows versions up to and including 7, the background only reaches the inside edge of the border when the element has a layout (p. 158). This means that for `dotted` or `dashed` borders, the background won't be visible through the spaces within the border. When the element doesn't have a layout, the background will extend under the borders.

When dotted borders are specified as the `border-style`, and the border's width is only 1px, Internet Explorer for Windows versions up to and including 6 will display the borders as `dashed` instead of `dotted`. At a width of 2px and above, the dotted borders will display correctly. This glitch was fixed in Internet Explorer Version 7 for cases when all four sides are set to 1px. However, if one of the sides is set to 2px or more, the 1px `dotted` borders revert to `dashed` in IE7.

The appearance of the borders may vary between user agents (within limits). The algorithms that define the relationship between the colors used to achieve an effect (for example, `groove`, `ridge`, `inset`, and `outset`) are not explicitly defined in the CSS specifications, so the colors may vary between user agents. In CSS2.1, the three-dimensional border styles (`groove`, `ridge`, `inset`, and `outset`) depend on the corresponding `border-color`, rather than on `color`.

Internet Explorer for Windows versions up to and including 7:

- don't support the value `hidden`
- don't support the value `inherit`

border-left-width

```
border-left-width: { thin | medium | thick | length
| inherit } ;
```

SPEC		
inherited	initial	version
NO	medium	CSS1
BROWSER SUPPORT		
IE5.5+	FF1+	Saf1.3+	Op9.2+
BUGGY	FULL	FULL	FULL

The property border-left-width sets the width of the border on the left-hand side of an element using the values specified.

Value

The property takes a CSS length (px, pt, em, and so on) or one of the allowed keywords; percentage values are not allowed.

Negative length values are illegal.

Example

This style rule assigns a 2px border width to the left of paragraphs within the element with ID "example":

```
#example p {
    border-left-width: 2px;
    border-left-style: solid;
}
```

The keyword width values of thin, medium, and thick aren't explicitly defined—their display will depend on the user agent—but have the following meaning: thin <= medium <= thick.

As an example, Internet Explorer versions (up to and including 7) size thin, medium, and thick borders at 2px, 4px, and 6px respectively, while Firefox 2.0 sizes them at 1px, 3px, and 5px.

Compatibility

Internet Explorer			Firefox			Safari			Opera
5.5	6.0	7.0	1.0	1.5	2.0	1.3	2.0	3.0	9.2
Buggy	Buggy	Buggy	Full	Full	Full	Full	Full	Full	Full

User agents are supposed to place borders on the element's background, but in Internet Explorer for Windows versions up to and including 7, the background only reaches the inside edge of the border when the element has a layout (p. 158). This means that for dotted or dashed borders, the background won't be visible through

the spaces within the border. When the element doesn't have a layout, the background will extend under the borders.

When dotted borders are specified as the `border-style`, and the border's width is only 1px, Internet Explorer for Windows versions up to and including 6 will display the borders as `dashed` instead of `dotted`. At a width of 2px and above, the dotted borders will display correctly. This glitch was fixed in Internet Explorer Version 7 for cases when all four sides are set to 1px. However, if one of the sides is set to 2px or more, the 1px `dotted` borders revert to `dashed` in IE7.

Internet Explorer for Windows versions up to and including 7 don't support the value `inherit`.

border-left

```
border-left: { [border-width] [border-style]
[border-color] | inherit } ;
```

SPEC		
inherited	initial	version
NO	see below	CSS1
BROWSER SUPPORT		
IE5.5+	FF1+	Saf1.3+	Op9.2+
BUGGY	FULL	FULL	FULL

The `border-left` shorthand property sets `border-left-width` and/or `border-left-style` and/or `border-left-color` to the left side of an element simultaneously.

Borders are placed on top of the element's background.

Value

Refer to the following individual properties for specific information on allowed and initial values: `border-width` (p. 254), `border-style` (p. 251), and `border-color` (p. 249).

Negative length values are illegal.

As with most shorthand properties, you don't need to specify all the properties listed, but any omitted properties will revert to their default values. In the case of

Example

This style rule assigns a 2px green border to the left-hand side of paragraphs within the element with ID "example":

```
#example p {
    border-left: 2px solid green;
}
```

`border-style`, if you omit a value no border will show at all, because the default value is `none`. A border will only be visible as long as the `border-style` property has been set to something other than `none` or `hidden`, or has been restated explicitly after the initial shorthand declaration. Otherwise, no border will show and the `border-width` will be reset to zero. Therefore, it's good practice to specify a value for the border's style when you're using shorthand notation.

Compatibility

Internet Explorer			Firefox			Safari			Opera
5.5	6.0	7.0	1.0	1.5	2.0	1.3	2.0	3.0	9.2
Buggy	Buggy	Buggy	Full	Full	Full	Full	Full	Full	Full

User agents are supposed to place borders on the element's background, but in Internet Explorer for Windows versions up to and including 7, the background only reaches the inside edge of the border when the element has a layout (p. 158). This means that for `dotted` or `dashed` borders, the background won't be visible through the spaces within the border. When the element doesn't have a layout, the background will extend under the borders.

When dotted borders are specified as the `border-style`, and the border's width is only 1px, Internet Explorer for Windows versions up to and including 6 will display the borders as `dashed` instead of `dotted`. At a width of 2px and above, the dotted borders will display correctly. This glitch was fixed in Internet Explorer Version 7 for cases when all four sides are set to 1px. However, if one of the sides is set to 2px or more, the 1px `dotted` borders revert to `dashed` in IE7.

Internet Explorer for Windows versions up to and including 6 do not support `transparent` borders.

Internet Explorer for Windows versions up to and including 7:

- don't support the value `hidden`
- don't support the value `inherit`

The appearance of the borders may vary between user agents (within limits). The algorithms that define the relationship between the colors used to achieve an effect (for example, `groove`, `ridge`, `inset`, and `outset`) are not explicitly defined in the

CSS specifications, so the colors may vary between user agents. In CSS2.1, the three-dimensional border styles (`groove`, `ridge`, `inset`, and `outset`) depend on the corresponding `border-color`, rather than on `color`.

border-color

```
border-color: { { color | transparent }   1 to 4 values
| inherit } ;
```

SPEC		
inherited	initial	version
NO	see below	CSS1, 2.1
BROWSER SUPPORT		
IE5.5+	FF1+	Saf1.3+	Op9.2+
BUGGY	FULL	FULL	FULL

The shorthand property `border-color` sets the border color on all four sides of an element using from one to four of the values specified. Each border can have its own value—refer to the mnemonic (TRouBLe) in Shorthand Properties (p. 39) for an easy way to remember the shorthand order.

Borders are placed on top of the element's background.

If no color value is specified for `border-color`, the border will use the `color` value of the element.

Example

This style rule assigns a red border to the top, a green border to the bottom, and blue borders to the left- and right-hand sides of paragraphs within the element with ID `"example"`:

```
#example p {
    border-color: red blue green;
    border-style: solid;
}
```

Value

This property takes any valid CSS color value or color keyword (p. 33). The initial value for this property is the value of the `color` property for the element.

The value `transparent` allows the border to be transparent, but it will still occupy the space set by the `border-width` property and allow the background of the element to show through the transparent border.

Note that a border will only be visible as long as a `border-style` has been set. The default for `border-style` is `none`, which means that no border will display, and the `border-width` will be reset to zero.

Compatibility

Internet Explorer			Firefox			Safari			Opera
5.5	6.0	7.0	1.0	1.5	2.0	1.3	2.0	3.0	9.2
Buggy	Buggy	Buggy	Full	Full	Full	Full	Full	Full	Full

Internet Explorer for Windows versions up to and including 6 do not support `transparent` borders.

User agents are supposed to place borders on the element's background, but in Internet Explorer for Windows versions up to and including 7, the background only reaches the inside edge of the border when the element has a layout (p. 158). This means that for `dotted` or `dashed` borders, the background won't be visible through the spaces within the border. When the element doesn't have a layout, the background will extend under the borders.

The appearance of the borders may vary between user agents (within limits). The algorithms that define the relationship between the colors used to achieve an effect (for example, `groove`, `ridge`, `inset`, and `outset`) are not explicitly defined in the CSS specifications, so the colors may vary between user agents. In CSS2.1, the three-dimensional border styles (`groove`, `ridge`, `inset`, and `outset`) depend on the corresponding `border-color`, rather than on `color`.

Internet Explorer for Windows versions up to and including 7 don't support the value `inherit`.

border-style

border-style: { { none | hidden | dotted | dashed |
solid | double | groove | ridge | inset | outset } [1]
to 4 values | inherit } ;

SPEC		
inherited	initial	version
NO	none	CSS1, 2.1
BROWSER SUPPORT		
IE5.5+	FF1+	Saf1.3+	Op9.2+
BUGGY	FULL	FULL	FULL

The shorthand property border-style sets the style of the border on all four sides of an element using the values specified. Each border can have its own value—refer to the mnemonic (TRouBLe) in Shorthand Properties (p. 39) for an easy way to remember the shorthand order.

Borders are placed on top of the element's background.

Example

This style rule assigns a solid border to the top, a dashed border to the bottom, and a dotted border to the left- and right-hand sides of paragraphs within the element with ID "example":

```
#example p {
  border-style: solid dotted
dashed;
}
```

Value

none   none means no border will show, and the computed border-width is zero.

hidden   hidden has the same meaning as none, except when it refers to table borders in cases where two cells share a border, and the table cells have collapsed borders (border-collapse:collapse;). The value hidden ensures that no border is drawn, since hidden takes precedence over all other border styles. If none had been used for one border in the cell, the border would still be drawn, as the adjacent cell's border would take precedence. See Table Formatting (p. 168) for more information.

dotted   dotted implements the border as a series of dots.

dashed   dashed implements the border as a series of dashes.

solid   solid implements the border as a solid line.

double   double implements the border as two solid lines. The sum of the two border widths and the space between them equals the value that has been set for border-width.

groove   groove is a three-dimensional effect that gives the impression that the border is carved into the canvas.

ridge   ridge is a 3D effect that has the opposite effect of groove, in that the border appears to protrude from the canvas.

inset   inset is a 3D effect that gives the impression that the box is embedded into the canvas. When it's used on tables to which the separated borders model has been applied, the inset value appears to make the whole box look as though it were embedded into the canvas. When used with the collapsing border model, it's treated the same as the value ridge.

outset   outset is a 3D effect that has the opposite effect of inset in that the border gives the impression that the box protrudes from the canvas. When it's used on tables to which the separated borders model has been applied, the border makes the whole box look as though it were coming out of the canvas. When it's used with the collapsing border model, it behaves the same way as groove.

Previously, in CSS1, user agents were allowed to interpret all dotted, dashed, double, groove, ridge, inset, and outset styles as solid.

Compatibility

Internet Explorer			Firefox			Safari			Opera
5.5	6.0	7.0	1.0	1.5	2.0	1.3	2.0	3.0	9.2
Buggy	Buggy	Buggy	Full	Full	Full	Full	Full	Full	Full

User agents are supposed to place borders on the element's background, but in Internet Explorer for Windows versions up to and including 7, the background only reaches the inside edge of the border when the element has a layout (p. 158). This means that for dotted or dashed borders, the background won't be visible through

the spaces within the border. When the element doesn't have a layout, the background will extend under the borders.

When dotted borders are specified as the border-style, and the border's width is only 1px, Internet Explorer for Windows versions up to and including 6 will display the borders as dashed instead of dotted. At a width of 2px and above, the dotted borders will display correctly. This glitch was fixed in Internet Explorer Version 7 for cases when all four sides are set to 1px. However, if one of the sides is set to 2px or more, the 1px dotted borders revert to dashed in IE7.

The appearance of the borders may vary between user agents (within limits). The algorithms that define the relationship between the colors used to achieve an effect (for example, groove, ridge, inset, and outset) are not explicitly defined in the CSS specifications, so the colors may vary between user agents. In CSS2.1, the three-dimensional border styles (groove, ridge, inset, and outset) depend on the corresponding border-color, rather than on color.

Internet Explorer for Windows versions up to and including 7:

- don't support the value hidden
- don't support the value inherit

border-width

border-width: { { thin | medium | thick | *length* }
to 4 values | inherit } ;

SPEC		
inherited	initial	version
NO	medium	CSS1
BROWSER SUPPORT		
IE5.5+	FF1+	Saf1.3+	Op9.2+
BUGGY	FULL	FULL	FULL

The shorthand property `border-width` sets the width of the border on all four sides of an element using the values specified. Each border can have its own value.

The shorthand `border-width` allows all four sides of an element's borders to be set using either one, two, three, or four specified values. Refer to the mnemonic (TRouBLe) in Shorthand Properties (p. 39) for an easy way to remember the shorthand order.

Example

This style rule assigns a 2px border to the top and bottom sides, and a four-pixel border to the left- and right-hand sides, of paragraphs within the element with ID `"example"`:

```
#example p {
    border-width: 2px 4px;
    border-style: solid;
}
```

Value

The property takes a CSS length (px, pt, em, and so on) or one of the allowed keywords; percentage values are not allowed.

Negative length values are illegal.

Note that a border will only be visible as long as a `border-style` has been set. The default for `border-style` is `none`, which means that no border will display, and the `border-width` will be reset to zero.

The keyword width values of `thin`, `medium`, and `thick` aren't explicitly defined—their display will depend on the user agent—but have the following meaning: `thin` <= `medium` <= `thick`.

As an example, Internet Explorer versions (up to and including 7) size `thin`, `medium`, and `thick` borders at 2px, 4px, and 6px respectively, while Firefox 2.0 sizes them at 1px, 3px, and 5px.

Compatibility

Internet Explorer			Firefox			Safari			Opera
5.5	6.0	7.0	1.0	1.5	2.0	1.3	2.0	3.0	9.2
Buggy	Buggy	Buggy	Full	Full	Full	Full	Full	Full	Full

User agents are supposed to place borders on the element's background, but in Internet Explorer for Windows versions up to and including 7, the background only reaches the inside edge of the border when the element has a layout (p. 158). This means that for `dotted` or `dashed` borders, the background won't be visible through the spaces within the border. When the element doesn't have a layout, the background will extend under the borders.

When dotted borders are specified as the `border-style`, and the border's width is only 1px, Internet Explorer for Windows versions up to and including 6 will display the borders as `dashed` instead of `dotted`. At a width of 2px and above, the dotted borders will display correctly. This glitch was fixed in Internet Explorer Version 7 for cases when all four sides are set to 1px. However, if one of the sides is set to 2px or more, the 1px `dotted` borders revert to `dashed` in IE7.

Internet Explorer for Windows versions up to and including 7 don't support the value `inherit`.

border

```
border: { [border-width] [border-style]
[border-color] | inherit } ;
```

SPEC		
inherited	initial	version
NO	see below	CSS1
BROWSER SUPPORT		
IE5.5+ FF1+ Saf1.3+ Op9.2+		
BUGGY FULL FULL FULL		

The shorthand property `border` sets the `border-width`, `border-style`, and `border-color` for all four sides of an element using the values specified. Unlike the shorthand `margin` property, you cannot set each border to a different width (or have different colors and styles for each border) using just the shorthand `border` property. To specify

Example

This style rule assigns a 2px red border to all four sides of paragraphs within the element with ID "example":

```
#example p {
   border: 2px solid red;
}
```

different values for each side, you'll need to refer to the property values for the shorthand styles border-width, border-style, and border-color.

It's also possible to be more specific, and apply an individual border-style, border-color, or border-width to a particular side. For example, to target the top border of an element you'd use the properties border-top-width, border-top-color, and border-top-style. (You can target other sides of the element in the same way, substituting "top" in the above property for "left," "right," or "bottom" as required.)

Borders are placed on top of the element's background.

Value

Refer to the following individual properties for specific information on allowed and initial values: border-width (p. 254), border-style (p. 251), and border-color (p. 249).

Negative length values are illegal.

As with most shorthand properties, you don't need to specify all the properties listed, but any omitted properties will revert to their default values. In the case of border-style, if you omit a value no border will show at all, because the default value is none. A border will only be visible as long as the border-style property has been set to something other than none or hidden, or has been restated explicitly after the initial shorthand declaration. Otherwise, no border will show and the border-width will be reset to zero. Therefore, it's good practice to specify a value for the border's style when you're using shorthand notation.

Compatibility

Internet Explorer			Firefox			Safari			Opera
5.5	6.0	7.0	1.0	1.5	2.0	1.3	2.0	3.0	9.2
Buggy	Buggy	Buggy	Full	Full	Full	Full	Full	Full	Full

User agents are supposed to place borders on the element's background, but in Internet Explorer for Windows versions up to and including 7, the background only reaches the inside edge of the border when the element has a layout (p. 158). This means that for dotted or dashed borders, the background won't be visible through

the spaces within the border. When the element doesn't have a layout, the background will extend under the borders.

When dotted borders are specified as the border-style, and the border's width is only 1px, Internet Explorer for Windows versions up to and including 6 will display the borders as dashed instead of dotted. At a width of 2px and above, the dotted borders will display correctly. This glitch was fixed in Internet Explorer Version 7 for cases when all four sides are set to 1px. However, if one of the sides is set to 2px or more, the 1px dotted borders revert to dashed in IE7.

Internet Explorer for Windows versions up to and including 6 do not support transparent borders.

Internet Explorer for Windows versions up to and including 7:

- don't support the value hidden
- don't support the value inherit

The appearance of the borders may vary between user agents (within limits). The algorithms that define the relationship between the colors used to achieve an effect (for example, groove, ridge, inset, and outset) are not explicitly defined in the CSS specifications, so the colors may vary between user agents. In CSS2.1, the three-dimensional border styles (groove, ridge, inset, and outset) depend on the corresponding border-color, rather than on color.

outline-color

`outline-color: { color | invert | inherit } ;`

SPEC		
inherited	initial	version
NO	invert	CSS2,2.1

BROWSER SUPPORT			
IE7	FF1.5+	Saf1.3+	Op9.2+
NONE	FULL	FULL	FULL

The `outline-style` property sets the style of the outline that's drawn around an element. See outline (p. 261) for more information about outlines.

Note that an outline will only show when `outline-style` has been set with a value other than `none`.

Value

`outline-color` accepts any valid CSS color value, as well as the keyword `invert`. `invert` does as its name suggests: it performs a pixel-color inversion of the outline in order that the outline remains visible regardless of any background colors that have been set. As of CSS2.1, user agents have been allowed to ignore the `invert` value, and instead use the element's `color` property.

Example

This style rule assigns a red outline color on focus to anchor elements within the element with ID "example":

```
#example a:focus {
    outline-color: red;
    outline-style: solid;
}
```

Compatibility

Internet Explorer			Firefox			Safari			Opera
5.5	6.0	7.0	1.0	1.5	2.0	1.3	2.0	3.0	9.2
None	None	None	None	Full	Full	Full	Full	Full	Full

Internet Explorer for Windows (up to and including version 7) and Firefox 1.0 provide no support for `outline`.

outline-style

```
outline-style: { none | dotted | dashed | solid |
double | groove | ridge | inset | outset |
inherit } ;
```

SPEC		
inherited	initial	version
NO	none	CSS2, 2.1
BROWSER SUPPORT		
IE7	FF1.5+	Saf1.3+ Op9.2+
NONE	FULL	FULL FULL

The `outline-style` property sets the style of the outline that's drawn around an element. See outline (p. 261) for more information about outlines.

Note that an outline will only show when `outline-style` has been set with a value other than `none`.

The property takes the same values as `border-style` (p. 251) with the exception of `hidden`, which is not allowed:

Example

This style rule assigns a `solid` outline (with the default width and color) on focus to anchor elements within the element with ID `"example"`:

```
#example a:focus {
    outline-style: solid;
}
```

Value

none	means no outline will show
dotted	implements the outline as a series of dots
dashed	implements the outline as a series of dashes
solid	implements the outline as a solid line
double	implements the outline as two solid lines (the sum of the two outline widths and the space between them equals the value that has been set for `outline-width`)
groove	a 3D effect that gives the impression that the outline is carved into the canvas
ridge	a 3D effect that has the opposite effect of `groove` in that the outline appears to protrude from the canvas

Box Properties

inset   a 3D effect that gives the impression that the outline is embedded into the canvas

outset   a 3D effect that has the opposite effect of inset in that the outline gives the impression of protruding from the canvas

In CSS1, user agents were allowed to interpret all dotted, dashed, double, groove, ridge, inset, and outset styles as solid.

Compatibility

Internet Explorer			Firefox			Safari			Opera
5.5	6.0	7.0	1.0	1.5	2.0	1.3	2.0	3.0	9.2
None	None	None	None	Full	Full	Full	Full	Full	Full

Internet Explorer for Windows (up to and including version 7) and Firefox 1.0 provide no support for outline.

outline-width

```
outline-width: { thin | medium | thick | length | inherit } ;
```

SPEC		
inherited	initial	version
NO	medium	CSS2, 2.1
BROWSER SUPPORT		
IE7	FF1.5+	Saf1.3+	Op9.2+
NONE	FULL	FULL	FULL

The outline-width property sets the width of the outline that's drawn around an element. See outline (p. 261) for more information about outlines.

Note that even though an outline-width has been set, outline-style must have a value other than none before the outline will show.

Example

This style rule assigns an outline with a 2px width on focus to anchor elements within the element with ID "example":

```
#example a:focus {
    outline-width: 2px;
    outline-style: solid;
}
```

Value

The property takes the same values as border-width (p. 254)—for example, a CSS length (px, pt, em, and so on) or one of the allowed keywords—but percentage or negative values are not allowed.

The keyword width values of thin, medium, and thick aren't explicitly defined—their display will depend on the user agent—but have the following meaning: thin <= medium <= thick.

Compatibility

Internet Explorer			Firefox			Safari			Opera
5.5	6.0	7.0	1.0	1.5	2.0	1.3	2.0	3.0	9.2
None	None	None	None	Full	Full	Full	Full	Full	Full

Internet Explorer for Windows (up to and including version 7) and Firefox 1.0 provide no support for outline.

outline

```
outline: { [outline-width] [outline-style]
[outline-color] | inherit } ;
```

SPEC		
inherited	initial	version
NO	none	CSS2, 2.1
BROWSER SUPPORT		
IE7	FF1.5+ Saf1.3+	Op9.2+
NONE	FULL FULL	FULL

The shorthand property outline sets the outline-color, outline-style, and outline-width around an element using the values specified.

An outline is similar to a border in that a line is drawn around the element; unlike borders, outlines won't allow us to set each edge to a different width, or set different colors and styles for each edge. An outline is the same on all sides.

Example

This style rule assigns a 2px red outline on focus to anchor elements within the element with ID "example":

```
#example a:focus {
    outline: 2px solid red;
}
```

Outlines do not take up space in the flow of the document (and will not cause overflow), which may cause them to overlap other elements on the page. The fact that outlines don't have any impact on surrounding elements (apart from overlapping) can be very useful in the debugging of layouts. We can apply an outline to all elements within a problematic section to see exactly what's going on, and where the elements are placed. Unlike borders, adding outlines won't disturb the flow of the document at all.

Outlines are usually drawn just outside the border edge of an element, although again the exact position isn't defined, and can vary between user agents. An outline placed around inline elements such as text will closely hug the edges of that text, even where the text flows over several lines and may result in a non-rectangular, jagged box. This behavior represents a significant difference from the `border` property, which has only a rectangular shape.

Outlines allow authors to apply visual cues to elements to make them stand out when they take focus. Some user agents apply an outline to web page link elements when they have focus—such as when the user's tabbing through a list of links. Changing an outline's appearance on focus won't cause the document to reflow.

Value

Refer to the `outline-width` (p. 260), `outline-style` (p. 259), and `outline-color` (p. 258) properties for information on their allowed values.

As with most shorthand properties, all the properties listed need not be specified, but any omitted properties will revert to their default values. In the case of `outline-style`, omitting a value will cause no outline to show at all (unless it's redefined subsequently) because the default value for `outline-style` is none.

Compatibility

Internet Explorer			Firefox			Safari			Opera
5.5	6.0	7.0	1.0	1.5	2.0	1.3	2.0	3.0	9.2
None	None	None	None	Full	Full	Full	Full	Full	Full

Internet Explorer for Windows (up to and including version 7) and Firefox 1.0 provide no support for `outline`.

Layout Properties

Layout properties allow authors to control the visibility, position, and behavior of the generated boxes for document elements. CSS layout is a complex topic and further information can be found in CSS Layout and Formatting (p. 139).

display

```
display: { block | inline | inline-block |
inline-table | list-item | run-in | table |
table-caption | table-cell | table-column |
table-column-group | table-footer-group |
table-header-group | table-row | table-row-group |
none | inherit } ;
```

SPEC		
inherited	initial	version
NO	inline	CSS1, 2, 2.1
BROWSER SUPPORT		
IE5.5+	FF1+	Saf1.3+ Op9.2+
PARTIAL	PARTIAL	FULL FULL

This property controls the type of box an element generates.

The computed value may differ from the specified value for the root element and for floated or absolutely positioned elements; see The Relationship Between display, position, and float (p. 184) for details about the relationship between the display, float (p. 269), and position (p. 267) properties.

Example

The following rule will cause a elements that are descendants of the .menu element to render as block elements instead of inline elements:

```
.menu a {
    display: block;
}
```

Note that a **user agent style sheet** may override the initial value of inline for some elements.

Value

block
    block makes the element generate a block box.

inline
    inline makes the element generate one or more inline boxes.

inline-block
    inline-block makes the element generate a block box that's laid out as if it were an inline box.

inline-table
    inline-table makes the element behave like a table that's laid out as if it were an inline box.

`list-item`	`list-item` makes the element generate a principal block box and a list-item inline box for the list marker.
`run-in`	A value of `run-in` makes the element generate either a block box or an inline box, depending on the context. If the run-in box doesn't contain a block box, and is followed by a sibling block box (except a table caption) in the normal flow that isn't, and doesn't contain, a run-in box, the run-in box becomes the first inline box of the sibling block box. Otherwise, the run-in box becomes a block box.
`table`	`table` makes the element behave like a table.
`table-caption`	`table-caption` makes the element behave like a table caption.
`table-cell`	`table-cell` makes the element behave like a table cell.
`table-column`	`table-column` makes the element behave like a table column.
`table-column-group`	`table-column-group` makes the element behave like a table column group.
`table-footer-group`	`table-footer-group` makes the element behave like a table footer row group.
`table-header-group`	`table-header-group` makes the element behave like a table header row group.
`table-row`	`table-row` makes the element behave like a table row.
`table-row-group`	`table-row-group` makes the element behave like a table body row group.

none   A value of none makes the element generate no box at all.
                                Descendant boxes cannot generate boxes either, even if
                                their display property is set to something other than none.

Compatibility

Internet Explorer			Firefox			Safari			Opera
5.5	6.0	7.0	1.0	1.5	2.0	1.3	2.0	3.0	9.2
Partial	Partial	Partial	Partial	Partial	Partial	Full	Full	Full	Full

Internet Explorer versions up to and including 7:

■ don't support the values inline-table, run-in, table, table-caption,
table-cell, table-column, table-column-group, table-row, and
table-row-group

■ only support the values table-footer-group and table-header-group for thead
and tfoot elements in HTML

■ only support the value inline-block for elements that are naturally inline or
have been set to inline outside the declaration block

■ treat block as list-item on li elements in HTML

■ will apply a layout (p. 158) to inline-block elements

■ don't support the value inherit

Firefox versions up to and including 2.0, and Opera 9.2 and prior versions:

■ only support the value table-column-group for colgroup elements in HTML

■ only support the value table-column for col elements in HTML

Firefox versions up to and including 2.0 don't support the values inline-block,
inline-table, or run-in.

position

```
position: { absolute | fixed | relative | static |
inherit } ;
```

SPEC		
inherited	initial	version
NO	static	CSS2
BROWSER SUPPORT		
IE5.5+	FF1+	Saf1.3+	Op9.2+
BUGGY	FULL	FULL	FULL

The `position` property, together with the `float` property, controls the way in which the position of the element's generated box is computed. See Positioning (p. 176) for details about element positioning.

Boxes with a `position` value other than `static` are said to be **positioned**. Their vertical placement in the stacking context is determined by the `z-index` (p. 279) property.

Example

This style rule makes the element with ID `"sidebar"` absolutely positioned at the top right-hand corner of its containing block:

```
#sidebar {
  position: absolute;
  top: 0;
  right: 0;
}
```

Value

absolute   The value `absolute` generates an absolutely positioned box that's positioned relative to its containing block. The position can be specified using one or more of the properties `top` (p. 275), `right` (p. 276), `bottom` (p. 277), and `left` (p. 278). Absolutely positioned boxes are removed from the flow and have no effect on later siblings. Margins on absolutely positioned boxes never collapse with margins on other boxes.

fixed   The value `fixed` generates an absolutely positioned box that's positioned relative to the initial containing block (normally the viewport). The position can be specified using one or more of the properties `top` (p. 275), `right` (p. 276), `bottom` (p. 277), and `left` (p. 278). In the print media type, the element is rendered on every page.

relative   The value `relative` generates a positioned box whose position is first computed as for the normal flow. The generated box is then offset from this position according to the properties `top` (p. 275) or `bottom` (p. 277) and/or `left` (p. 278) or `right` (p. 276). The position of the following box is computed as if the relatively positioned box occupied the position that was computed before the box was offset. This value cannot be used for table cells, columns, column groups, rows, row groups, or captions.

static   The value `static` generates a box that isn't positioned, but occurs in the normal flow. The properties `top` (p. 275), `right` (p. 276), `bottom` (p. 277), `left` (p. 278), and `z-index` (p. 279) are ignored for static boxes.

Compatibility

Internet Explorer			Firefox			Safari			Opera
5.5	6.0	7.0	1.0	1.5	2.0	1.3	2.0	3.0	9.2
Buggy	Buggy	Buggy	Full	Full	Full	Full	Full	Full	Full

Internet Explorer for Windows versions up to and including 6 don't support the value `fixed`.

Internet Explorer for Windows versions up to and including 6 have problems with margin calculations for absolutely positioned boxes. Percentages for dimensions are computed relative to the parent block, rather than the containing block. Consider this example:

```
<div id="containing">
  <div id="parent">
    <div id="child"></div>
  </div>
</div>
```

```
#containing {
  position: relative;
  width: 200px;
  height:200px;
}
#parent {
  width: 100px;
  height: 100px;
}
#child {
  position: absolute;
```

```
    top: 10px;
    left: 10px;
    width: 50%;
    height: 50%;
}
```

Here, the element with ID "child" is absolutely positioned, and therefore its containing block is the one generated by the element with the (convenient) ID "containing"—the "child" element's nearest positioned ancestor. IE6 and earlier versions will make the "child" element 50 pixels square—50% of the element with the ID "parent"—instead of the expected 100 pixels, since they base the calculation on the dimensions of the *parent* block rather than the *containing* block.

Internet Explorer versions up to and including 7:

■ always generate a new stacking context (p. 179) for positioned boxes, even if z-index is auto

■ don't support the value inherit

In Internet Explorer for Windows versions up to and including 7, a position value of absolute will cause an element to gain a layout (p. 158), as will a value of fixed in version 7.

float

```
float: { left | right | none | inherit } ;
```

SPEC		
inherited	initial	version
NO	none	CSS1
BROWSER SUPPORT			
IE5.5+	FF1+	Saf1.3+	Op9.2+
BUGGY	BUGGY	FULL	BUGGY

This property specifies whether or not a box should float and, if so, if it should float to the left or to the right. A floating box is shifted to the left or to the right as far as it can go, and non-floating content in the normal flow will flow around it on the opposite side. The float property is ignored for elements

Example

This style rule makes the box generated by the element with ID "nav" float to the left:

```
#nav {
  float: left;
}
```

that are absolutely positioned. User agents are also allowed to ignore it when it's applied to the root element.

See Floating and Clearing (p. 180) for more information about the behavior of floated elements.

Value

left   makes the element generate a block box that is floated to the left

right   makes the element generate a block box that is floated to the right

none   makes the element generate a box that is not floated

Compatibility

Internet Explorer			Firefox			Safari			Opera
5.5	6.0	7.0	1.0	1.5	2.0	1.3	2.0	3.0	9.2
Buggy	Buggy	Buggy	Buggy	Buggy	Buggy	Full	Full	Full	Buggy

Internet Explorer versions up to and including 6 add three pixels of padding (in the floated direction) to adjacent line boxes.

In Internet Explorer versions up to and including 6, the left or right margins are doubled on floated elements that touch their parents' side edges. The margin value is doubled on the side that touches the parent. A simple fix for this problem is to set `display` to `inline` for the floated element.

Internet Explorer for Windows versions up to and including 7:

- will place a floated box below an immediately preceding line box
- will expand a left-floated box to the width of the containing block if it has a right-floated child and a computed width of `auto`
- will apply a layout (p. 158) to a floated element
- don't support the value `inherit`

In Firefox versions up to and including 2.0, a floated box appears below an immediately preceding line box. A left-floated box with a right-floated child and a computed width of `auto` expands to the width of the containing block.

In Opera up to and including version 9.2, if the computed width of the floated box is `auto` and it has floated children, its width is computed as if the floats don't wrap and aren't cleared.

Other Relevant Stuff

clear (p. 271)

prevents a box from being adjacent to floated boxes

clear

`clear: { none | left | right | both | inherit } ;`

SPEC		
inherited	initial	version
NO	none	CSS1
BROWSER SUPPORT			
IE5.5+	FF1+	Saf1.3+	Op9.2+
BUGGY	FULL	FULL	FULL

This property specifies which sides of an element's box (or boxes) can't be adjacent to any floated boxes. This property can clear an element only from floated boxes within the same block formatting context (p. 164). It doesn't clear the element from floated child boxes within the element itself.

Example

This style rule prevents all `pre` elements in an HTML document from being adjacent to a previously floated box:

```
pre {
    clear: both;
}
```

The clearance is achieved by adding space above the top margin of the element, if necessary, until the top of the element's border edge is below the bottom edge of any boxes floated in the specified direction or directions.

When `clear` is specified for a run-in box, it applies to the block box to which the run-in box eventually belongs.

See Floating and Clearing (p. 180) for more information about the behavior of cleared elements.

Layout Properties

Value

left   The value left adds space above the element's generated box, if necessary, to put its top border edge below the bottom edge of any left-floating boxes previously generated by elements in the same block formatting context.

right   The value right adds space above the element's generated box, if necessary, to put its top border edge below the bottom edge of any right-floating boxes previously generated by elements in the same block formatting context.

both   The value both adds space above the element's generated box, if necessary, to put its top border edge below the bottom edge of any floating boxes that were previously generated by elements in the same block formatting context.

none   The value none doesn't clear any previously floated boxes.

Compatibility

Internet Explorer			Firefox			Safari			Opera
5.5	6.0	7.0	1.0	1.5	2.0	1.3	2.0	3.0	9.2
Buggy	Buggy	Buggy	Full	Full	Full	Full	Full	Full	Full

Internet Explorer for Windows versions up to and including 6 exhibit a bug known as the peekaboo bug, wherein a cleared element that touches the floating box(es) it clears may become invisible.

Internet Explorer for Windows version 7:

- doesn't clear elements with an unshared ancestor whose height value is anything other than auto

- doesn't clear floated elements if the clear property is specified for an element floating in the opposite direction

Internet Explorer for Windows versions up to and including 7 don't support the value inherit.

Other Relevant Stuff

 float (p. 269)

specifies whether a box should float to the left or right, or not float at all

 # visibility

`visibility: { visible | hidden | collapse | inherit } ;`

SPEC		
inherited	initial	version
YES	visible	CSS2, 2.1
BROWSER SUPPORT		
IE5.5+	FF1+	Saf1.3+ Op9.2+
PARTIAL	FULL	PARTIAL BUGGY

This property specifies whether an element is visible—that is, whether the box(es) that are generated by an element are rendered.

Note that even if a box in the normal flow is hidden, it still affects the layout of other elements, unlike the behavior that occurs when we suppress box generation altogether by setting `display` to `none`. Descendant boxes of a hidden box will be visible if their `visibility` is set to `visible`, whereas descendants of an element for which `display` is set to `none` can never generate boxes of their own.

The initial value and the inheritability were changed in CSS2.1 to address the previously undefined state for the root element.

Example

This style rule makes the element with ID `"dynamic"` generate an invisible box. It can be made visible using client-side scripting:

```
#dynamic {
    visibility: hidden;
}
```

Value

visible   The value `visible` makes the generated boxes visible.

hidden   The value `hidden` makes the generated boxes invisible without removing them from the layout. Descendant boxes can be made visible.

collapse   The value `collapse` is only meaningful for certain internal table objects: rows, row groups, columns, and column groups. It causes the object to be removed from the display; the space it occupied will be filled by subsequent siblings. This doesn't affect the table layout in any other way, so the user agent doesn't have to recompute the layout of the table. If a spanned row or column intersects the collapsed object, it is clipped. When it's specified for any other element than these internal table objects, `collapse` causes the same behavior as `hidden`.

Compatibility

Internet Explorer			Firefox			Safari			Opera
5.5	6.0	7.0	1.0	1.5	2.0	1.3	2.0	3.0	9.2
Partial	Partial	Partial	Full	Full	Full	Partial	Partial	Partial	Buggy

Internet Explorer for Windows versions up to and including 7:

- don't support the value `collapse`
- don't support the value `inherit`
- don't allow descendant boxes of an element whose `visibility` value is `hidden` to be made visible if the ancestor has a layout (p. 158)

Opera 9.2 and prior versions treat the value `collapsed` as `hidden` for all elements.

Safari versions up to and including 2.0 don't support the value `collapse`.

top

`top: { length | percentage | auto | inherit } ;`

SPEC		
inherited	initial	version
NO	auto	CSS2
BROWSER SUPPORT		
IE7+	FF1+	Saf1.3+ Op9.2+
FULL	FULL	FULL FULL

For absolutely positioned boxes, this property specifies how far the top margin edge of the box is offset below the top padding edge of its containing block. However, should the value for `top` be `auto` (the initial value), the top margin edge of the box will be positioned at the top content edge of its containing block.

Example

This style rule makes the element with ID `"logo"` generate a relatively positioned box that's shifted down by ten pixels:

```
#logo {
   position: relative;
   top: 10px;
}
```

For relatively positioned boxes, this property specifies how far the top edge of the box is offset below the position it would have had in the normal flow.

Compatibility

Internet Explorer			Firefox			Safari			Opera
5.5	6.0	7.0	1.0	1.5	2.0	1.3	2.0	3.0	9.2
Buggy	Buggy	Full	Full	Full	Full	Full	Full	Full	Full

Internet Explorer for Windows versions up to and including 6:

- compute percentage values on the basis of the height of the parent block, rather than of the containing block

- don't support the specification of both the position and the dimensions of an absolutely positioned element using `top`, `right`, `bottom`, and `left` together; they'll use the last vertical and horizontal position specified, and need the dimensions to be specified using `width` and `height`

Internet Explorer for Windows versions up to and including 7 don't support the value `inherit`.

right

`right: { length | percentage | auto | inherit } ;`

	SPEC	
inherited	initial	version
NO	auto	CSS2
BROWSER SUPPORT		
IE7+	FF1+	Saf1.3+	Op9.2+
FULL	FULL	FULL	FULL

For absolutely positioned boxes, this property specifies how far the right margin edge of the box is offset from the left of the right padding edge of its containing block.

For relatively positioned boxes, this property specifies how far the right edge of the box is offset from the left of the position it would have had in the normal flow.

Example

This style rule makes the element with ID "sidebar" generate an absolutely positioned box at the top right-hand corner of its containing block:

```
#sidebar {
    position: absolute;
    top: 0;
    right: 0;
}
```

If both `right` and `left` have a value other than `auto`, the offset is over-constrained. If the `direction` property is `ltr`, `right` will be ignored. If `direction` is `rtl`, `left` will be ignored.

Compatibility

Internet Explorer			Firefox			Safari			Opera
5.5	6.0	7.0	1.0	1.5	2.0	1.3	2.0	3.0	9.2
Buggy	Buggy	Full	Full	Full	Full	Full	Full	Full	Full

Internet Explorer for Windows versions up to and including 6:

- compute percentage values on the basis of the width of the parent block, rather than that of the containing block

- don't support the specification of both the position and the dimensions of an absolutely positioned element using `top`, `right`, `bottom`, and `left` together; they'll use the last vertical and horizontal position specified, and need the dimensions to be specified using `width` and `height`

Internet Explorer for Windows versions up to and including 7 don't support the value `inherit`.

bottom

`bottom: { length | percentage | auto | inherit } ;`

SPEC		
inherited	initial	version
NO	auto	CSS2
BROWSER SUPPORT		
IE7+ FF1+ Saf1.3+ Op9.2+		
FULL FULL FULL FULL		

For absolutely positioned boxes, this property specifies how far the bottom margin edge of the box is offset above the bottom padding edge of its containing block.

For relatively positioned boxes, this property specifies how far the bottom edge of the box is offset above the position it would have had in the normal flow.

Example

This style rule makes the element with ID "logo" generate a relatively positioned box that's shifted ten pixels upward:

```
#logo {
    position: relative;
    bottom: 10px;
}
```

If both `top` and `bottom` have a value other than `auto`, `bottom` is ignored.

Compatibility

Internet Explorer			Firefox			Safari			Opera
5.5	6.0	7.0	1.0	1.5	2.0	1.3	2.0	3.0	9.2
Buggy	Buggy	Full	Full	Full	Full	Full	Full	Full	Full

Internet Explorer for Windows versions up to and including 6:

- compute percentage values on the basis of the height of the parent block, rather than of the containing block
- are one pixel off when `bottom` and `right` are used to specify the position, and the offset is an odd number of pixels
- don't support the specification of both the position and the dimensions of an absolutely positioned element using `top`, `right`, `bottom`, and `left` together; they'll use the last vertical and horizontal position specified, and need the dimensions to be specified using `width` and `height`

Internet Explorer for Windows versions up to and including 7 don't support the value `inherit`.

Layout Properties

left

`left: { length | percentage | auto | inherit } ;`

SPEC		
inherited	initial	version
NO	auto	CSS2
BROWSER SUPPORT		
IE7+	FF1+	Saf1.3+	Op9.2+
FULL	FULL	FULL	FULL

For absolutely positioned boxes, this property specifies how far the left margin edge of the box is offset to the right of the left padding edge of its containing block. However, should the value for `left` be `auto` (the initial value), the left margin edge of the box is positioned at the left content edge of its containing block.

For relatively positioned boxes, this property specifies how far the left edge of the box is offset to the right of the position it would have had in the normal flow. If both `right` and `left` have a value other than `auto`, the offset is over-constrained. If the `direction` property is `ltr`, `right` will be ignored. If `direction` is `rtl`, `left` will be ignored.

Example

This style rule makes the element with ID `"nav"` generate an absolutely positioned box at the top left-hand corner of its containing block:

```
#nav {
    position: absolute;
    top: 0;
    left: 0;
}
```

Compatibility

Internet Explorer			Firefox			Safari			Opera
5.5	6.0	7.0	1.0	1.5	2.0	1.3	2.0	3.0	9.2
Buggy	Buggy	Full	Full	Full	Full	Full	Full	Full	Full

Internet Explorer for Windows versions up to and including 6:

■ compute percentage values on the basis of the width of the parent block, rather than that of the containing block

■ don't support the specification of both the position and the dimensions of an absolutely positioned element using `top`, `right`, `bottom`, and `left` together; they'll use the last vertical and horizontal position specified, and need the dimensions to be specified using `width` and `height`

Internet Explorer for Windows versions up to and including 7 don't support the value `inherit`.

z-index

```
z-index: { integer | auto | inherit } ;
```

SPEC		
inherited	initial	version
NO	auto	CSS2
BROWSER SUPPORT		
IE5.5+	FF1+	Saf1.3+	Op9.2+
BUGGY	BUGGY	FULL	FULL

This property specifies the stack level of a box whose `position` value is one of `absolute`, `fixed`, or `relative`.

The **stack level** refers to the position of the box along the *z* axis, which runs perpendicular to the display. The higher the value, the closer the box is to the user; in other words, a box with a high `z-index` will obscure a box with a lower `z-index` occupying the same location along the *x* and *y* axes.

Example

This style rule makes the element with ID `"warning"` absolutely positioned and assigns it a higher stack level than its siblings:

```
#warning {
    position: absolute;
    z-index: 1;
}
```

See Stacking Contexts (p. 179) for more information about stacking contexts.

Value

An integer value—which can be negative—sets the stack level of the box in the current stacking context, and also establishes a new stacking context. The box itself has stack level 0 (zero) in the new context.

The value `auto` gives the box the same stack level as its parent, and doesn't establish a new stacking context.

Compatibility

Internet Explorer			Firefox			Safari			Opera
5.5	6.0	7.0	1.0	1.5	2.0	1.3	2.0	3.0	9.2
Buggy	Buggy	Buggy	Buggy	Buggy	Buggy	Full	Full	Full	Full

Layout Properties

In Internet Explorer for Windows versions up to and including 6, `select` elements always appear on top of everything else; their stack level can't be changed.

Internet Explorer for Windows versions up to and including 7 always use the nearest positioned ancestor to determine the stacking context for the element in question.

Internet Explorer for Windows version 7 treats the value `auto` as if it were 0 (zero).

Internet Explorer for Windows versions up to and including 7 don't support the value `inherit`.

In Firefox versions up to and including 2, a negative stack level positions the box behind the stacking context, rather than above the context's background and borders and below block-level descendants in the normal flow.

Other Relevant Stuff

 position (p. 267)

specifies the positioning scheme used to position an element

overflow

```
overflow: { auto | hidden | scroll | visible |
inherit } ;
```

	SPEC	
inherited	initial	version
NO	visible	CSS2
BROWSER SUPPORT		
IE7+	FF1+	Saf1.3+	Op9.2+
FULL	FULL	FULL	FULL

This property specifies the behavior that occurs when an element's content overflows the element's box.

The default behavior is to make the overflowing content visible, but it can be changed so that the content is clipped to the confines of the element's box, optionally providing a mechanism for scrolling the content.

Example

This style rule makes the `pre` element type in HTML generate a fixed-sized box with visible scrollbars:

```
pre {
    width: 40em;
    height: 20em;
    overflow: scroll;
}
```

If the `overflow` property is applied to the `body` or `html` elements in an HTML document, the user agent may apply it to the viewport. This does not apply to XHTML, though.

If a scrollbar needs to be provided, the user agent should insert it between the element's outer padding edge and its inner border edge. The space occupied by the scrollbar should be subtracted (by the user agent) from the computed width or height, so that the inner border edge is preserved.

Boxes with an `overflow` value other than `visible` will expand vertically to enclose any floated descendant boxes.

Margins will never collapse for a box with an `overflow` value other than `visible`.

Value

auto   The behavior of `auto` isn't specified in any detail in the CSS2.1 specification. In existing implementations it provides scrollbar(s) when necessary, but it doesn't show scrollbars unless the content overflows the element's box.

hidden   `hidden` causes content that overflows the element's box to be clipped. No scrolling mechanism will be provided, so the overflow will be invisible and inaccessible.

scroll   `scroll` clips overflowing content, just like `hidden`, but provides a scrolling mechanism so that the overflow can be accessed. This scrolling mechanism is present whether the content overflows the element's box or not, to prevent it from appearing and disappearing in a dynamic layout. When the output medium is `print`, this value allows overflowing content to be printed (as if the value were `visible`).

visible   `visible` allows overflowing content to be visible. It will be rendered *outside* the element's box, and may thus overlap other content.

Compatibility

Internet Explorer			Firefox			Safari			Opera
5.5	6.0	7.0	1.0	1.5	2.0	1.3	2.0	3.0	9.2
Buggy	Buggy	Full	Full	Full	Full	Full	Full	Full	Full

Internet Explorer for Windows versions up to and including 6:

■ will not apply a value specified for the body element to the viewport, if the computed value for the html element is visible

■ will increase the width and height of the element when the value is specified as visible, instead of rendering the overflow outside the element's box; if the value is auto, hidden, or scroll, and the element's width is specified as auto, the width will increase to avoid overflow

In Internet Explorer for Windows versions up to and including 7:

■ a relatively positioned child of an element whose overflow value is auto or scroll will behave as if the position were specified as fixed; if overflow is hidden, a relatively positioned element will be visible if the generated box lies outside the parent's box

■ the value inherit is unsupported

In Internet Explorer for Windows version 7, the values auto, hidden, and scroll cause an element to gain a layout (p. 158).

Firefox versions up to and including 2 apply overflow to table row groups.

clip

`clip: { shape | auto | inherit } ;`

	SPEC	
inherited	initial	version
NO	auto	CSS2, 2.1
BROWSER SUPPORT		
IE5.5+	FF1+	Saf1.3+	Op9.2+
PARTIAL	FULL	FULL	FULL

This property sets the clipping region for an absolutely positioned element.

Any part of an element that would render outside the clipping region will be invisible. This includes the content of the element and its children, backgrounds, borders, outlines, and even any visible scrolling mechanism.

Clipping may be further influenced by any clipping regions that are set for the element's ancestors, and whether or not those have a `visibility` property whose value is something other than `visible`. Clipping may also occur at the edges of the browser window, or the margins of the paper (when printing).

Example

This style rule assigns a clipping region of 200×100 pixels for the element with ID "`tunnel-vision`". The upper left-hand corner of the clipping region is at position (50,50) with respect to the element's box:

```
#tunnel-vision {
  width: 400px;
  height: 200px;
  clip: rect(50px, 250px, 150px,
➥    50px);
}
```

The default clipping region is a rectangle with the same dimensions as the element's border box.

Value

If the value is specified as `auto`, no clipping will be applied.

The only shape value that's allowed in CSS2.1 is a rectangle, which must be specified using the `rect()` functional notation. The function takes four comma-separated arguments—top, right, bottom, and left—in the usual TRouBLe order. Each argument is either `auto` or a length, and negative length values are allowed. The top and bottom positions are relative to the top border edge of the element's box. The left and right positions are relative to the left border edge in a left-to-right environment, or to the right border edge in a right-to-left environment. When specified as `auto`, the position is that of the corresponding border edge.

Layout Properties

Note that the interpretation of positions specified in the rect() functional notation changed between CSS2 and CSS2.1. In CSS2, each value specified the offset from the corresponding border edge.

Compatibility

Internet Explorer			Firefox			Safari			Opera
5.5	6.0	7.0	1.0	1.5	2.0	1.3	2.0	3.0	9.2
Partial	Partial	Partial	Full	Full	Full	Full	Full	Full	Full

Internet Explorer for Windows versions up to and including 7 do not support the recommended syntax for the rect() notation. However, they do support a deprecated syntax where the arguments are separated by whitespace rather than commas.

Internet Explorer for Windows versions up to and including 7 don't support the value inherit.

Chapter

List Properties

These properties allow the author to control the presentation of list item markers. For further information about list formatting, see List Formatting (p. 168).

list-style-type

```
list-style-type: { circle | disc | square | armenian
| decimal | decimal-leading-zero | georgian |
lower-alpha | lower-greek | lower-latin | lower-roman
| upper-alpha | upper-latin | upper-roman | none |
inherit } ;
```

SPEC		
inherited	initial	version
YES	disc	CSS1, 2
BROWSER SUPPORT		
IE5.5+	FF1+	Saf1.3+	Op9.2+
PARTIAL	FULL	FULL	FULL

This property specifies the type of list marker for an item in a list—an element whose `display` property has the value `list-item`.

The list style type only applies if `list-style-image` is set to `none`, or to a URI that can't be displayed.

Example

This style rule applies roman numerals as the numbering scheme to items in an ordered list:

```
ol li {
    list-style-type: upper-roman;
}
```

List markers can either be glyphs (that is, bullets), or comprise a numeric or alphabetic numbering system. The CSS2.1 specification doesn't define how alphabetic numbering wraps at the end of the alphabet sequence.

The color of the list markers is the same as the computed value of the `color` property for the list items.

The exact position of the list marker can't be specified beyond the styling allowed by the `list-style-position` (p. 288) property.

Value

The values `circle`, `disc`, and `square` generate glyphs as list markers. The exact appearance of these glyphs isn't defined by the CSS2.1 specification, but is left to the user agent.

Numeric numbering systems include:

- `armenian`: traditional Armenian numbering
- `decimal`: decimal numbers (1, 2, 3, ...)

- `decimal-leading-zero`: decimal numbers where values less than ten are padded by an initial zero (01, 02, 03, …)

- `georgian`: traditional Georgian numbering

- `lower-roman`: lowercase roman numerals (i, ii, iii, …)

- `upper-roman`: uppercase roman numerals (I, II, III, …)

Alphabetic numbering systems:

- `lower-greek`: lowercase Greek letters

- `lower-latin` or `lower-alpha`: lowercase Latin letters (a, b, c, …)

- `upper-latin` or `upper-alpha`: uppercase Latin letters (A, B, C, …)

Compatibility

Internet Explorer			Firefox			Safari			Opera
5.5	6.0	7.0	1.0	1.5	2.0	1.3	2.0	3.0	9.2
Partial	Partial	Partial	Full	Full	Full	Full	Full	Full	Full

Internet Explorer for Windows versions up to and including 7 don't support the values `armenian`, `decimal-leading-zero`, `georgian`, or `lower-greek`. Nor do they support the values `lower-latin` or `upper-latin`, although they do support the alternative forms `lower-alpha` and `upper-alpha`.

These browsers will not increment the list markers in numbering systems if the list item has a layout.

Internet Explorer for Windows versions up to and including 7 don't support the value `inherit`.

list-style-position

`list-style-position: { inside | outside | inherit } ;`

SPEC		
inherited	initial	version
YES	outside	CSS1
BROWSER SUPPORT		
IE5.5+	FF1+	Saf1.3+ Op9.2+
FULL	FULL	FULL FULL

This property specifies where the list marker is rendered with respect to the list item's principal block box.

Value

outside The value `outside` causes the list marker to be rendered outside the principal block box. Its precise location isn't defined by the CSS2.1 specification. Contemporary browsers seem to render it approximately 1.5em to the left of the principal block box in a left-to-right environment, or 1.5em to the right of the principal block box in a right-to-left environment. Some browsers use padding on the list to make room for the marker box, while others use a margin.

inside The value `inside` makes the list marker the first inline box in the principal block box. Its exact location is not defined by the CSS2.1 specification.

Example

This style rule makes the markers for all items within the list with ID `"compact"` appear on the inside:

```
#compact li {
  list-style-position: inside;
}
```

Compatibility

Internet Explorer			Firefox			Safari			Opera
5.5	6.0	7.0	1.0	1.5	2.0	1.3	2.0	3.0	9.2
Full	Full	Full	Full	Full	Full	Full	Full	Full	Full

Internet Explorer for Windows versions up to and including 7 don't support the value `inherit`.

list-style-image

`list-style-image: { uri | none | inherit } ;`

SPEC		
inherited	initial	version
YES	none	CSS1
BROWSER SUPPORT		
IE5.5+ FF1+	Saf1.3+	Op9.2+
BUGGY FULL	FULL	FULL

This property specifies the image to use as a list marker for an item in a list (an element whose `display` property has the value `list-item`). If the specified image is available, it will replace any marker specified by the `list-style-type` property.

The exact position of the list marker image can't be specified beyond what the `list-style-position` (p. 288) property allows.[1]

Example

This style rule assigns an image as the list marker for all items in the list with ID `"links"`:

```
#links li {
  list-style-image:
➥     url("/images/link.png");
}
```

Value

If the property value is specified as `none`, no list marker image will be used. Instead, the `list-style-type` property will control what type of list marker—if any—will be rendered.

If the value is specified as a URI using the `url()` functional notation (p. 38), the image at that URI will be used as the list marker if it's available.

Compatibility

Internet Explorer			Firefox			Safari			Opera
5.5	6.0	7.0	1.0	1.5	2.0	1.3	2.0	3.0	9.2
Buggy	Buggy	Buggy	Full	Full	Full	Full	Full	Full	Full

In Internet Explorer for Windows versions up to and including 7, a floated list item will not display any list marker image.

---

[1] It has become common practice, however, to apply a background image to the list items in order to gain precise control over list item marker image positioning.

Internet Explorer for Windows versions up to and including 7 don't support the value `inherit`.

list-style

```
list-style: { list-style-type list-style-position
list-style-image | inherit } ;
```

SPEC		
inherited	initial	version
YES	see below	CSS1
BROWSER SUPPORT		
IE5.5+	FF1+	Saf1.3+	Op9.2+
BUGGY	FULL	FULL	FULL

This shorthand property sets all three list style properties simultaneously. Note that an omitted property value will be set to that property's initial value.

Value

Refer to the individual properties for information on allowed and initial values.

Example

This style rule uses inheritance to set the list marker for items within the element with ID `"legal"` to be uppercase Latin letters that appear inside the list items' principal block boxes:

```
#legal {
  list-style: upper-latin inside;
}
```

Compatibility

Internet Explorer			Firefox			Safari			Opera
5.5	6.0	7.0	1.0	1.5	2.0	1.3	2.0	3.0	9.2
Buggy	Buggy	Buggy	Full	Full	Full	Full	Full	Full	Full

Internet Explorer for Windows versions up to and including 7 will only recognize a list image URI if it's immediately followed by whitespace, or the end of the declaration.

Internet Explorer for Windows versions up to and including 7 don't support the value `inherit`.

Chapter 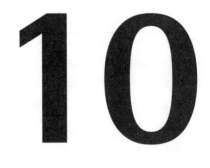 **10**

Table Properties

These properties allow us to control the layout and presentation of table elements. For further information about table formatting, see Table Formatting (p. 168).

table-layout

`table-layout: { auto | fixed | inherit } ;`

SPEC		
inherited	initial	version
NO	auto	CSS2
BROWSER SUPPORT		
IE5.5+	FF1+	Saf1.3+ Op9.2+
FULL	FULL	FULL FULL

This property specifies the layout algorithm that's used to lay out a table or an inline table (an element whose `display` property has one of the values `table` or `inline-table`). Two table layout algorithms are available: automatic and fixed. See Table Formatting (p. 168) for details of these algorithms.

Example

This style rule ensures that the table element with the ID "`results`" is laid out using the fixed layout algorithm:

```
#results {
    width: 24em;
    table-layout: fixed;
}
```

Note that the automatic algorithm will normally be used if the table's `width` is specified as `auto`, although user agents are allowed (but not required) to attempt to use the fixed algorithm in these cases if so specified by the CSS author. This special case only applies to tables, however, not inline tables.

Value

auto   selects the automatic table layout algorithm

fixed   selects the fixed table layout algorithm, if applicable

Compatibility

Internet Explorer			Firefox			Safari			Opera
5.5	6.0	7.0	1.0	1.5	2.0	1.3	2.0	3.0	9.2
Full	Full	Full	Full	Full	Full	Full	Full	Full	Full

Internet Explorer for Windows versions up to and including 7 don't support the value `inherit`.

Other Relevant Stuff

display (p. 264)

controls the type of box generated by an element

 width (p. 194)

sets the content width of a block or a replaced element

border-collapse

`border-collapse: { collapse | separate | inherit } ;`

SPEC		
inherited	initial	version
YES	separate	CSS2, 2.1
BROWSER SUPPORT		
IE5.5+ FF1+ Saf1.3+ Op9.2+		
FULL FULL FULL FULL		

This property specifies the border model that's to be used for a table or an inline table—that is, an element whose `display` property has one of the values `table` or `inline-table`.

See Table Formatting (p. 168) for details about the table border models.

Example

This style rule makes the table element with the ID `"results"` use the collapsing borders model:

```
#results {
  border-collapse: collapse;
}
```

Value

collapse   selects the collapsing borders model (the `border-spacing` and `empty-cells` properties will be ignored)

separate   selects the separated borders model (the `border-spacing` and `empty-cells` properties will be taken into account)

Note that the initial value was `collapse` in CSS2, but it was changed to `separate` in CSS2.1.

Compatibility

Internet Explorer			Firefox			Safari			Opera
5.5	6.0	7.0	1.0	1.5	2.0	1.3	2.0	3.0	9.2
Full	Full	Full	Full	Full	Full	Full	Full	Full	Full

Internet Explorer for Windows versions up to and including 7 don't support the value `inherit`.

Other Relevant Stuff

 display (p. 264)

controls the type of box generated by an element

border-spacing (p. 294)

sets the cell spacing for a table element that uses the separated borders model

empty-cells (p. 295)

controls the rendering of empty cells in a table that uses the separated borders model

 # border-spacing

border-spacing: { *length* [*length*] | inherit } ;

SPEC		
inherited	initial	version
YES	0	CSS2
BROWSER SUPPORT		
IE7	FF1+	Saf1.3+	Op9.2+
NONE	FULL	FULL	FULL

This property sets the spacing between adjacent table cells' borders using the separated borders model. If the collapsing borders model is used, this property is ignored.

Note that the distance between a cell border and the table border is the corresponding border spacing plus the table's padding for that side.

See Table Formatting (p. 168) for details about the table border models.

Example

This style rule sets 1em of horizontal spacing and 0.5em of vertical spacing between the cells of the table element with the ID "results":

```
#results {
  border-collapse: separate;
  border-spacing: 1em 0.5em;
}
```

The CSS2.1 specification states that user agents may apply this property to frameset elements (therefore replacing the framespacing attribute).

Value

Negative values are not allowed.

The border spacing can be specified using one or two length values. If two values are given, the first sets the horizontal spacing, and the second sets the vertical spacing. If only one value is given, it sets both the horizontal and vertical spacing to the specified value.

Compatibility

Internet Explorer			Firefox			Safari			Opera
5.5	6.0	7.0	1.0	1.5	2.0	1.3	2.0	3.0	9.2
None	None	None	Full	Full	Full	Full	Full	Full	Full

Internet Explorer for Windows versions up to and including 7 do not support this property.

Other Relevant Stuff

 `border-collapse` (p. 293)

specifies the border model for a table element

`display` (p. 264)

controls the type of box generated by an element

empty-cells

`empty-cells: { hide | show | inherit } ;`

	SPEC	
inherited	initial	version
YES	show	CSS2
BROWSER SUPPORT		
IE7	FF1+	Saf1.3+	Op9.2+
NONE	BUGGY	FULL	BUGGY

This property controls the rendering of the borders and backgrounds of cells that have no visible content in a table that's using the separated borders model. If the collapsing model is used, this property is ignored.

The property applies only to elements whose `display` property has the value `table-cell`, but since it's inherited, it can also be set on the whole table, a row group, or a row.

Example

This style rule hides empty cells in the table element with the ID `"results"`:

```
#results {
  empty-cells: hide;
}
```

A cell is considered to have no visible content if any of the following cases apply:

- It has no content at all.
- It contains only carriage returns, line feeds, tab characters, or blank spaces.
- Its `visibility` property is set to `hidden`.

A non-breaking space is considered to be visible content.

Value

show The value `show` means borders will be drawn around empty cells, and backgrounds will be drawn behind them.

hide The value `hide` means that no borders or backgrounds will display empty cells. If all the cells in a row have this setting for `empty-cells`, and none of them have any visible content, the entire row will behave as if it had `display:none`.

Compatibility

Internet Explorer			Firefox			Safari			Opera
5.5	6.0	7.0	1.0	1.5	2.0	1.3	2.0	3.0	9.2
None	None	None	Buggy	Buggy	Buggy	Full	Full	Full	Buggy

Internet Explorer for Windows versions up to and including 7 don't support this property, and will behave as if all tables had `empty-cells` set to `hide`.

Firefox versions up to and including 2 don't hide the row if all the cells have `empty-cells:hide` and none of them have any visible content.

Opera versions up to and including 9.2 won't hide the row, and will display cell backgrounds, if `empty-cells:hide` is applied to all the cells, and none of them have any visible content.

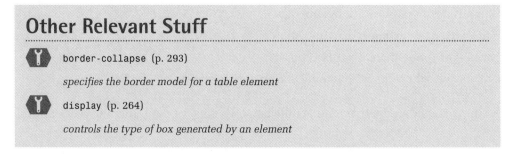

Other Relevant Stuff

border-collapse (p. 293)

specifies the border model for a table element

display (p. 264)

controls the type of box generated by an element

caption-side

`caption-side: { bottom | top | inherit } ;`

SPEC		
inherited	initial	version
YES	top	CSS2, 2.1
BROWSER SUPPORT		
IE7	FF1+	Saf1.3+	Op9.2+
NONE	FULL	FULL	FULL

This property sets the vertical position of a table caption box (an element whose `display` property has the value `table-caption`).

To affect the horizontal alignment of the caption text, use the `text-align` property.

The caption box is positioned relative to the table box. See Table Formatting (p. 168) for details.

Example

This style rule positions all table captions below their parent tables:

```
caption {
    caption-side: bottom;
}
```

Value

bottom   puts the caption below the table box

top   puts the caption above the table box

CSS2 also defined the values `left` and `right` for this property, but they were removed in CSS2.1.

Compatibility

Internet Explorer			Firefox			Safari			Opera
5.5	6.0	7.0	1.0	1.5	2.0	1.3	2.0	3.0	9.2
None	None	None	Full	Full	Full	Full	Full	Full	Full

Internet Explorer for Windows versions up to and including 7 don't support this property.

Other Relevant Stuff

 display (p. 264)

controls the type of box generated by an element

text-align (p. 330)

sets the horizontal text alignment

Chapter 11

Color and Backgrounds

These properties allow the author to control the foreground and background color of elements and the placement of background images.

background-color

```
background-color: { color | transparent | inherit } ;
```

SPEC		
inherited	initial	version
NO	transparent	CSS1
BROWSER SUPPORT		
IE5.5+	FF1+	Saf1.3+	Op9.2+
BUGGY	FULL	FULL	FULL

This property sets the background-color of an element; it's good practice to specify a foreground color (color) at the same time, to ensure that conflicts don't arise with colors or backgrounds that are defined elsewhere.

The background of an element is the area covered by the width and height of that element (whether those

Example

This style rule assigns a white background (#fff) to the element with ID "example":

```
#example{
   background-color: #fff;
}
```

dimensions are set explicitly, or the content dictates them); it also includes the area covered by padding and borders. A `background-color` (or `background-image`) that's applied to an element will appear beneath the foreground content of that element, and the area covered by the `padding` and `border` properties for the element. This coverage area is evident where an element has `transparent` (or `dotted` or `dashed`) borders, and the `background` is seen beneath the borders (or between the dots). Note that Internet Explorer versions up to and including 6 don't support `transparent` borders.

Some area of the element in question must be visible if the `background-color` is to show through. If the element has no intrinsic height (defined either by its content or its dimensions), the background will not be seen. If an element contains only floated children which haven't been cleared—see clear (p. 271)—then again the background won't show, as the element's height will be zero.

Value

`color` takes any valid CSS color value or color keyword.

The keyword `transparent` sets the `background-color` to be transparent. This value ensures that the content of any element that's beneath the current element will be visible through the transparent background. The default for `background-color` is `transparent`, so there is no need to specify this value unless you're overwriting previous definitions.

Compatibility

Internet Explorer			Firefox			Safari			Opera
5.5	6.0	7.0	1.0	1.5	2.0	1.3	2.0	3.0	9.2
Buggy	Buggy	Buggy	Full	Full	Full	Full	Full	Full	Full

Internet Explorer for Windows versions up to and including 7 will only apply the `background` from inside the border's edge when the element in question has a layout (p. 158). If the element does not have a layout, the `background-color` or `background-image` will slide under the borders as per the specifications.

Internet Explorer for Windows versions up to and including 7 don't support the value `inherit`.

Other Relevant Stuff

 The CSS Box Model (p. 142)

background-image

`background-image: { uri | none | inherit } ;`

	SPEC	
inherited	initial	version
NO	none	CSS1
BROWSER SUPPORT		
IE5.5+	FF1+	Saf1.3+	Op9.2+
BUGGY	FULL	FULL	FULL

This property sets the background image of an element via the specified URI. The image is placed on top of the `background-color`, and if the image is opaque, the `background-color` will not be visible beneath it. When you're setting a `background-image`, also set a `background-color`, where possible, in case the image is unavailable.

Example

This style rule assigns a background image to the element with ID `"example"` :

```
#example {
  background-image:
    ➥    url(images/bg.gif);
}
```

The background of an element is the area covered by the `width` and `height` of that element (whether those dimensions are set explicitly, or the content dictates them); it also includes the area covered by padding and borders. A `background-color` (or `background-image`) that's applied to an element will appear beneath the foreground content of that element, and the area covered by the `padding` and `border` properties for the element. This coverage area is evident where an element has `transparent` (or `dotted` or `dashed`) borders, and the `background` is seen beneath the borders (or between the dots). Note that Internet Explorer versions up to and including 6 don't support `transparent` borders.

Some area of the element in question must be visible so that the `background-image` can show through. If the element has no intrinsic height (either defined by its content or dimensions), the background won't have any space in which to display. If an element contains only floated children which haven't been cleared—see clear (p. 271)—again, the background won't display, since the element's height will be zero.

By default, the background-image is placed at the top-left (background-position) of the element; it's repeated along the x and y axes (background-repeat) and will scroll with the document. These are the default settings that apply if you haven't explicitly set any others, and can be adjusted with the other background properties. Refer to the other relevant stuff below for methods you can use to position and control the image.

Value

A URI value (p. 38) specifies a location at which the image can be found.

The value none ensures that no background-image will be displayed; this is the default setting, so you don't need to define it explicitly unless you want to override previous background-image declarations.

The value inherit would cause the element to inherit the background-image of its parent. This approach would not normally be taken, as the element's inherited background image would most likely overlap the parent's image. In most cases, the parent's background-image will be visible through the element's transparent background unless another background-image or background-color has been set.

Compatibility

Internet Explorer			Firefox			Safari			Opera
5.5	6.0	7.0	1.0	1.5	2.0	1.3	2.0	3.0	9.2
Buggy	Buggy	Buggy	Full	Full	Full	Full	Full	Full	Full

Internet Explorer for Windows versions up to and including 7 will only apply the background from inside the border's edge when the element in question has a layout (p. 158). If the element does not have a layout, the background-color or background-image will slide under the borders as per the specifications.

Internet Explorer for Windows versions up to and including 7 don't support the value inherit.

Other Relevant Stuff

The CSS Box Model (p. 142)

background-repeat

```
background-repeat: { repeat | repeat-x | repeat-y |
no-repeat | inherit } ;
```

SPEC		
inherited	initial	version
NO	repeat	CSS1
BROWSER SUPPORT			
IE5.5+	FF1+	Saf3+	Op9.2+
FULL	FULL	FULL	FULL

The `background-repeat` property controls whether or not a `background-image` is repeated (tiled), and if it is repeated, the property defines along which of the specified axes (*x*, *y*, or both) the image is to be repeated.

By default, a `background-image` is repeated along both vertical and horizontal axes, and is repeated in both directions. We use the `background-repeat` property to specify the axis along which an image should be repeated.

Example

This style rule causes a `background-image` assigned to the element with ID `"example"` to repeat along the *x* axis:

```
#example{
    background-repeat: repeat-x;
}
```

When a background image is repeated, it's first placed according to the `background-position` property, and then begins repeating from that point in both directions. For example, a `background-image` that's placed at a `background-position` of `center center` (the center of the element), and which has a `background-repeat` value of `repeat`, will repeat in both directions along the *x* and *y* axes—that is, up and down, left and right, starting from the center.

The background of an element is the area covered by the `width` and `height` of that element (whether those dimensions are set explicitly, or the content dictates them); it also includes the area covered by padding and borders. A `background-color` (or `background-image`) that's applied to an element will appear beneath the foreground content of that element, and the area covered by the `padding` and `border` properties for the element. This coverage area is evident where an element has `transparent` (or `dotted` or `dashed`) borders, and the `background` is seen beneath the borders (or between the dots). Note that Internet Explorer versions up to and including 6 don't support `transparent` borders.

Some area of the element in question must be visible if the background-image is to show through. If the element has no intrinsic height (either as defined by its content, or by its dimensions), the background won't be visible. If an element contains only floated children that haven't been cleared—see clear (p. 271)—no background will show, as the element's height will be zero.

The tiling and positioning of the background-image on inline elements isn't defined in the CSS2.1 specification, but it might be addressed in future versions.

Value

repeat   The value repeat ensures that the background-image is repeated in both directions (that is, left and right, and up and down), and along both axes, until the element's background is fully covered.

repeat-x   The value repeat-x ensures that the background-image is repeated only along the *x* axis (that is, the horizontal axis in both directions—left and right) until the element's background is fully covered along that axis.

repeat-y   The value repeat-y ensures that the background-image is repeated only along the *y* axis (that is, the vertical axis in both directions—up and down) until the element's background is fully covered along that axis.

no-repeat   The value no-repeat ensures that the background-image is not repeated in any direction, and that only a single instance of the image will be placed at the coordinates specified by the background-position.

If no background-position has been specified, the image is placed at the element's default left-top position (0,0).

Compatibility

Internet Explorer			Firefox			Safari			Opera
5.5	6.0	7.0	1.0	1.5	2.0	1.3	2.0	3.0	9.2
Full	Full	Full	Full	Full	Full	Buggy	Buggy	Full	Full

Safari versions up to and including 2.0 exhibit a `background-repeat` bug: the image is repeated incorrectly when `no-repeat` has been applied. This bug is evident when the image's height exceeds that of the element to which it's applied, and when the image is offset from the top position. In these cases, the image will repeat upwards, filling in the area immediately above the point at which the image was initially placed.

Internet Explorer for Windows versions up to and including 7 will only apply the `background` from inside the border's edge when the element in question has a layout (p. 158). If the element does not have a layout, the `background-color` or `background-image` will slide under the borders as per the specifications.

Internet Explorer for Windows versions up to and including 7 don't support the value `inherit`.

background-position

```
background-position: { { percentage | length | left
| center | right } 1 or 2 values | inherit } ;
```

SPEC		
inherited	initial	version
NO	0% 0%	CSS1, 2.1
BROWSER SUPPORT		
IE5.5+	FF1+	Saf1.3+ Op9.2+
FULL	FULL	FULL FULL

The `background-position` property defines the initial position of a `background-image`. We can repeat the image from this position using the `background-repeat` property, which will cause the image to be repeated in both directions along the specified axis—see background-repeat (p. 303).

The background of an element is the area covered by the `width` and `height`

Example

This style rule places a `background-image` at a position that's 100 pixels from the left and 200 pixels from the top of the element with ID `"example"`:

```
#example{
  background-position: 100px 200px;
}
```

of that element (whether those dimensions are set explicitly, or the content dictates them); it also includes the area covered by padding and borders. A `background-color` (or `background-image`) that's applied to an element will appear beneath the foreground content of that element, and the area covered by the `padding` and `border` properties for the element. This coverage area is evident where an element has transparent (or dotted or dashed) borders, and the background is seen beneath the borders (or between the dots). Note that Internet Explorer versions up to and including 6 don't support transparent borders.

Some area of the element must be visible so that the background-image is able to show through. If the element has no intrinsic height (defined either by its content or by its dimensions), there will be no space in which the background can be seen. Similarly, if an element contains only floated children that haven't been cleared—see clear (p. 271)—there will be no background to show, as the element's height will be zero.

If no background-position has been specified, the image is placed at the default top-left position of the element (0,0), which is located within the top-left corner of the element, just inside the border at the outside edge of the padding box.

The tiling and positioning of the background-image on inline elements isn't defined in the CSS2.1 specification, but it might be addressed in future versions.

Value

This property accepts one or two length values, percentages, or keywords.

If only one value is specified for background-position, the second value is assumed to be center. Where two values are used, and at least one is not a keyword, the first value represents the horizontal position, and the second represents the vertical position.

A length value (p. 29) places the top-left corner of the background-image at the exact horizontal and vertical position specified.

Note that when the background-position is defined with a percentage value, that position refers to both the element itself and the corresponding point on the background-image. For example, a background-image with background-position values of 50% 50% will place the point of the image that's located at 50% of the image's width and 50% of the image's height at a corresponding position within the element that contains the image. In the above case, this causes the image to be perfectly centered. This is an important point to grasp—using `background-position` isn't the same as placing an element with absolute position using percentages where the top-left corner of the element is placed at the position specified.

> 📓 **`background-position` and `background-attachment`**
>
> If the `background-image` has been placed using a `fixed` `background-attachment` value, the `background-position` refers to the viewport, rather than the element's padding box.

CSS2 didn't allow us to mix keywords and length values for `background-position` values. This point was amended in CSS2.1, and it's now quite valid to specify an image's `background-position` as follows:

```
.example {
  background-position: 200px bottom;
}
```

That said, in the interests of achieving the greatest browser compatibility, it's still advisable to avoid mixing keywords and length values. Besides, it's easier to use the equivalent percentage measurement, like so:

```
.example {
  background-image: 200px 100%;
}
```

Specify the horizontal position using one of the following keywords: `left`, `center`, or `right`. To set the vertical position, the following values are used: `top`, `center`, and `bottom`. Unlike length units, keywords don't have to be kept in a horizontal–vertical order—the browser is able to determine what they refer to—but, for the sake of clarity and consistency, it's best to keep them in that order.

The horizontal keyword `left` refers to the left-hand side of the element's padding box (it corresponds to 0%). If only one keyword is specified, the vertical position equates to 50% (that is, `0% 50%` or `left center`).

The horizontal keyword `center` refers to the horizontal position in the middle of the element's padding box (it corresponds to 50%). If only one keyword is specified, the vertical position equates to 50% (that is, `50% 50%` or `center center`).

The horizontal keyword `right` refers to the right-hand side of the element's padding box (corresponds to 100%). If only one keyword is specified, the vertical position equates to 50% (that is, `100% 50%` or `right center`).

The vertical keyword `top` refers to the top of the element's padding box (it corresponds to 0%). If only one keyword is specified, the horizontal position equates to 50% (that is, `50% 0%` or `center top`).

The vertical keyword `center` refers to the vertical position in the middle of the element's padding box (it corresponds to 50%). If only one keyword is specified, the horizontal position equates to 50% (that is, `50% 50%` or `center center`).

The vertical keyword `bottom` refers to the bottom of the element's padding box (it corresponds to 100%). If only one keyword is specified, the horizontal position equates to 50% (that is, `50% 100%` or `center bottom`).

The following example illustrates how the keywords refer to their equivalent percentage values:

```
background-position: left top;      /* same as 0% 0% */
background-position: left center;   /* same as 0% 50% */
background-position: left bottom;   /* same as 0% 100% */

background-position: right top;     /* same as 100% 0% */
background-position: right center;  /* same as 100% 50% */
background-position: right bottom;  /* same as 100% 100% */

background-position: center top;    /* same as 50% 0% */
background-position: center center; /* same as 50% 50% */
background-position: center bottom; /* same as 50% 100% */
```

Negative length and percentage values are allowed. Their effect is to shift the image's position outside the confines of the element it's placed in, although, of course, none of the negative part of the image will be visible. The image will be visible only inside the element itself, even though its starting position may be outside the element.

Compatibility

Internet Explorer			Firefox			Safari			Opera
5.5	6.0	7.0	1.0	1.5	2.0	1.3	2.0	3.0	9.2
Full	Full	Full	Full	Full	Full	Full	Full	Full	Full

Internet Explorer versions 6 and 7 will not base a background-position em length value on the parent element's font-size when that background-image is applied to the body element. Instead, these browsers will act as if the font-size has not been set on the html element. This issue only applies to the body element; other elements on the page remain unaffected.

Internet Explorer for Windows versions up to and including 7 don't support the value inherit.

background-attachment

`background-attachment: { scroll | fixed | inherit } ;`

SPEC		
inherited	initial	version
NO	scroll	CSS1, 2.1
BROWSER SUPPORT		
IE5.5+ FF1+ Saf1.3+ Op9.2+		
BUGGY FULL FULL FULL		

The background-attachment property defines whether the background-image scrolls with the document, or remains fixed to the viewing area. Its default value is scroll, which dictates that as the document is scrolled up or down, the image scrolls with it.

The background of an element is the area covered by the width and height of that element (whether those dimensions are set explicitly, or the content dictates them); it also includes the area covered by padding and borders. A background-color (or background-image) that's applied to an element will appear beneath the foreground content of that element, and the area covered by the padding and border properties for the element. This coverage area is evident where an element has transparent (or dotted or dashed) borders, and the background is seen beneath the borders (or between the dots). Note

Example

This style rule sets a fixed background-image to the element with ID "example":

```
#example{
    background-attachment: fixed;
}
```

that Internet Explorer versions up to and including 6 don't support `transparent` borders.

Value

The value `scroll` allows the `background-image` to scroll along with the document. When it's used on an element that has a scrollbar—see overflow (p. 280)—the value `scroll` ensures that the `background-image` doesn't move with that element's scrolling mechanism, but instead scrolls with the document's scrolling mechanism.

The value `fixed` stops the `background-image` from scrolling with its containing block. Note that although the `fixed` `background-image` may be applied to elements throughout the document, its `background-position` is always placed in relation to the viewport. This means the `background-image` is only visible when its `background-position` coincides with the content, padding, or border area of the element to which it is applied. Thus, a `fixed` `background-image` doesn't move with elements that have a scrollbar—see overflow (p. 280)—because it's placed in relation to the viewport.

Previously, user agents were allowed to treat the value `fixed` as `scroll`, but this changed in CSS2.1: if the user agent does not implement the value `fixed`, it should be ignored as if it were an invalid value.

Compatibility

Internet Explorer			Firefox			Safari			Opera
5.5	6.0	7.0	1.0	1.5	2.0	1.3	2.0	3.0	9.2
Buggy	Buggy	Buggy	Full	Full	Full	Full	Full	Full	Full

Internet Explorer for Windows versions up to and including 6 incorrectly implement the value `fixed` for the property `background-attachment` and place the `background-image` in relation to its containing block instead of the viewport. The result is that `fixed` only really works when the `background-image` is applied to the `html` or `body` elements, since they're effectively equivalent to the viewport. When a `background-position` value of `fixed` is applied to other elements on the page, it will fix the image to that element, not the viewport.

Internet Explorer version 7 implemented the `scroll` value incorrectly in cases where it's used on a container that has a scroll mechanism—when `overflow` is set to a value other than `visible`. In such cases, the `background-image` scrolls with the content when it should in fact remain in view at the position specified. Internet Explorer versions 6 and below exhibit the same behavior as IE 7 in this respect; however, using the value `fixed` instead of `scroll` will cause IE versions 6 and below to exhibit the behavior defined in the specifications for `scroll`.

Internet Explorer for Windows versions up to and including 7 will only apply the `background` from inside the border's edge when the element in question has a layout (p. 158). If the element does not have a layout, the `background-color` or `background-image` will slide under the borders as per the specifications.

Internet Explorer for Windows versions up to and including 7 don't support the value `inherit`.

Other Relevant Stuff

The Viewport, the Page Box, and the Canvas (p. 141)

background

```
background: { background-color background-image
background-repeat background-attachment
background-position | inherit } ;
```

SPEC		
inherited	initial	version
NO	see below	CSS1, 2.1
BROWSER SUPPORT			
IE5.5+	FF1+	Saf3+	Op9.2+
BUGGY	FULL	FULL	FULL

The background property is a shorthand property that allows all the individual background properties to be set in a single declaration (including background-color, background-image, background-repeat, background-attachment, and background-position).

Example

This style rule simultaneously assigns values to all the individual background properties of the element with ID "example":

```
#example{
  background: #fff url(image.gif)
➡      no-repeat fixed left top;
}
```

Using this shorthand property, we can set the color of the background (the background-color), and supply the URI of an image to be used on the background at the same time. The remaining properties dictate how and where the image is placed.

As with other shorthand properties, any values that aren't specified will be set to their defaults. This has implications if, for instance, the background-color is defined as follows:

```
#example{
  background: red;
}
```

In the above example, all the omitted values will be set to their default states—for background-image, the default is none. If the element already had a background image defined, that specification would be negated, and no image would appear. Therefore, when you're using the shorthand property, take care to ensure that no conflicts exist. That said, it's common practice to use background rather than background-color because the former property is shorter. There's no problem in doing this—as long as you realize the consequences.

The background of an element is the area covered by the `width` and `height` of that element (whether those dimensions are set explicitly, or the content dictates them); it also includes the area covered by padding and borders. A `background-color` (or `background-image`) that's applied to an element will appear beneath the foreground content of that element, and the area covered by the `padding` and `border` properties for the element. This coverage area is evident where an element has `transparent` (or `dotted` or `dashed`) borders, and the `background` is seen beneath the borders (or between the dots). Note that Internet Explorer versions up to and including 6 don't support `transparent` borders.

The tiling and positioning of the `background-image` on inline elements isn't defined in the CSS2.1 specification, but it might be addressed in future versions.

Value

- `background-color` sets the color of the background.

- `background-image` supplies the address of an image to be used on the background.

- `background-repeat` specifies whether a `background-image` is repeated (tiled) or not, and also defines the axis along which the image will repeat.

- `background-attachment` determines whether the `background-image` is to `scroll` with the document or remain `fixed` to the viewport (p. 141).

- `background-position` specifies the initial starting position of the `background-image`.

Refer to the individual properties for their specific details, and the initial and allowed values for each.

Compatibility

Internet Explorer			Firefox			Safari			Opera
5.5	6.0	7.0	1.0	1.5	2.0	1.3	2.0	3.0	9.2
Buggy	Buggy	Buggy	Full	Full	Full	Buggy	Buggy	Full	Full

Internet Explorer for Windows versions up to and including 6 incorrectly implement the value `fixed` for the property `background-attachment` and place the `background-image` in relation to its containing block instead of the viewport. The result is that `fixed` only really works when the `background-image` is applied to the `html` or `body` elements, since they're effectively equivalent to the viewport. When a `background-position` value of `fixed` is applied to other elements on the page, it will fix the image to that element, not the viewport.

Internet Explorer version 7 implemented the `scroll` value incorrectly in cases where it's used on a container that has a scroll mechanism—when `overflow` is set to a value other than `visible`. In such cases, the `background-image` scrolls with the content when it should in fact remain in view at the position specified. Internet Explorer versions 6 and below exhibit the same behavior as IE 7 in this respect; however, using the value `fixed` instead of `scroll` will cause IE versions 6 and below to exhibit the behavior defined in the specifications for `scroll`.

Internet Explorer for Windows versions up to and including 7 will only apply the `background` from inside the border's edge when the element in question has a layout (p. 158). If the element does not have a layout, the `background-color` or `background-image` will slide under the borders as per the specifications.

Safari versions up to and including 2.0 exhibit a `background-repeat` bug: the image is repeated incorrectly when `no-repeat` has been applied. This bug is evident when the image's height exceeds that of the element to which it's applied, and when the image is offset from the top position. In these cases, the image will repeat upwards, filling in the area immediately above the point at which the image was initially placed.

Internet Explorer for Windows versions up to and including 7 don't support the value `inherit`.

Other Relevant Stuff

The CSS Box Model (p. 142)

color

```
color: { color | inherit } ;
```

SPEC		
inherited	initial	version
YES	see below	CSS1, 2.1
BROWSER SUPPORT			
IE5.5+	FF1+	Saf1.3+	Op9.2+
FULL	FULL	FULL	FULL

The `color` property defines the foreground color of an element; in essence, this means it defines the color of the text content. If a `border-color` value hasn't been defined explicitly for the element, the `color` value will be used instead.

It's always good practice to set a `background-color`, as we set `color` to ensure that conflicts don't arise between these values and any previous declarations or styles contained within user style sheets.

Example

This style rule sets the color `red` for text within the element with ID `"example"` :

```
#example {
  color: red;
}
```

Value

`color` takes any valid CSS color value (p. 33). The initial value for this property depends on the user agent.

Compatibility

	Internet Explorer			Firefox			Safari			Opera
5.5	6.0	7.0	1.0	1.5	2.0	1.3	2.0	3.0	9.2
Full	Full	Full	Full	Full	Full	Full	Full	Full	Full

Internet Explorer for Windows versions up to and including 7 don't support the value `inherit`.

Chapter 12

Typographical Properties

Typographical properties allow the author to customize the presentation and layout of textual content.

font-family

`font-family: { family name ,… | inherit } ;`

	SPEC	
inherited	initial	version
YES	see below	CSS1, 2
BROWSER SUPPORT		
IE5.5+	FF1+	Saf1.3+	Op9.2+
FULL	FULL	FULL	FULL

The property `font-family` sets a
prioritized list of font family names
and/or generic family names to be used
to display a given element's text
content.

A user agent will use the first family
that's available. Since there's no
guarantee that any particular font will
be available, a generic family name
should always be the last value in the
list.

Note that it's meaningless to list any
font family names after a valid generic
family name, since the latter will always
match an available font.

Example

This style rule sets the list of font families
to be used for the root element, and,
through inheritance, all elements in a given
HTML document (unless overridden). If
Helvetica isn't available, the user agent will
try Arial. If Arial isn't available, Luxi Sans
will be tried. If none of the font families
are available, the user agent will resort to
its default sans-serif font family:

```
html {
    font-family: Helvetica, Arial,
➥      "Luxi Sans", sans-serif;
}
```

While an element's `font-family` value will be inherited if it's not explicitly
specified, if it is specified, and none of the specified font families match an available
font (this case only arises if the list doesn't include a generic family name), the
resulting property value will default to the user agent's *initial* value (p. 39), not
the value inherited from the parent element, as you might expect.

Value

Note that the values are separated by commas, not the spaces that are used in most
other CSS properties. Comma separators are used because the values are
alternatives—at most, one of them will be used.

The values are either font family names or generic family names. Font family names
are quoted or unquoted strings, while generic family names are keywords and
shouldn't be quoted.

It's a good idea to quote any font family name that contains spaces or other non-alphanumeric characters. Special characters must be escaped if the value isn't quoted. Whitespace characters will be ignored at the beginning or end of an unquoted name, and multiple white space characters inside the name will collapse to a single space.

Also, if a font family name happens to be the same as a generic family name or any other CSS keyword, it must be quoted to avoid confusion.

Note that font family names may be case sensitive on some operating systems. Generic family names, being CSS keywords, are always case insensitive.

CSS2.1 defines five generic family name keywords:

- `cursive` (a cursive script font)
- `fantasy` (a special, decorative font)
- `monospace` (a monospaced font)
- `sans-serif` (a sans-serif font)
- `serif` (a serif font)

Those generic family names are mapped to actual font families by the user agent. Most browsers allow the user to modify this mapping via software preferences or options.

The initial value for this property depends on the user agent.

Compatibility

Internet Explorer			Firefox			Safari			Opera
5.5	6.0	7.0	1.0	1.5	2.0	1.3	2.0	3.0	9.2
Full	Full	Full	Full	Full	Full	Full	Full	Full	Full

Internet Explorer for Windows versions up to and including 7 don't support the value `inherit`.

Other Relevant Stuff

 `@font-face` (p. 54)

defines custom font properties

font-size

```
font-size: { absolute-size | relative-size | length
| percentage | inherit } ;
```

SPEC		
inherited	initial	version
YES	medium	CSS1, 2
BROWSER SUPPORT		

IE5.5+	FF1+	Saf1.3+	Op9.2+
FULL	FULL	FULL	FULL

This property specifies the font size to be applied to the text content of an element.

Value

An absolute size (sometimes referred to as a **T-shirt size**) is specified using one of the following keywords:

- xx-small
- x-small
- small
- medium
- large
- x-large
- xx-large

Example

These style rules set the font size for paragraphs to be 80% of the parent element's font size for screen output, and to be ten points for print output:

```
@media screen {
  p {
    font-size: 80%;
  }
}
@media print {
  p {
    font-size: 10pt;
  }
}
```

The exact sizes to which those keywords map aren't defined, but each one in the list above must be larger than or equal to the keyword that precedes it. User agents are recommended never to map any of those keywords to a physical size that's less than nine pixels for screen use.

A relative size is specified using one of the following keywords:

- smaller
- larger

Those keywords will make the font size smaller or larger than the inherited value, by some factor that isn't exactly defined. Most modern browsers seem to use a factor of 1.2, but the result may be adjusted to match a table of font sizes.

A length specified with a unit of em or ex refers to the computed font size that's inherited from the parent element. This also applies to percentages.

Negative length values and percentages are illegal.

Compatibility

Internet Explorer			Firefox			Safari			Opera
5.5	6.0	7.0	1.0	1.5	2.0	1.3	2.0	3.0	9.2
Full	Full	Full	Full	Full	Full	Full	Full	Full	Full

Internet Explorer for Windows up to and including versions 5.5 use an initial value of small, rather than medium.

Internet Explorer for Windows versions up to and including 7 don't support the value inherit.

font-weight

```
font-weight: { 100 | 200 | 300 | 400 | 500 | 600 |
700 | 800 | 900 | bold | bolder | lighter | normal
| inherit } ;
```

SPEC		
inherited	initial	version
YES	normal	CSS1, 2
BROWSER SUPPORT		
IE5.5+	FF1+	Saf1.3+	Op9.2+
FULL	FULL	FULL	FULL

This property sets the font weight that's applied to the text content of an element.

Note that many common computer fonts are only available in a limited number of weights (often, the only options are normal and bold).

Example

This style rule makes emphasized elements display with a bolder weight than that of their parent elements:

```
em {
  font-weight: bolder;
}
```

Value

The numeric values 100–900 specify font weights where each number represents a weight equal to or darker than its predecessor. 400 is considered the "normal" weight. If the specified font isn't available in the specified weight, the font weight will be mapped to a suitable existing value.

The following keywords can also be used for this property:

bold   is a synonym for 700

bolder   selects a font weight that's darker than that inherited from the parent element

lighter   selects a font weight that's lighter than that inherited from the parent element

normal   is a synonym for 400

Compatibility

Internet Explorer			Firefox			Safari			Opera
5.5	6.0	7.0	1.0	1.5	2.0	1.3	2.0	3.0	9.2
Full	Full	Full	Full	Full	Full	Full	Full	Full	Full

Internet Explorer for Windows versions up to and including 7 don't support the value inherit.

font-style

`font-style: { italic | normal | oblique | inherit } ;`

SPEC		
inherited	initial	version
YES	normal	CSS1, 2
BROWSER SUPPORT		
IE5.5+ FF1+ Saf1.3+ Op9.2+		
FULL FULL FULL FULL		

This property sets the font style to be applied for the text content of an element.

Value

italic   This value specifies a font that's labeled "italic" in the user agent's font database. If such a font isn't available, it will use one labeled "oblique."

normal   This value specifies a font classified as "normal" in the user agent's font database. This is typically a Roman (upright) font for Latin characters.

oblique   This value specifies a font labeled "oblique" in the user agent's font database. This may not be a true oblique font, but may be generated by slanting a Roman font.

Example

This style rule makes all elements that belong to the `"ship"` class render as italics:

```
.ship {
    font-style: italic;
}
```

Compatibility

Internet Explorer			Firefox			Safari			Opera
5.5	6.0	7.0	1.0	1.5	2.0	1.3	2.0	3.0	9.2
Full	Full	Full	Full	Full	Full	Full	Full	Full	Full

In Internet Explorer for Windows versions up to and including 7, the calculation of widths for inline blocks is incorrect when an italic or oblique font is used. This can cause the element to overflow, which may break float-based layouts due to the incorrect handling of overflow in those browsers.

Internet Explorer for Windows versions up to and including 7 don't support the value `inherit`.

Typographical Properties

font-variant

`font-variant: { normal | small-caps | inherit } ;`

SPEC		
inherited	initial	version
YES	normal	CSS1, 2

BROWSER SUPPORT			
IE5.5+	FF1+	Saf3	Op9.2+
FULL	FULL	NONE	FULL

`font-variant` sets the font variant that will be used for the text content of an element.

Small-caps fonts are fonts in which lowercase letters appear as smaller versions of the corresponding uppercase letters.

Example

This style rule makes **h1** headings render with small-caps:

```
h1 {
    font-variant: small-caps;
}
```

Value

normal　The value `normal` specifies a font that is not a small-caps font.

small-caps　The value `small-caps` specifies a font that is a small-caps font. CSS2.1 allows a user agent to use scaled-down versions of uppercase letters in lieu of true small-caps lowercase letters, and even to use ordinary uppercase letters as a replacement.

Compatibility

Internet Explorer			Firefox			Safari			Opera
5.5	6.0	7.0	1.0	1.5	2.0	1.3	2.0	3.0	9.2
Full	Full	Full	Full	Full	Full	None	None	None	Full

In Internet Explorer for Windows versions up to and including 7, setting `font-variant` to `small-caps` causes the values `lowercase` and `uppercase` for the `text-transform` property to behave as if they were set to `none`. The computed intrinsic height of an inline box will be incorrect for small-caps text if the text consists solely of lowercase letters, and contains no whitespace or punctuation characters.

Internet Explorer for Windows versions up to and including 7 don't support the value `inherit`.

Safari versions up to and including 3 don't support this property.

font

```
font: { [font-style] [font-variant] [font-weight]
font-size [ /line-height ]  font-family | caption |
icon | menu | message-box | small-caption |
status-bar | inherit } ;
```

SPEC		
inherited	initial	version
YES	see below	CSS1, 2
BROWSER SUPPORT		
IE5.5+	FF1+	Saf1.3+	Op9.2+
FULL	FULL	FULL	FULL

This property sets the font size and the font family, plus, optionally, the font style, font variant, font weight, and line height, for an element's text content.

Value

The font size and font family must be specified. The font style, variant, and weight may be specified (in arbitrary order) before the font size. The line height may be specified, preceded by a slash character, between the font size and the font family.

Any omitted value will be set to its *initial* value, not its *inherited* value. See the individual properties for information on their initial values.

Example

This style rule sets some font properties for the element with ID "sidebar":

```
#sidebar {
    font: bold small-caps 0.8em/1.4
➡       Helvetica, Arial,
➡       "Luxi Sans", sans-serif;
}
```

This style rule sets the font for the class "dialog" to be the system font used for dialog boxes, but changes the font size to twice that of the parent element's:

```
.dialog {
    font: message-box;
    font-size: 200%;
}
```

As an alternative to the aforementioned syntax, the value can be specified using one of the special keywords for system fonts. These keywords imply all of the font properties in one go, and can't be combined with other property values such as a font weight or font size, although those traits can be modified in subsequent declarations. The keywords are:

caption   selects the font used for captioned controls such as buttons

icon   selects the font used to label icons

menu   selects the font used in menus

message-box   selects the font used in dialog boxes

small-caption   selects the font used for labeling small controls, or a smaller version of the caption font

status-bar   selects the font used in window status bars

Note that the system fonts can only be set with this shorthand property; not with the font-family property.

Compatibility

Internet Explorer			Firefox			Safari			Opera
5.5	6.0	7.0	1.0	1.5	2.0	1.3	2.0	3.0	9.2
Full	Full	Full	Full	Full	Full	Full	Full	Full	Full

Internet Explorer for Windows versions up to and including 7 don't support the value inherit.

letter-spacing

letter-spacing: { *length* | normal | inherit } ;

SPEC		
inherited	initial	version
YES	normal	CSS1, 2
BROWSER SUPPORT		
IE5.5+	FF1+	Saf1.3+	Op9.2+
FULL	FULL	FULL	FULL

This property sets the extra spacing between characters in the text content of an element.

Value

A length value specifies extra space to be inserted between characters *in addition to* the default inter-character space. This space may not be adjusted by the user agent in order to justify text.

Negative length values are legal.

Example

This style rule tightens the letter spacing in h1 headings by one pixel:

```
h1 {
    letter-spacing: -1px;
}
```

normal means there will be no extra space between characters. The space may be adjusted by the user agent in order to justify text.

Note that `normal` and 0 are not fully equivalent. If the value is `normal`, the user agent is allowed to adjust the letter spacing for justified text; if the value is 0, it cannot.

Compatibility

Internet Explorer			Firefox			Safari			Opera
5.5	6.0	7.0	1.0	1.5	2.0	1.3	2.0	3.0	9.2
Full	Full	Full	Full	Full	Full	Full	Full	Full	Full

Internet Explorer for Windows versions up to and including 7 exhibit an exotic bug whereby every other `br` element within an element whose `letter-spacing` is a length value will be ignored.

Internet Explorer for Windows versions up to and including 7 don't support the value `inherit`.

word-spacing

`word-spacing: { length | normal | inherit } ;`

SPEC		
inherited	initial	version
YES	normal	CSS1, 2
BROWSER SUPPORT		
IE6+	FF1+	Saf1.3+ Op9.2+
FULL	BUGGY	FULL BUGGY

The `word-spacing` property sets the extra spacing between words in the text content of an element.

Word spacing can be affected by text justification (see the `text-align` (p. 330) property).

When whitespace is preserved—see `white-space` (p. 341)—all space characters are affected by word spacing.

Example

This style rule adds half an em square of spacing between words in paragraph elements:

```
p {
    word-spacing: 0.5em;
}
```

Value

A length value specifies extra space to be inserted between words *in addition to* the default inter-word space.

Negative length values are legal.

A value of `normal` means no extra space will appear between words.

Compatibility

	Internet Explorer			Firefox			Safari			Opera
5.5	6.0	7.0	1.0	1.5	2.0	1.3	2.0	3.0	9.2
None	Full	Full	Buggy	Buggy	Buggy	Full	Full	Full	Buggy

Internet Explorer for Windows versions up to and including 7 don't support the value `inherit`.

In Firefox versions up to and including 2, and in Opera versions up to and including 9.2, the whitespace between inline child elements has a minimum width of zero.

line-height

```
line-height: { length | number | percentage | normal
| inherit } ;
```

SPEC		
inherited	initial	version
YES	normal	CSS1, 2
BROWSER SUPPORT		
IE5.5+	FF1.5+ Saf1.3+ Op9.2+	
BUGGY	FULL FULL FULL	

This property sets the line height, providing an indirect means to specify the leading or half-leading.

The **leading** is the difference between the content height and the (used) value of `line-height`. Half the leading is known as the **half-leading**—an old typographic term.

Example

This style rule sets the default line height in an HTML document to 1.5:

```
html {
    line-height: 1.5;
}
```

Glyphs (the visual representations of a character) are centered vertically within an inline box. If the line height is larger than the content height, half the difference—the half-leading—is added as space at the top; the same amount is also added at the bottom.

When it's set on a block-level element, a table cell, a table caption, or an inline block that consists solely of inline boxes, this property specifies the *minimal* height of descendant line boxes.

When set on a non-replaced inline element, it specifies the height used to calculate the height of the surrounding line box.

See Formatting Concepts (p. 163) for more information about block and inline formatting.

Value

A specified length value will be the computed value for this property, and will be used in the calculation of the final height for the line box. Negative length values are illegal.

A number value is used as a multiplier in the calculation of the value used for this property, which equals the specified number multiplied by the element's computed font size. Child elements will inherit the specified value, not the resulting used value for this property. Negative values are illegal.

A percentage is used as a multiplier in the same way as a number value—the computed value for the property equals the specified percentage value of the element's computed font size. However, child elements will inherit the computed value for the property, not the specified percentage value. Again, negative values are illegal.

`normal` is the normal line height, which depends on the user agent. In this case, it's the specified value, `normal`, rather than the resulting used value for the property, which will be inherited by child elements.

As you can see, the way the value is specified has great implications for the inheritance of line height by child elements. A unitless number is inherited as specified, so the declaration `line-height: 2;` will make child elements double-spaced even if their font sizes are different from the parent's. For a length or percentage, however, the value is first computed as an absolute value, then this absolute value is inherited. This means that child elements will have the same absolute line height as their parents, regardless of their font sizes.

Typographical Properties

Compatibility

Internet Explorer			Firefox			Safari			Opera
5.5	6.0	7.0	1.0	1.5	2.0	1.3	2.0	3.0	9.2
Buggy	Buggy	Buggy	Buggy	Full	Full	Full	Full	Full	Full

Internet Explorer for Windows versions up to and including 7 will use the wrong line height if the line box contains a replaced inline element, such as an image or a form control. The line height will shrink-wrap to the intrinsic height of the replaced element, and will also collapse with the half-leading of adjacent line boxes.

Firefox versions up to 1.0.0.8 do not handle number values correctly, but will use a computed value that's too large. This is especially noticeable on Macintosh systems.

Internet Explorer for Windows versions up to and including 7 don't support the value inherit.

Other Relevant Stuff

vertical-align (p. 338)

controls vertical alignment

Inline Formatting (p. 166)

text-align

```
text-align: { center | justify | left | right |
inherit } ;
```

SPEC		
inherited	initial	version
YES	see below	CSS1, 2
BROWSER SUPPORT			

IE5.5+	FF1+	Saf1.3+	Op9.2+
BUGGY	FULL	FULL	FULL

This property specifies how the inline content of a block is aligned, when the sum of the widths of the inline boxes is less than the width of the line box.

Value

The initial value is left if direction is ltr, and right if direction is rtl.

Example

This style rule makes text in h1 headings centered:

```
h1 {
    text-align: center;
}
```

center   This value makes the text center justified.

justify   This value makes the text left and right justified. In this case, inline
boxes may be stretched in addition to being repositioned. If `white-space`
is `pre` or `pre-line`, the alignment is set to the initial value.

left   This value makes the text left justified.

right   This value makes the text right justified.

Compatibility

Internet Explorer			Firefox			Safari			Opera
5.5	6.0	7.0	1.0	1.5	2.0	1.3	2.0	3.0	9.2
Buggy	Buggy	Buggy	Full	Full	Full	Full	Full	Full	Full

Internet Explorer for Windows versions up to and including 7 incorrectly align
block-level boxes according to the `text-align` property, although it should only
affect inline boxes. The value `justify` behaves like `center` for table caption boxes.

Internet Explorer for Windows versions up to and including 7 don't support the
value `inherit`.

text-decoration

```
text-decoration: { { blink | line-through | overline
| underline } ... | none | inherit } ;
```

SPEC		
inherited	initial	version
NO	none	CSS1, 2
BROWSER SUPPORT		
IE5.5+	FF1+	Saf1.3+ Op9.2+
BUGGY	BUGGY	FULL FULL

This property specifies the decorations that will be applied to the text content of an element. These decorations are rendered in the color specified by the element's `color` property.

The text decorations are not technically inherited, but the effect is similar to inheritance. If they're set on an inline element, they apply to all boxes generated by that element. If they're set on a block-level element, the setting is applied to an anonymous inline box that encompasses all inline children in the normal flow, and also to all block-level descendants in the normal flow. The decorations are not propagated to floated or absolutely positioned descendants, or to descendant inline tables or inline blocks.

Also, text decorations on inline boxes are rendered along the entire box, even if it contains descendant boxes. This, too, may appear similar to inheritance. Any text decoration setting on a descendant box can never "undo" the text decorations of an ancestor box.

Example

With the following rules applied, unvisited anchor links are bold, but have no underline, visited links have a line through them, and links in the hover or focus state have a line above and below them:

```
a:link {
  font-weight: bold;
  text-decoration: none;
}
a:visited {
  font-weight: bold;
  text-decoration: line-through;
}
a:hover, a:focus {
  text-decoration: underline
overline;
}
```

Value

blink   This value makes the text blink. (Conforming user agents are allowed to ignore this value, since blinking content can be detrimental to a page's accessibility.)

line-through This value draws a horizontal line through the text.

none   This value produces no text decoration (although it doesn't undo a decoration that's set on an ancestor element).

overline   This value draws a horizontal line above the text.

underline   This value draws a horizontal line below the text.

Compatibility

Internet Explorer			Firefox			Safari			Opera
5.5	6.0	7.0	1.0	1.5	2.0	1.3	2.0	3.0	9.2
Buggy	Buggy	Buggy	Buggy	Buggy	Buggy	Full	Full	Full	Full

Internet Explorer for Windows versions up to and including 7 don't support the `blink` property. Setting the value to `none` will remove all text decorations from an element, even if one or more decorations are specified for its parent element. Text decorations are propagated to floating and absolutely positioned descendants.

Internet Explorer for Windows versions up to and including 6 place the `line-through` line noticeably higher above the baseline than other browsers.

Internet Explorer for Windows versions up to and including 7 don't support the value `inherit`.

Firefox versions up to and including 2 propagate text decoration values to floating descendants.

text-indent

`text-indent: { length | percentage | inherit } ;`

SPEC		
inherited	initial	version
YES	0	CSS1, 2
BROWSER SUPPORT			
IE5.5+	FF1+	Saf1.3+	Op9.2+
FULL	FULL	FULL	FULL

This property specifies the indentation of the first line of text in a block. Whether the text is indented from the left or from the right depends on the element's `direction` (p. 343) property.

Whereas margins and padding affect the whole block, `text-indent` only applies to the first rendered line of text in the element.

Example

These rules style paragraphs in a way that's common in novels—there's no vertical space between the paragraphs, and each paragraph except the first is indented 1.5 em squares:

```
p {
  margin: 0;
  text-indent: 1.5em;
}
p:first-child {
  text-indent: 0;
}
```

Using `text-indent` to Hide Text

Setting `text-indent` to a large negative value is a technique commonly used to "hide" short texts—such as structural headings—in visual browsers without hiding them from screen readers (as is the case with `display:none`). For example, a `text-indent` value of `-9999px` is high enough to push the text far off the screen—even for large viewport sizes.

Value

Negative values are legal.

A length specifies an indentation of a fixed length.

A percentage specifies an indentation that's a percentage of the containing block's (p. 147) width.

Compatibility

Internet Explorer			Firefox			Safari			Opera
5.5	6.0	7.0	1.0	1.5	2.0	1.3	2.0	3.0	9.2
Full	Full	Full	Full	Full	Full	Full	Full	Full	Full

Internet Explorer for Windows versions up to and including 5.5 will indent text in inline elements that have been assigned a `width` value other than `auto`.

Internet Explorer for Windows versions up to and including 7 don't support the value `inherit`.

Opera browsers will ignore "extreme" values. So, when you're using `text-indent` to hide text, don't go beyond `-999em` or `-9999px`.

Other Relevant Stuff

 `direction` (p. 343)

specifies the writing direction

text-transform

```
text-transform: { capitalize | lowercase | none |
uppercase | inherit } ;
```

SPEC		
inherited	initial	version
YES	none	CSS1, 2
BROWSER SUPPORT		
IE5.5+	FF1+	Saf1.3+	Op9.2+
BUGGY	FULL	FULL	FULL

This property controls if and how an element's text content is capitalized.

Value

capitalize   transforms the first character in each word to uppercase; all other characters remain

Example

These style rules make h1 headings use only uppercase letters, while the first letter of each word in h2 headings will be uppercased:

```
h1 {
    text-transform: uppercase;
}
h2 {
    text-transform: capitalize;
}
```

unaffected—they're not transformed to lowercase, but will appear as written in the document

lowercase   transforms all characters to lowercase

none   produces no capitalization effect at all

uppercase   transforms all characters to uppercase

Compatibility

Internet Explorer			Firefox			Safari			Opera
5.5	6.0	7.0	1.0	1.5	2.0	1.3	2.0	3.0	9.2
Buggy	Buggy	Buggy	Full	Full	Full	Full	Full	Full	Full

Note that the concept of what constitutes a word depends on the language in which the content is presented, and differs between browsers. Opera and Firefox will capitalize text-transform as Text-transform, while Internet Explorer for Windows will capitalize it as Text-Transform.

In Internet Explorer for Windows versions up to and including 7, the values lowercase and uppercase behave like none if the font-variant property is set to small-caps.

Internet Explorer for Windows versions up to and including 7 don't support the value inherit.

text-shadow

`text-shadow: { shadow,… | none | inherit } ;`

SPEC		
inherited	initial	version
NO	none	CSS2, 3
BROWSER SUPPORT		
IE7	FF2	Saf1.3+	Op9.2
NONE	NONE	PARTIAL	NONE

The property specifies one or more text shadow effects to be added to the text content of an element. `text-shadow` was originally specified in CSS2 but removed from CSS2.1 due to the lack of implementation among browsers. It's currently also included in the CSS3 Text module.

Shadow effects are applied in the order in which they are specified. They don't increase the size of a box, though they can extend past its boundaries, and their stack order is the same as the element itself.

`text-shadow` is inherited in CSS3.

Example

This rule specifies a text shadow effect that's black, extends 2px to the right of and below the text, and has a 2px blur:

```
.title {
    text-shadow: 2px 2px 2px #000;
}
```

Value

Each shadow value must specify a shadow offset and, optionally, a blur radius and color.

The offset is specified using two length values; the first value represents the horizontal distance to the right of the text (if it's positive), or to the left of the text (if the value's negative); the second value represents the vertical distance below the text (if it's positive) or above the text (if it's negative).

The blur radius is specified after the offset values; it's a length value that represents the size of the blur effect. If no radius is specified, the shadow will not be blurred.

The color can be specified before or after the offset and blur radius values. According to CSS2, if no color value is specified, the shadow will use the value of the `color` property instead. However, in CSS3 the specification states that the user agent determines the shadow color in the absence of a specified value.

Compatibility

Internet Explorer			Firefox			Safari			Opera
5.5	6.0	7.0	1.0	1.5	2.0	1.3	2.0	3.0	9.2
None	None	None	None	None	None	Partial	Partial	Partial	None

This property is currently only supported by Safari up to and including version 3 and Opera 9.5 beta. However, Safari doesn't support multiple shadows.

vertical-align

```
vertical-align: { length | percentage | baseline |
bottom | middle | sub | super | text-bottom |
text-top | top | inherit } ;
```

SPEC		
inherited	initial	version
NO	baseline	CSS1, 2
BROWSER SUPPORT		
IE5.5+	FF1+	Saf1.3+	Op9.2+
BUGGY	BUGGY	FULL	FULL

This property controls the vertical alignment of inline boxes within a line box, or of table cells within a row.

Value

The following values apply to inline boxes:

> ### Example
>
> This style rule makes images within table cells align to the bottom of the cell, to eliminate the gap that otherwise occurs:
>
> ```
> td img {
>     vertical-align: bottom;
> }
> ```

- A length value raises or lowers (depending on its sign) the box by the specified distance.

- A percentage value raises or lowers (depending on its sign) the box by the distance specified as the percentage applied to the element's `line-height`.

- The following keyword values can be specified for inline boxes:

  baseline   aligns the baseline of the box with the baseline of the parent box; if the box doesn't have a baseline (for instance, an image) the bottom margin edge is aligned with the parent's baseline

`bottom`	aligns the bottom of the aligned subtree with the bottom of the line box[1]
`middle`	aligns the vertical midpoint of the box with a point that's half the parent's x-height above the baseline of the parent box
`sub`	lowers the baseline of the box to a position suitable for subscripts of the parent's box
`super`	raises the baseline of the box to a position suitable for superscripts of the parent's box
`text-bottom`	aligns the bottom of the box with the bottom of the parent element's font
`text-top`	aligns the top of the box with the top of the parent element's font
`top`	aligns the top of the aligned subtree with the top of the line box

For inline blocks, the baseline is the baseline of the last line box in the normal flow. If there isn't one, the element's bottom margin edge is used.

The baseline of an inline table is the baseline of the first row of the table.

The following values apply to table cells:

`baseline`	aligns the baseline of the cell with the baseline of the first of the rows it spans
`bottom`	aligns the bottom of the cell box with the bottom of the last row it spans
`middle`	aligns the center of the cell with the center of the rows it spans
`top`	aligns the top of the cell box with the top of the first row it spans

---

[1] An aligned subtree includes the element and the aligned subtrees of all child elements, except those whose `vertical-align` value is top or bottom.

Any other value, including lengths and percentages, won't apply to cells. The computed vertical alignment will be `baseline`.

The baseline of a table cell is the baseline of the first line box in the cell. If there is none, the bottom of the cell box is used.

Compatibility

Internet Explorer			Firefox			Safari			Opera
5.5	6.0	7.0	1.0	1.5	2.0	1.3	2.0	3.0	9.2
Buggy	Buggy	Buggy	Buggy	Buggy	Buggy	Full	Full	Full	Full

In Internet Explorer for Windows versions up to and including 7, some elements behave as if the declaration `vertical-align: inherit;` was in the user agent style sheet. The values `bottom` and `top` are treated like `text-bottom` and `text-top`, respectively. Length values, percentages, and the values `sub`, `super`, `text-bottom`, and `text-top` don't compute to `baseline` for table cells.

Internet Explorer for Windows versions up to and including 7 don't support the value `inherit`.

In Firefox up to and including version 2, some elements behave as if the declaration `vertical-align: inherit;` was in the user agent style sheet.

As an example, in both Firefox and Internet Explorer for Windows, a `vertical-align` value specified for a table row will be applied to all the cells in that row. This is incorrect, because `vertical-align` doesn't apply to table rows, and isn't inherited, so such a setting should have no effect.

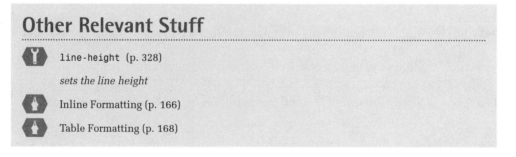

Other Relevant Stuff

`line-height` (p. 328)

sets the line height

Inline Formatting (p. 166)

Table Formatting (p. 168)

white-space

```
white-space: { normal | nowrap | pre | pre-line |
pre-wrap | inherit } ;
```

SPEC		
inherited	initial	version
YES	normal	CSS1, 2
BROWSER SUPPORT		
IE5.5+	FF1+	Saf1.3+	Op9.2+
PARTIAL	PARTIAL	FULL	PARTIAL

This property controls the handling of whitespace inside an element.

Whitespace is a collective name for one or more occurrences of the characters space, tab, line feed, carriage return, and form feed. Typically, within an HTML element, user agents will collapse a sequence of whitespace characters into a single space character.

Example

This style rule makes elements that belong to the `"poetry"` class retain and render all whitespace in the document markup:

```
.poetry {
  white-space: pre;
}
```

Note that this property only handles whitespace characters; a common beginner's mistake is to try to use it to prevent floated elements from dropping down if there isn't enough room on a line.

Value

normal   A value of normal dictates that sequences of whitespace will collapse into a single space character. Line breaks will occur wherever necessary to fill line boxes.

nowrap   Specifying nowrap ensures that sequences of whitespace will collapse into a single space character, but line breaks will be suppressed.

pre   Specifying pre ensures that sequences of whitespace won't collapse. Lines are only broken at new lines in the markup (or at occurrences of "\a" in generated content).

pre-line   This value will cause sequences of whitespace to collapse into a single space character. Line breaks will occur wherever necessary to fill line boxes, and at new lines in the markup (or at occurrences of "\a" in generated content). In other words, it's like normal except that it'll honor explicit line breaks.

pre-wrap   Specify pre-wrap to ensure that sequences of whitespace won't collapse. Line breaks will occur wherever necessary to fill line boxes, and at new lines in the markup (or at occurrences of "\a" in generated content). In other words, it's like pre except that it'll wrap the text at the end of line boxes.

Compatibility

Internet Explorer			Firefox			Safari			Opera
5.5	6.0	7.0	1.0	1.5	2.0	1.3	2.0	3.0	9.2
Partial	Partial	Partial	Partial	Partial	Partial	Full	Full	Full	Partial

Internet Explorer for Windows versions up to and including 7 don't support the values pre-line or pre-wrap. The values normal and pre behave like pre-wrap on textarea elements. The value nowrap behaves like pre-line on textarea elements.

Internet Explorer for Windows versions up to and including 7 don't support the value inherit.

Firefox versions up to and including 2 don't support the values pre-line and pre-wrap (although -moz-pre-wrap is similar to the latter). The values normal, nowrap, and pre behave like pre-wrap on textarea elements.

Opera 9.2 and prior versions don't support the value pre-line. The values normal and pre behave like pre-wrap on textarea elements. The value nowrap behaves like pre-line on textarea elements.

direction

`direction: { ltr | rtl | inherit } ;`

SPEC		
inherited	initial	version
YES	ltr	CSS2
BROWSER SUPPORT			
IE5.5+	FF1+	Saf1.3+	Op9.2+
FULL	FULL	FULL	FULL

This property specifies the following:

- the base writing direction of blocks
- the direction of embeddings and overrides—see `unicode-bidi` (p. 344)—for the Unicode bidirectional algorithm
- the direction of table column layout
- the direction of horizontal overflow
- the position of an incomplete last line in a block, when the `text-align` property has the value `justify`

Example

This style rule causes the columns in tables belonging to the `"arabic"` class to be laid out from right to left:

```
table.arabic {
    direction: rtl;
}
```

For the `direction` property to affect content reordering in inline elements, the `unicode-bidi` property must be set to `embed` or `override`.

The CSS2.1 specification[2] emphasizes that this property should normally be used only by DTD designers. In particular, authors, web designers, and users shouldn't override it.

Value

ltr   sets a left-to-right direction

rtl   sets a right-to-left direction

Compatibility

Internet Explorer			Firefox			Safari			Opera
5.5	6.0	7.0	1.0	1.5	2.0	1.3	2.0	3.0	9.2
Full	Full	Full	Full	Full	Full	Full	Full	Full	Full

[2] http://www.w3.org/TR/REC-CSS2/visuren.html#direction

Typographical Properties

Other Relevant Stuff

 unicode-bidi (p. 344)

controls embeddings and overrides for the Unicode bidirectional algorithm

unicode-bidi

unicode-bidi: { bidi-override | embed | normal | inherit } ;

SPEC		
inherited	initial	version
NO	normal	CSS2
BROWSER SUPPORT		
IE5.5+	FF1+	Saf3	Op9.2+
BUGGY	FULL	NONE	FULL

Along with `direction` (p. 343), this property relates to the handling of bidirectional text within a given document. If a paragraph contains both left-to-right text and right-to-left text, the user agent applies a complex algorithm defined by the Unicode standard[3] to determine how the text should appear. This property specifically controls the embedding levels and overrides for the Unicode bidirectional algorithm.

Example

This style rule creates a new embedding level with a right-to-left writing direction for `bible-quote` elements (assumed to be in Hebrew) in an XML document:

```
bible-quote {
  direction: rtl;
  unicode-bidi: embed;
}
```

The CSS2.1 specification[4] emphasizes that this property should normally be used only by DTD designers. In particular, authors, web designers, and users shouldn't override it.

Value

bidi-override   This value creates an override for inline elements. For block-level elements, table cells, table captions, or inline blocks, it creates an override for (some) inline-level descendants. In other words, the implicit part of the bidirectional algorithm is ignored and

---

[3] http://www.unicode.org/reports/tr9/
[4] http://www.w3.org/TR/REC-CSS2/visuren.html#direction

the value of the `direction` property is used for reordering content within the element.

embed   This value offers an additional level of embedding for inline elements. The direction of the embedding level is determined by the `direction` property.

normal   This value doesn't offer an additional level of embedding with respect to the bidirectional algorithm. For inline elements, implicit reordering works across element boundaries.

Compatibility

Internet Explorer			Firefox			Safari			Opera
5.5	6.0	7.0	1.0	1.5	2.0	1.3	2.0	3.0	9.2
Buggy	Buggy	Buggy	Full	Full	Full	None	None	None	Full

Internet Explorer for Windows versions up to and including 7 have some serious bugs relating to floated elements used in combination with the declarations `direction: rtl;` and `unicode-bidi: embed;`.

Internet Explorer for Windows versions up to and including 7 don't support the value `inherit`.

Safari versions up to and including 3 don't support this property.

Other Relevant Stuff

direction (p. 343)

specifies the writing direction

Chapter  13

Generated Content

These properties allow the author to insert generated content into a document. More specifically, it allows the control and presentation of extra content, counters, and quote characters through the use of the `:before` and `:after` pseudo-elements.

content

```
content: { { string | uri | counter |
attr(identifier) | open-quote | close-quote |
no-open-quote | no-close-quote } ... | normal | none
| inherit } ;
```

SPEC		
inherited	initial	version
NO	normal	CSS2, 2.1
BROWSER SUPPORT			
IE7	FF1.5+	Saf1.3+	Op9.2+
NONE	PARTIAL	PARTIAL	PARTIAL

The content property, used in conjunction with the `:before` (p. 113) or `:after` (p. 114) pseudo-elements, inserts generated content.

Use the `display` property to control the type of box that's generated for the content.

Example

This style rule inserts the text "You are here:" before the element with the ID "breadcrumbs":

```
#breadcrumbs:before {
    content: "You are here:";
    margin-right: 0.5em;
}
```

Note that the generated content is only rendered—it doesn't appear in the DOM tree. In other words, generated content doesn't alter the document as such—only the presentation.

That said, generated content is still matched by pseudo-elements like :first-letter (p. 107) and :first-line (p. 110).

Here are some additional examples that demonstrate more advanced usage of generated content, including the use of the `counter-increment` (p. 352) and `counter-reset` (p. 354) properties.

This style rule adds the URI, enclosed in angle brackets, after links when the document's printed to paper:

```
@media print {
  a[href]:after {
    content: "<" attr(href) ">";
  }
}
```

These CSS3 style rules format paragraphs within a block quotation in the way that's common in (American) English novels:

```
blockquote p {
  margin: 0;
  text-indent: 1em;
  quotes: "\201c" "\201d";
}
blockquote p:first-of-type {
  text-indent: 0;
}
blockquote p::before {
  content: open-quote;
}
blockquote p::after {
  content: no-close-quote;
}
blockquote p:last-of-type::after {
  content: close-quote;
}
```

These style rules add the word "Chapter" and a chapter number before every h1 heading, and prefix every h2 heading with the chapter number and a section number:

```
body {
  counter-reset: chapter;
}
h1 {
  counter-increment: chapter;
  counter-reset: section;
}
h2 {
  counter-increment: section;
}
h1:before {
  content: "Chapter " counter(chapter) ": ";
}
h2:before {
  content: counter(chapter) "." counter(section) " ";
}
```

These style rules apply a hierarchical numbering system to items in ordered lists (for example, 1, 1.1, 1.1.1 ... and so on):

```
ol {
  counter-reset: item;
  margin: 0;
  padding: 0;
}
```

```
ol>li {
  counter-increment: item;
  list-style: none inside;
}
ol>li:before {
  content: counters(item, ".") " - ";
}
```

Value

The value of `content` is either the keyword `none`, the keyword `normal`, the keyword `inherit`, or one or more content specifications (strings, URIs, counters, or quote characters) separated by whitespace.

Using the value `normal`, we can reset or clear a previously specified `content` declaration. From an authoring standpoint, there's no real difference between the values `normal` and `none`, except that there's currently no browser support for `none`. According to the CSS2.1 specification,[1] if `none` is specified, the pseudo-element isn't generated, and if `normal` is specified for the `:before` (p. 113) or `:after` (p. 114) pseudo-elements, it acts like `none`. Furthermore, if `content` is specified for other element types, the computed value should aways be `normal`. However, these kinds of details are targeted towards browser makers rather than CSS authors, so you shouldn't worry if they're confusing.

A string value inserts the specified string. If you want a newline character in the generated content, you can use the `\a` escape, but the generated content is subject to the `white-space` property, so you'll need to modify its value for the newline to be rendered as such.

A URI value inserts content read from the specified external resource. The Changes section in the CSS2.1 specification says that this value type has been dropped, but it's still listed in the normative section for the `content` property.[2]

A counter value inserts the current value(s) of the specified counter(s). It can be expressed using two different functional notations, both of which have two forms. The `counter(name)` notation inserts the current value of the counter with the specified

---

[1] http://www.w3.org/TR/CSS21/generate.html#content
[2] http://www.w3.org/TR/CSS21/generate.html#propdef-content

name. The counters(*name*,*separator*) notation inserts the values of all counters with the specified name, separated by the specified separator string. Both notations also take an optional list style argument (decimal by default) as the last argument, to control the style of the output—for example, counter(item, upper-roman). The keywords available for the list style argument match those available for the list-style-type (p. 286) property.

See counter-reset (p. 354) and counter-increment (p. 352) for details about counters.

The *identifier* notation inserts the value of the attribute whose name is specified by the identifier. Note that the argument is an identifier (p. 43); it shouldn't be enclosed in quotes.

The open-quote and close-quote values insert the corresponding quotation mark specified in the quotes (p. 355) property. These values also increment or decrement the nesting level for quotes.

The no-open-quote and no-close-quote values don't insert any content, but they'll increment or decrement the nesting level for quotes.

See quotes (p. 355) for details about quotes.

Compatibility

Internet Explorer			Firefox			Safari			Opera
5.5	6.0	7.0	1.0	1.5	2.0	1.3	2.0	3.0	9.2
None	None	None	None	Partial	Partial	Partial	Partial	Partial	Partial

Internet Explorer for Windows versions up to and including 7 don't support generated content at all.

Firefox versions up to and including 2, and Opera versions up to and including 9.2 don't support the value none. Safari versions up to and including 3 don't support the values none or normal. An empty string can be used instead to reset a previous declaration.

In Opera, up to and including version 9.2:

- Counters used without a `counter-reset` have global scope instead of the scope of the elements for which they are used.

- When the quote nesting level isn't within the number of pairs defined for the `quotes` property, `open-quote` inserts the last-defined *close* quote character, while `close-quote` inserts the default close quote character.

Opera and Safari 3 (partially) also support `content` in contexts other than the `:before` and `:after` pseudo-elements. In these cases, the content of the element is replaced by the value of the `content` property.

Other Relevant Stuff

 `:before` (p. 113)

specifies content to be inserted before another element

 `:after` (p. 114)

specifies content to be inserted after another element

 # counter-increment

```
counter-increment: { identifier [integer]¹ or more pairs
| none | inherit } …;
```

SPEC		
inherited	initial	version
NO	none	CSS2
BROWSER SUPPORT		
IE7	FF1+	Saf3	Op9.2+
NONE	FULL	NONE	BUGGY

This property increments one or more counter values.

A counter is identified by a name that's normally established by using the counter in the `counter-reset` (p. 354) property. Counters can be nested: if an element has the counter *C*, and a child element resets that counter name, it won't reset the parent's counter, but instead will create a new, nested counter, *C*.

Example

These style rules prepend a number to all h2 headings, incrementing the value for each heading:

```
h1 {
    counter-reset: section;
}
h2:before {
    counter-increment: section;
    content: counter(section) ". ";
}
```

Value

The value none indicates that no counters will be incremented.

If one or more identifiers are specified, each named counter will be incremented. If an integer value is specified after the identifier, the counter value is incremented by that amount. The default increment is 1; zero, or negative values, are allowed.

If an identifier refers to a counter that hasn't been initialized by counter-reset, the default initial value is 0.

Compatibility

Internet Explorer			Firefox			Safari			Opera
5.5	6.0	7.0	1.0	1.5	2.0	1.3	2.0	3.0	9.2
None	None	None	Full	Full	Full	None	None	None	Buggy

Internet Explorer for Windows versions up to and including 7 don't support generated content or counters.

Safari versions up to and including 3 don't support this property.

In Opera versions up to and including 9.2, counters used without a counter-reset property have global scope, instead of the scope of the elements for which they're used.

Other Relevant Stuff

content (p. 348)

inserts content before or after an element

counter-reset

```
counter-reset: { identifier [integer]¹ or more pairs |
none | inherit } ...;
```

SPEC		
inherited	initial	version
NO	none	CSS2
BROWSER SUPPORT		
IE7	FF1+	Saf3	Op9.2+
NONE	FULL	NONE	FULL

This property creates or resets one or more counters. The created counters have a scope: the element for which the counter is created, its following siblings, and all descendants of the element and its following siblings.

The `counter-reset` property is usually used in conjunction with `counter-increment` (p. 352) to handle automatic numbering, and with `content` (p. 348) to display the generated counter values.

Value

The value none ensures that no counters will be reset.

If one or more identifiers are specified, each named counter will be reset. If an integer value is specified after the identifier, the counter is reset to that value. The default reset value is 0.

Example

These style rules assign a two-level numbering system for tables. One counter is incremented for body row groups, and the other for each row. The value in the first cell in each row is prepended with the two counters, such as A.1, A.2, A.3, and so on.

```
table {
    counter-reset: group;
}
tbody {
    counter-increment: group;
    counter-reset: row;
}
tbody tr {
    counter-increment: row;
}
tbody td:first-child:before {
    content: counter(group,
upper-latin) "." counter(row);
}
```

Compatibility

Internet Explorer			Firefox			Safari			Opera
5.5	6.0	7.0	1.0	1.5	2.0	1.3	2.0	3.0	9.2
None	None	None	Full	Full	Full	None	None	None	Full

Internet Explorer for Windows versions up to and including 7 don't support generated content or counters.

Safari versions up to and including 3 don't support this property.

In Opera, counters used without a `counter-reset` have global scope, instead of the scope of the elements for which they're used.

Other Relevant Stuff

 content (p. 348)

inserts content before or after an element

quotes

```
quotes: { string string¹ or more pairs | none |
inherit } …;
```

SPEC		
inherited	initial	version
YES	see below	CSS2
BROWSER SUPPORT		
IE7	FF1+	Saf3	Op9.2+
NONE	FULL	NONE	BUGGY

This property specifies the quote characters to use for generated content.

The quote characters specified for this property are those used for the `open-quote` and `close-quote` values of the `content` property.

Quotes can be specified for a number of nesting levels. Each use of `open-quote` or `no-open-quote` increments the nesting level, while each use of `close-quote` or `no-close-quote` decrements the nesting level.

Note that the nesting level has nothing to do with the markup; it's only the use of the aforementioned `content` values that affect the nesting level.

Example

These style rules define the traditional sequence of quote characters for q elements in American and British English.

For American English, quotes are normally surrounded by double quotation marks, while nested quotes use single quotation marks. For British English, it's the other way around.

```
:lang(en-us)>q {
  quotes: "\201c" "\201d" "\2018"
"\2019";
}
:lang(en-gb)>q {
quotes: "\2018" "\2019" "\201c"
"\201d";
}
```

Value

If specified as none, the values open-quote and close-quote won't insert any quote character when they're used with the content property.

If the values are specified as string pairs, each pair represents a nesting level. The first pair is used for the outermost quotation level, the second pair for the first embedded quote, and so on through nesting levels. The first string in each pair is the open quote, and the second string is the close quote.

The initial value for this property depends on the user agent.

Compatibility

Internet Explorer			Firefox			Safari			Opera
5.5	6.0	7.0	1.0	1.5	2.0	1.3	2.0	3.0	9.2
None	None	None	Full	Full	Full	None	None	None	Buggy

Internet Explorer for Windows versions up to and including 7 don't support generated quotes.

Safari versions up to and including 3 don't support this property.

In Opera versions up to and including 9.2, when the quote nesting level isn't represented by the number of pairs defined for the quotes property, open-quote inserts the last defined close quote character, while close-quote inserts the default close quote character.

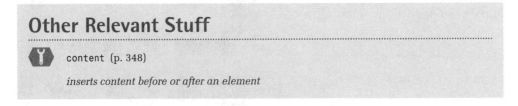

Other Relevant Stuff

content (p. 348)

inserts content before or after an element

User Interface Properties

User interface properties allow the author to control the presentation of the user interface elements of user agents.

cursor

```
cursor: { [ uri ],⁰ ᵒʳ ᵐᵒʳᵉ ᵗⁱᵐᵉˢ { auto | crosshair |
default | e-resize | help | move | n-resize |
ne-resize | nw-resize | pointer | progress | s-resize
| se-resize | sw-resize | text | w-resize | wait }
| inherit } ;
```

SPEC		
inherited	initial	version
YES	auto	CSS2, 2.1
BROWSER SUPPORT			
IE5.5+	FF1+	Saf1.3+	Op9.2+
BUGGY	FULL	PARTIAL	PARTIAL

This property sets the type of cursor to be displayed for a pointing device.

Value

We can specify a comma-separated list of URI values from which we want CSS to retrieve the cursor. And in a similar way to the method by which a list of font family names is used, the browser will use the first URI it successfully retrieves. Note that you must also specify a fallback cursor-type keyword.

Example

This style rule sets the cursor to take the appearance of the text cursor for the element whose ID is "current":

```
#current {
    cursor: text;
}
```

Descriptions for all the valid **cursor** keywords are provided here:

auto   the browser's default cursor in the current context

crosshair   a crosshair cursor

default   the default cursor for the platform, without regard for the context

e-resize   a cursor that indicates that a right-hand ("east") edge will be moved

help   a cursor that indicates that help is available for the object under the cursor

move   a cursor that indicates that something will be moved

n-resize   a cursor that indicates that a top ("north") edge will be moved

ne-resize	a cursor that indicates that top ("north") and right-hand ("east") edges will be moved
nw-resize	a cursor that indicates that top ("north") and left-hand ("west") edges will be moved
pointer	a cursor that indicates a link (commonly a hand with an extended index finger)
progress	a cursor that indicates progress: the application is busy doing something, but the user can still interact with it
s-resize	a cursor that indicates that a bottom ("south") edge will be moved
se-resize	a cursor that indicates that bottom ("south") and right-hand ("east") edges will be moved
sw-resize	a cursor that indicates that bottom ("south") and left-hand ("west") edges will be moved
text	a cursor that indicates that text may be selected (commonly an I-beam)
w-resize	a cursor that indicates that a left-hand ("west") edge will be moved
wait	a cursor that indicates that the application is busy and that the user should wait (commonly an hourglass)

Compatibility

Internet Explorer			Firefox			Safari			Opera
5.5	6.0	7.0	1.0	1.5	2.0	1.3	2.0	3.0	9.2
Buggy	Buggy	Buggy	Full	Full	Full	Partial	Partial	Partial	Partial

Internet Explorer for Windows versions up to and including 5.5 don't support the pointer value; instead, they use the non-standard value hand.

In Internet Explorer for Windows up to and including version 7, if a relative URI value is specified in an external style sheet file the base URI is considered to be the URI of the document containing the element and not the URI of the style sheet in which the declaration appears.

Internet Explorer for Windows versions up to and including 7 don't support the value `inherit`.

Opera versions up to and including 9.2 don't support URI values.

Safari versions up to and including 3 don't support URI values.

Paged Media Properties

Paged media properties allow the author to control the presentation of content when displayed on paged media like print, as opposed to continuous media like a computer screen.

page-break-before

```
page-break-before: { always | auto | avoid | left |
right | inherit } ;
```

SPEC		
inherited	initial	version
NO	auto	CSS2
BROWSER SUPPORT		
IE5.5+	FF1+	Saf1.3+	Op9.2+
PARTIAL	PARTIAL	PARTIAL	FULL

This property specifies whether a page break may, must, or shouldn't occur before a block-level element's generated box.

Example

This style rule makes every h2 element start at the top of a new page:

```
h2 {
    page-break-before: always;
}
```

Value

always   forces a page break before the box

auto   allows a page break before the box, but doesn't require it

avoid   tells the user agent to avoid inserting a page break before the box, if at all possible

left   forces one or two page breaks before the box, so that the next page will be a left-hand page

right   forces one or two page breaks before the box, so that the next page will be a right-hand page

Compatibility

Internet Explorer			Firefox			Safari			Opera
5.5	6.0	7.0	1.0	1.5	2.0	1.3	2.0	3.0	9.2
Partial	Partial	Partial	Partial	Partial	Partial	Partial	Partial	Partial	Full

Internet Explorer for Windows versions up to and including 7 do not support the values left and right; either value is interpreted as the value always.

Internet Explorer for Windows versions up to and including 7 don't support the value inherit.

Firefox versions up to and including 2 don't support the avoid, left, or right values.

Safari versions up to and including 3 don't support the `avoid`, `left`, or `right` values.

page-break-inside

`page-break-inside: { auto | avoid | inherit } ;`

SPEC		
inherited	initial	version
YES	auto	CSS2
BROWSER SUPPORT		
IE7	FF2	Saf3	Op9.2+
NONE	NONE	NONE	FULL

This property specifies whether a page break may or shouldn't occur inside a block-level element's generated box.

Value

auto   allows a page break inside the box

avoid   tells the user agent to avoid inserting a page break inside the box, if at all possible

Example

This style rule tells the user agent to avoid splitting unordered lists over two pages:

```
ul {
    page-break-inside: avoid;
}
```

Compatibility

Internet Explorer			Firefox			Safari			Opera
5.5	6.0	7.0	1.0	1.5	2.0	1.3	2.0	3.0	9.2
None	None	None	None	None	None	None	None	None	Full

Internet Explorer for Windows versions up to and including 7 don't support this property.

Firefox versions up to and including 2 don't support this property.

Safari versions up to and including 3 don't support this property.

page-break-after

`page-break-after: { always | auto | avoid | left | right | inherit } ;`

SPEC		
inherited	initial	version
NO	auto	CSS2
BROWSER SUPPORT		
IE5.5+	FF1+	Saf1.3+	Op9.2+
PARTIAL	PARTIAL	PARTIAL	FULL

This property specifies whether a page break may, must, or shouldn't occur after a block-level element's generated box.

Value

always   forces a page break after the box

auto   allows a page break after the box, but doesn't require it

avoid   tells the user agent to avoid inserting a page break after the box, if at all possible

left   forces one or two page breaks after the box, so that the next page will be a left-hand page

right   forces one or two page breaks after the box, so that the next page will be a right-hand page

Example

This style rule ensures that an h3 element never ends up at the bottom of a page:

```
h3 {
    page-break-after: avoid;
}
```

Compatibility

Internet Explorer			Firefox			Safari			Opera
5.5	6.0	7.0	1.0	1.5	2.0	1.3	2.0	3.0	9.2
Partial	Partial	Partial	Partial	Partial	Partial	Partial	Partial	Partial	Full

Internet Explorer for Windows versions up to and including 7 do not support the values `left` and `right`; either value is interpreted as the value `always`.

Internet Explorer for Windows versions up to and including 7 don't support the value `inherit`.

Firefox versions up to and including 2 don't support the `avoid`, `left`, or `right` values.

Safari versions up to and including 3 don't support the `avoid`, `left`, or `right` values.

orphans

`orphans: { integer | inherit } ;`

	SPEC	
inherited	initial	version
YES	2	CSS2
BROWSER SUPPORT		
IE7	FF2	Saf3	Op9.2+
NONE	NONE	NONE	FULL

Orphans are the lines of text that remain on the previous page when an element is split over two pages. It's usually undesirable to display only the first line of a paragraph at the bottom of a page. This property allows the designer to specify the minimum number of lines that must display at the bottom of a page.

Example

This style rule ensures that at least three lines of text display at the bottom of the page when a page break occurs inside a paragraph:

```
p {
    orphans: 3;
}
```

Value

An integer value specifies the minimum number of lines that must display at the bottom of a page when a page break occurs inside an element.

Negative values are illegal.

Compatibility

Internet Explorer			Firefox			Safari			Opera
5.5	6.0	7.0	1.0	1.5	2.0	1.3	2.0	3.0	9.2
None	None	None	None	None	None	None	None	None	Full

Internet Explorer for Windows versions up to and including 7 don't support this property.

Firefox versions up to and including 2 don't support this property.

Safari versions up to and including 3 don't support this property.

widows

`widows: { integer | inherit } ;`

SPEC		
inherited	initial	version
YES	2	CSS2
BROWSER SUPPORT		
IE7	FF2	Saf3	Op9.2+
NONE	NONE	NONE	FULL

Widows are the lines of text that are shifted to the next page when an element is split over two pages. It's usually undesirable to display only the last line of a paragraph at the top of a page. This property allows the designer to specify the minimum number of lines that must display at the top of a page.

Value

An integer value specifies the minimum number of lines that must display at the top of a page when a page break occurs inside an element.

Negative values are illegal.

Example

This style rule ensures that at least three lines of text display at the top of the second page when a page break occurs inside a paragraph:

```
p {
    widows: 3;
}
```

Compatibility

Internet Explorer			Firefox			Safari			Opera
5.5	6.0	7.0	1.0	1.5	2.0	1.3	2.0	3.0	9.2
None	None	None	None	None	None	None	None	None	Full

Internet Explorer for Windows versions up to and including 7 don't support this property.

Firefox versions up to and including 2 don't support this property.

Safari versions up to and including 3 don't support this property.

Chapter

16

Vendor-specific Properties

Vendors—browser makers—are free to implement extensions to the CSS specifications that, in most cases, are proprietary to their browser. They may do this for a number of reasons, such as adding new features for users, or for experiments and debugging. Most often, though, the extensions are used to release and test browser features that have been developed in the preparation of W3C drafts that have not yet reached Candidate Recommendation status—the extensions allow these new properties to be widely tested before they become available as standard CSS properties.

In order to accommodate the release of vendor-specific extensions, the CSS specifications[1] define a specific format that vendors should follow.

The format is quite simple: keywords and property names beginning with - (dash) or _ (underscore) are reserved for vendor-specific extensions. As such, vendors should use the following formats:

---

[1] http://www.w3.org/TR/CSS21/syndata.html#vendor-keywords

```
'-' + vendor specific identifier + '-' + meaningful name

'_' + vendor specific identifier + '-' + meaningful name
```

This approach allows any vendor-specific extension to coexist with any future (or current) CSS properties without causing conflicts because, according to the W3C specifications, a CSS property name will never begin with a dash or an underscore:

"An initial dash or underscore is guaranteed never to be used in a property or keyword by any current or future level of CSS. Thus, typical CSS implementations may not recognize such properties, and may ignore them according to the rules for handling parsing errors. However, because the initial dash or underscore is part of the grammar, CSS2.1 implementers should always be able to use a CSS-conforming parser, whether or not they support any vendor-specific extensions."[2]

A number of extensions are known to exist. Their prefixes are outlined in Table 16.1.

Table 16.1: Vendor Extension Prefixes

Prefix	Organisation
-ms-	Microsoft
mso-	Microsoft Office
-moz-	Mozilla Foundation (Gecko-based browsers)[4]
-o-	Opera Software
-atsc-	Advanced Television Standards Committee
-wap-	The WAP Forum
-webkit-	Safari (and other WebKit-based browsers)[5]

---

[2] http://www.w3.org/TR/CSS21/syndata.html#vendor-keywords
[4] http://en.wikipedia.org/wiki/Gecko_(layout_engine)
[5] http://trac.webkit.org/projects/webkit/wiki/Applications%20using%20WebKit

Prefix	Organisation
`-khtml-`	Konqueror browser

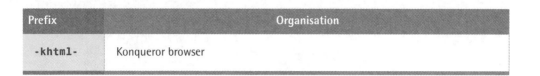 **Use these Extensions with Care!**

Even though vendor-specific extensions are guaranteed not to cause conflicts (unless two vendors happen to choose the same identifier, of course), it should be recognized that these extensions may also be subject to change at the vendor's whim, as they don't form part of the CSS specifications, even though they often mimic the proposed behavior of existing or forthcoming CSS properties.

Although these extensions can be useful at times, it's still recommended that you avoid using them unless it's absolutely necessary. It's also worth noting that, as is usually the case with proprietary code, the extensions will not pass CSS validation.

If you must use extensions, you should use those that are closely related to equivalent CSS properties (be that CSS1, 2, or 3), so that you can switch to the standard property later on, and remove the extension when the browser implements the correct specification.

Bearing this in mind, let's go back a few years and take as an example the `opacity` property, which is part of CSS3 (Candidate Recommendation May 2003), which few browsers actually supported (`opacity` was implemented in Firefox 1.0, Opera 9, and Safari 1.2). Therefore, authors resorted to using vendor-specific extensions to cater for the lack of CSS3 opacity support at the time. Gecko-based browsers (like Mozilla) used the `—moz-opacity` property, and Safari 1.1 used `-khtml-opacity`. Internet Explorer versions 5.5 and above used the non-standard `filter` property (p. 381).

Bringing together the above extensions, the following method was (and is still) commonly used to apply opacity to a range of browsers:

```
.test{
  background: red;
  /* IE filter extension */
  filter: progid:DXImageTransform.Microsoft.Alpha(opacity=60);
  width:100%;               /* Required for IE filter */
  -moz-opacity: 0.6;        /* Mozilla extension */
```

```
    -khtml-opacity:0.6;        /* Konqueror extension (Safari 1.1)*/
    opacity: 0.6;              /* the correct CSS3 syntax */
}
```

In the code fragment above, Internet Explorer will use the `filter` property and ignore the other opacity declarations. Older Gecko browsers that don't understand the CSS3 `opacity` property will respect the `–moz-opacity` property instead, and Safari 1.1 will respect the `-khtml-opacity` property. Finally, if it's supported, the CSS3 `opacity` property will be respected by other browsers and browser versions. Of course, a browser that doesn't support element opacity will ignore the lot.

The Internet Explorer `filter` property is a proprietary Microsoft extension to CSS that clearly doesn't follow the correct naming rules for vendor-specific extensions. On the other hand, the Mozilla and Safari (`-moz-opacity` and `–khtml-opacity`) properties do follow the rules, and although the code won't validate, you can be sure these properties will be relatively safe from conflicts.

Even though browsers such as Firefox, Opera, and Safari eventually implemented the CSS3 `opacity` property, the style rules like the one in the example above still continued to work, ensuring a seamless transition between the old and the new.

As you can see, extensions can be useful, and can provide a measure of longevity; however, it's not advisable to rely on the availability of extensions. It's also possible that CSS3 properties may be changed before they become the standard. Therefore, as the W3C states, "Authors should avoid vendor-specific extensions."

Due to the very nature of vendor-specific extensions, they're not well documented for public use, so it's difficult to provide full and accurate listings of all the available extensions. The following links may be used as a guide, but we urge you to carry out your own research if you want to use these extensions:

■ Internet Explorer CSS Attributes: Index[6]

■ CSS Reference: Mozilla Extensions[7]

■ CSS3 Columns in Mozilla[8]

---

[6] http://msdn.microsoft.com/workshop/author/css/reference/attributes.asp
[7] http://developer.mozilla.org/en/docs/CSS_Reference:Mozilla_Extensions
[8] http://developer.mozilla.org/en/docs/CSS3_Columns

- Safari CSS Reference[9]

- Webkit CSS Styles[10]

- Opera 9 CSS Support[11]

- Opera CSS Extensions[12]

As we already mentioned, we don't recommend that you use these extensions in a real application. It's fine to use them for testing purposes, and for trying out CSS properties that haven't been implemented yet. This will prepare and educate you for the time when the correct CSS syntax becomes available for general use.

While an explanation of all the properties is beyond the scope of this book, we will look at a few that you might find useful, and investigate a few extensions that you might find in use elsewhere.

Mozilla Extensions

Here's a very small selection of the available Mozilla CSS extensions.

---

[9] http://tinyurl.com/26e9vl
[10] http://qooxdoo.org/documentation/general/webkit_css_styles
[11] http://www.opera.com/docs/specs/opera9/css/
[12] http://www.blooberry.com/indexdot/css/properties/extensions/operaextensions.htm

-moz-border-radius

-moz-border-radius: { { *length* | *percentage* } ¹ to ⁴
ᵛᵃˡᵘᵉˢ | inherit } ;

SPEC		
inherited	initial	version
NO	0	N/A
BROWSER SUPPORT		
IE7	FF1+	Saf3	Op9.2
NONE	FULL	NONE	NONE

-moz-border-radius [14] is Gecko's equivalent to CSS3's border-radius [15] property, although it differs in a few respects that are discussed below. This property allows us to specify rounded borders, or rounded backgrounds if no borders have been defined.

Example

This rule applies rounded corners to the .test element:

```
.test{
  -moz-border-radius: 10px;
}
```

The main differences are that the Gecko shorthand property −moz-border-radius will allow each individual corner to have a different radius, whereas the CSS3 property defines all four corners to be the same size, but caters for elliptical rounding by allowing two values to be specified. It's possible to specify the radius of individual corners in the CSS3 version of this property using more specific properties such as border-top-right-radius. The Gecko version also allows individual corners to be set using the following properties:

- -moz-border-radius-bottomleft (rounds the bottom-left curve)
- -moz-border-radius-bottomright (rounds the bottom-right curve)
- -moz-border-radius-topleft (rounds the top-left curve)
- -moz-border-radius-topright (rounds the top-right curve)

Gecko doesn't support elliptical rounding at all, and this is likely to be a source of confusion when defining different values for the corners using the shorthand −moz-border-radius. Gecko will see the specified values in the order top left, top right, bottom right, and bottom left. If fewer than four values are provided, the list of values is repeated to fill the remaining values. Consider the following rule:

---

[14] http://developer.mozilla.org/en/docs/CSS:-moz-border-radius
[15] http://www.w3.org/TR/css3-background/#the-border-radius

```
.test{
  background-color: #ffffcc;
  -moz-border-radius: 10px 30px;
  border-radius: 10px 30px;
  border: 1px solid #000;
  padding: 10px;
}
```

The above code would produce different results in different browsers. CSS3-capable browsers would apply a corner that has a horizontal radius of 10px and a vertical radius of 30px to each corner. Gecko browsers, on the other hand, will display top-left and bottom-right corners with a 10px radius (horizontal and vertical radii), and top-right and bottom-left corners with a 30px radius, as is shown in Figure 16.1.

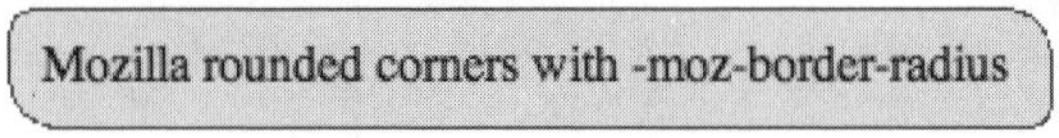

Mozilla rounded corners with -moz-border-radius

Figure 16.1: Rounded corners with —moz-border-radius

Therefore, to be safe in the future, it would be wise to specify for the —moz-border-radius property, and the CSS3 border-radius properties, values that will produce the same results in both types of browsers. The following example demonstrates this:

```
.test{
  background-color: #ffffcc;
  -moz-border-radius: 10px;
  border-radius: 10px;
  border: 1px solid #000;
  padding: 10px;
}
```

In this case, every one of the border's corners to which this rule is applied will have a horizontal radius of 10px and a vertical radius of 10px, as shown in Figure 16.2.

Rounded corners with -moz-border-radius

Figure 16.2: Equal radius for both properties

Using an approach that respects the CSS3 specifications ensures that we have a better chance of maintaining future compatibility than using the non-standard features of the −moz-border-radius property.

The CSS3 border-radius property will also round backgrounds so that they're contained within the border of the element. If no border has been set, the background is still rounded, but no border is applied. The Mozilla extension will only round background colors, not background images.

> ### 📝 border-radius in Other Browsers
>
> Safari 3 supports the -webkit-border-radius property and seems to follow the CSS3 specifications for the border-radius property.

Value

This property accepts between one and four length values in the order top-left, top-right, bottom-right, and bottom-left. If less than four values are provided, the list of values is repeated to fill the remaining values.

Compatibility

Internet Explorer			Firefox			Safari			Opera
5.5	6.0	7.0	1.0	1.5	2.0	1.3	2.0	3.0	9.2
None	None	None	Full	Full	Full	None	None	None	None

This is a proprietary Mozilla extension to the CSS standard.

-moz-box-sizing

```
-moz-box-sizing: { content-box | border-box |
padding-box } ;
```

SPEC		
inherited	initial	version
NO	content-box	N/A
BROWSER SUPPORT		
IE7	FF1+	Saf3	Op9.2
NONE	FULL	NONE	NONE

This property can be used to specify the CSS box model that's used to calculate the widths and heights of elements. -moz-box-sizing[16] is similar to the CSS3 proposal called box-sizing[17] but, again, exhibits differences: the CSS3 proposal doesn't include the value padding-box.

Example

This rule will cause the browser to render the .example element using the padding-box box sizing model:

```
.example {
  -moz-box-sizing: padding-box;
}
```

In the following example, we specify that the border-box box model is to be used to calculate the dimensions of matching elements, where the padding and borders will be included within the dimensions, rather than added to them:

```
.example {
  -moz-box-sizing: border-box;
  box-sizing: border-box;
  width: 200px;
  height: 120px;
  padding: 30px;
  border: 5px solid #000;
  background: #ffffcc;
  text-align: center;
}
```

The results of the CSS above can be seen in Figure 16.3.

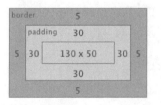

Figure 16.3: Mozilla border-box dimensions

---

16 http://developer.mozilla.org/en/docs/CSS:-moz-box-sizing
17 http://www.w3.org/TR/css3-ui/#box-model

As you can see, the padding and borders have not added to the element's overall width or height. Instead, the content area has been reduced by the size of the padding. The result is the same behavior that Internet Explorer versions 6 and 7 exhibit while in quirks mode, and that Internet Explorer for Windows versions 5 and 5.5 will display at all times. There are merits in both box models, as we've already discussed in The Internet Explorer 5 Box Model (p. 156).

---

box-sizing in Other Browsers

Opera, since version 8.5, has supported the CSS3 box-sizing property. Safari 3 supports the -webkit-box-sizing property, which matches the specifications for the CSS3 property.

Value

content-box If this value is specified, the width and height properties represent only the dimensions of the content—they don't include the border, margin, or padding. This reflects the default CSS2 box model (p. 142).

padding-box If the value padding-box is specified, the width and height properties include the padding size with the content dimensions, but don't include the border or margin. This value isn't included in the CSS3 box-sizing property specifications.

border-box If the value border-box is specified, the width and height properties represent the sum of the padding size, border size, and the content dimensions, but don't include the margin. This box sizing model reflects the IE5 box model (p. 156).

Compatibility

Internet Explorer			Firefox			Safari			Opera
5.5	6.0	7.0	1.0	1.5	2.0	1.3	2.0	3.0	9.2
None	None	None	Full	Full	Full	None	None	None	None

This is a proprietary Mozilla extension to the CSS standard.

The `display` Property Value: `-moz-inline-box`

The value `-moz-inline-box` is the Mozilla equivalent to CSS2.1's inline-block[18] `display` value. It will allow an element to generate a block box that can be flowed as a single inline box, similar to the way replaced elements, such as images, are handled. This allows the box to sit on the same line as other inline or inline-block boxes, though it will still be able to take height and width dimensions in the way that block level boxes can.

This facility would be useful in the case of a group of horizontal elements of varying dimensions that we wanted to center horizontally in the available width. This effect would not be possible with floated elements, which would just float to one side or the other; dimensions cannot be defined for inline elements.

The following example creates three inline-block boxes that are centered in the available width:

```
<!DOCTYPE HTML PUBLIC "-//W3C//DTD HTML 4.01//EN"
    "http://www.w3.org/TR/html4/strict.dtd">
<html>
<head>
<meta http-equiv="Content-Type"
    content="text/html; charset=iso-8859-1">
<title>moz-inline-box</title>
<style type="text/css">
.outer{
  width: 500px;
  text-align: center;
  border: 1px solid #000;
  padding: 1em;
}
.box {
  display: -moz-inline-box;
  display: inline-block;
  padding: 1em;
  background-color: #ccc;
  border: 1px dotted #000;
}
#box1 {
  width: 150px;
  height: 100px;
```

---

[18] http://www.w3.org/TR/CSS21/visuren.html#propdef-display

```
}
#box2 {
  width: 100px;
  height: 150px;
  margin: 0 5px
}
#box3 {
  width: 75px;
  height: 75px;
}
</style>
<!--[if IE ]>
<style type="text/css">
.box {
  display: inline;
  vertical-align: top;
}
</style>
<![endif]-->
</head>
<body>
<div class="outer">
  <div id="box1" class="box">Box 1</div>
  <div id="box2" class="box">Box 2</div>
  <div id="box3" class="box">Box 3</div>
</div>
</body>
</html>
```

The result of this code is shown in Figure 16.4.

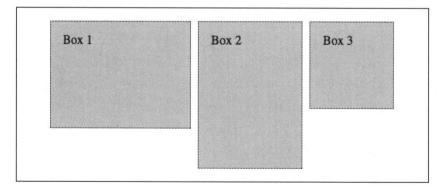

Figure 16.4: `inline-block` example

> ### 📓 `inline-block` in Other Browsers
>
> The above example will work in the latest versions of Safari and Opera too, because they support the CSS2.1 `display` property value `inline-block`.
>
> Internet Explorer for Windows versions 5 and upwards have also been catered for: we can use conditional comments (p. 394) to supply them with the `display` value `inline`. Without straying too far from the original topic, we can have IE can make block-level elements behave as inline-block boxes simply by setting one of the properties that trigger an element to gain a layout and then, in a separate style block, declaring the element to display `inline`. The element will behave in most respects as though the `display` value was `inline-block`.
>
> Internet Explorer for Windows only understands the `display` value `inline-block` when it's applied to inline elements, which rather defeats the purpose in most cases. However, using the method above, we can coax IE into displaying block-level elements as inline-block boxes. The layout trigger is actually the `display: inline-block;` declaration, but it could equally well be any of the other properties that cause an element to gain a layout. See The Internet Explorer hasLayout Property (p. 158) for more information on IE and layout.

Internet Explorer Extensions

These are some of the CSS extensions available for Internet Explorer.

zoom

```
zoom: { number | percentage | normal } ;
```

SPEC		
inherited	initial	version
NO	normal	N/A
BROWSER SUPPORT		
IE5.5+	FF2	Saf3	Op9.2
FULL	NONE	NONE	NONE

Internet Explorer for Windows versions 5.5 and above support the non-standard property zoom,[19] which sets the magnification scale of an element. There's no CSS3 equivalent to this property (as yet).

The zoom property isn't inherited, but it will affect the children of the element to which it is applied, which will be magnified along with the parent. The content surrounding an element that has zoom applied will reflow to account for the resizing that will occur when zoom is set to a value other than normal.

Example

In the following example, all images in the document have their magnification levels increased by 150%:

```
img {
    zoom: 150%;
}
```

One of the main uses for zoom has been to ensure that an element has a layout. It's commonly used with a value of 1.0 (normal), so that no other changes are evident on the page. Refer to The Internet Explorer hasLayout Property (p. 158) for a longer discussion of the usage that the zoom property can be put to when debugging CSS issues in Internet Explorer.

Value

The value normal is the default, and produces no magnification.

Number values are specified as floating-point numbers that represent the magnification scale where 1.0 is equivalent to normal.

Percentage values represent a percentage of the magnification scale where 100% is equal to normal (note that decimals of percentages are ignored).

---

[19] http://msdn2.microsoft.com/en-us/library/ms535169.aspx

Compatibility

Internet Explorer			Firefox			Safari			Opera
5.5	6.0	7.0	1.0	1.5	2.0	1.3	2.0	3.0	9.2
Full	Full	Full	None	None	None	None	None	None	None

This property is a proprietary Microsoft extension to the CSS standard.

filter

`filter:filter;`

SPEC		
inherited	initial	version
NO	N/A	N/A
BROWSER SUPPORT		
IE5.5+	FF2	Saf3	Op9.2
FULL	NONE	NONE	NONE

Since version 4, Internet Explorer for Windows has implemented a range of visual effects and transitions through the use of the proprietary `filter` property. Many weird and wonderful filters[20] are available (there are too many to mention here!) but it's worth documenting some of them. The syntax used in the examples of `filter` provided here, however, will only function in Internet Explorer 5.5 or later.

Example

This example applies a filter called `MotionBlur` to the element with the ID `"example"`:

```
#example {
    filter: progid:DXImageTransform
    ➥   .Microsoft.MotionBlur(
    ➥   strength=10,
    ➥   direction=310);
}
```

📖 Filters and Layout

For filters to work, the element in question must have a layout—a requirement that can be achieved most simply by setting a dimension such as `width`. See The Internet Explorer hasLayout Property (p. 158) for more information on IE and layout, and other properties that cause an element to gain a layout.

As we saw in Vendor-specific Properties (p. 367), the Alpha filter[21] is a popular filter that can be used to control the opacity levels of elements in Internet Explorer. The

---

20   http://msdn2.microsoft.com/en-us/library/ms532847.aspx
21   http://msdn2.microsoft.com/en-us/library/ms532967.aspx

AlphaImageLoader[22] is another popular filter which can be used to provide support for PNG (Portable Network Graphic)[23] transparency in IE5.5 and IE6 (IE7 already offers native support for PNG transparency). IE6 and earlier versions don't natively support alpha transparency (partial levels of transparency)—they support only binary transparency, where pixels are either fully opaque or fully transparent.

The AlphaImageLoader filter will display an image within an element between that element's background and its content. The filter doesn't have the same features as CSS background images, so its use is limited: you will be able to stretch or shrink the image, crop the image, or leave the image at its initial size, but you won't be able to specify the equivalent of `background-repeat` or `background-position` for it.

When you use this filter, you set the URI of the image to be used via the `src` attribute. You then have three options for displaying that image using the `sizingMethod` attribute:

crop   This setting clips the image to fit the dimensions of the containing object.

image   This is the default value, and enlarges or reduces the border of the object to fit the dimensions of the image; the image remains at its original size.

scale   This setting will stretch or shrink the image according to the element's size.

In the following example, a background image on an element with the ID `"outer"` is stretched to the size of the container in which it resides:

```
#outer {
  filter: progid:DXImageTransform.Microsoft.AlphaImageLoader(
      src='images/transparent-border.png',
      sizingMethod='scale');
}
```

As you can see, the filter syntax is a bit of a mouthful, but the only parts that need concern us are the `src` and `sizingMethod` values, as explained above.

---

[22] http://msdn2.microsoft.com/en-us/library/ms532969.aspx
[23] http://en.wikipedia.org/wiki/Portable_Network_Graphics

Relative Image Paths

Unlike normal background images in CSS, the path to the image file is relative to the HTML page location, not the CSS file. For that reason, it's safer to use an absolute address for the image, so that no conflicts arise.

For the filter to work, the element in question must have a layout, which can be achieved most simply by setting a dimension. See The Internet Explorer hasLayout Property (p. 158) for more information on IE and layout, and other properties that cause an element to gain a layout. It's also important to note that IE shouldn't have a background image specified, as that would conflict with the filter and ruin the effect. Therefore, when you're using the filter, you'll need to use some other sort of filter, such as conditional comments (p. 394), or a hack like the one below.

Here's an example that uses the star selector hack (p. 402) to supply the required declarations to IE6 and under (IE7 will ignore the rule):

```
#outer{
  width: 796px;
  margin: auto;
  background: url(images/transparent-border.png) repeat-y left top;
}
* html #outer {
  background: none; /*Remove background*/
  filter: progid:DXImageTransform.Microsoft.AlphaImageLoader(
      src='images/transparent-border.png',
      sizingMethod='scale');
}
```

In the above CSS, we add a rule targeted to IE6 and earlier versions, using the selector `* html #outer`, in which we set the `background-image` property to `none` and specify the AlphaImageLoader filter. The result of the above CSS is that browsers that support PNG transparency will repeat the background image along the *y* axis, whereas the AlphaImageLoader filter will just stretch the image to the whole size of the element. This will cause the image to appear differently from what was expected, as you can see in Figure 16.5.

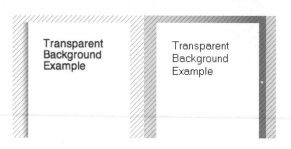

Figure 16.5: Firefox 2 and Internet Explorer 6

The intended effect is accurately displayed in Firefox 2 (on the left): a transparent border down the left-hand side. The transparent border has been stretched in IE6 (on the right) to cover the entire area. If we want to create this effect in IE6 and under, our only other choice is to use a very long image (to cover expansion of the element) and set the `sizingMethod` to `"crop"`, but this approach may not always be feasible.

For an image that doesn't need to stretch or scale with the layout, where `sizingMethod` can be set to `"image"` the effect will be much better, as can be seen Figure 16.6.

Figure 16.6: Transparency with no scaling

Firefox 2 is pictured on the left, while IE6 is on the right. There's very little difference between the two since the image size remains unchanged.

Another issue arises from the filter's use: anchors can't be clicked when the anchor lies on a background that's been created by the filter. Usually, what happens is that the filter is applied to an element that has `position` set to `relative`, and the links suddenly stop working. Sometimes, we can fix the issue by setting `position` to `relative` for the anchors in question, and setting a `z-index` appropriately. This isn't a foolproof method, though, and the solution is often to remove the filter from the original element, and instead to place it on a nested element that doesn't have `position` set to `relative`.

It has also been noted[24] that the size of the image used can have an impact on whether or not the anchors are clickable, but in most cases the solutions already mentioned above are enough to resolve the issue.

The Shadow[25] and DropShadow[26] filters can be used to create shadow effects for HTML elements. The following example uses the DropShadow filter to create a shadow around an `h1` element that has a `class` of `"shadow"`:

```
<h1 class="shadow">Shadow Heading</h1>
```

Here's the rule with which we specify the filter:

```
h1.shadow {
  width: 260px;
  color: gray;
  filter: progid:DXImageTransform.Microsoft.DropShadow(
      offx=2, offy=1, color=#000000);
}
```

The DropShadow filter accepts `offx` and `offy` attribute values, which represent the offset distance in pixels along the *x* and *y* axes respectively, and a `color` attribute value for the shadow color.

The result of that CSS can be seen in Figure 16.7.

Shadow Heading

Figure 16.7: Applying the DropShadow filter

If we keep the HTML the same as the previous example, we can specify the Shadow filter like this:

---

[24] http://www.daltonlp.com/view/217
[25] http://msdn2.microsoft.com/en-us/library/ms533086.aspx
[26] http://msdn2.microsoft.com/en-us/library/ms532985.aspx

```
h1.shadow {
  width: 260px;
  color: gray;
  filter: progid:DXImageTransform.Microsoft.Shadow(
      color=#000000,direction=45);
}
```

The Shadow filter also accepts a `color` attribute value, but instead of offsets, a `direction` is specified. The `direction` value is an integer between "0" and "360", representing degrees; the default value is "225".

The result of this CSS can be seen in Figure 16.8.

Figure 16.8: Applying the Shadow filter

Value

The value of the filter property begins with the filter name followed by any applicable attributes and values. Each filter has a different set of attributes available, so you'll need to check the Microsoft Developer Network site for their details.

Compatibility

Internet Explorer			Firefox			Safari			Opera
5.5	6.0	7.0	1.0	1.5	2.0	1.3	2.0	3.0	9.2
Full	Full	Full	None	None	None	None	None	None	None

This property is a proprietary Microsoft CSS extension.

behavior

```
behavior:URI;
```

SPEC		
inherited	initial	version
NO	N/A	N/A
BROWSER SUPPORT		
IE5.5+ FF2 Saf3 Op9.2		
FULL NONE NONE NONE		

Internet Explorer versions 5 and later support the `behavior` property.[27] The `behavior` property lets you use CSS to attach a script to a specific element in order to implement DHTML (Dynamic HTML) components.

The script resides in an HTC (HTML Component) file. HTC files have the extension .htc, and are HTML files that contain a script plus a set of HTC-specific elements that define the components.

Example

The following CSS attaches the component file **iepngfix.htc** to all images in a web page:

```
img {
    behavior: url(iepngfix.htc);
}
```

It's beyond the scope of this reference to explain the ins and outs of HTC files, but if you visit the Microsoft Developers Network,[28] you'll find a wealth of information that'll keep you occupied for hours.

An example of an HTML component, the IE PNG Fix component can be found at TwinHelix Designs.[29] This component implements alpha transparency for PNG images in IE5.5 and 6. It's the one you'll find referenced in the example.

Value

The `behavior` property requires the URI to the HTC file to be specified using the `url()` syntax. Multiple HTC files can be referenced with a space-delimited list.

Compatibility

Internet Explorer			Firefox			Safari			Opera
5.5	6.0	7.0	1.0	1.5	2.0	1.3	2.0	3.0	9.2
Full	Full	Full	None	None	None	None	None	None	None

---

[27] http://msdn2.microsoft.com/en-us/library/ms530723.aspx
[28] http://msdn2.microsoft.com/en-us/library/ms531078.aspx
[29] http://www.twinhelix.com/css/iepngfix/

This property is a proprietary Microsoft extension to CSS.

The expression Property Value

Internet Explorer 5 for Windows introduced CSS expressions,[30] an extension that allows us to use Microsoft JScript[31] to assign a dynamic value to a CSS property value.[32] This value could be something as simple as a mathematical calculation, or something as complicated as an expression to calculate an appropriate width based on the size of the browser window.

Active Scripting Must Be Enabled

In order for expressions to work they do need JavaScript to be enabled on the client browser. Even though they are called from within a CSS style sheet they'll fail if JavaScript is disabled.

Without getting into too much detail about scripting, here are a couple of examples to give you an idea of how CSS expressions work.

The first example demonstrates how we can use an expression to imitate the min-width and max-width CSS properties that aren't supported by Internet Explorer 6 and earlier versions. The following example applies to Internet Explorer Windows versions 5 and above:

```
#outer{
  width: expression(
      (d = document.compatMode == "CSS1Compat" ?
          document.documentElement : document.body) &&
      (d.clientWidth > 1024 ? "1024px" :
          d.clientWidth < 600 ? "600px" : "auto")
  );
  background: red;
}
```

---

[30] http://msdn2.microsoft.com/en-us/library/ms537634.aspx#Implement
[31] http://msdn2.microsoft.com/en-us/library/hbxc2t98.aspx
[32] JScript is Microsoft's implementation of JavaScript. While JScript's core language implementation is basically the same as JavaScript's, the DOM implementation is quite different.

This expression results in a value that's applied to the `width` property. The element with an ID of `"outer"` will be restricted to a maximum width of 1024 pixels, and a minimum width of 600 pixels, depending on the size of the browser window. The width value is automatically monitored and updated, so the user's resizing of the browser window will trigger whether the minimum or maximum width should be in effect. Note that the expression needs to take into account whether the element is being rendered in quirks or standards mode in order to ascertain the correct value for `clientWidth`, as the method for obtaining this value varies between these two modes.

In the next example, we imitate the `position` property value `fixed`, which, again, isn't supported in Internet Explorer for Windows versions 6 and earlier:

```
h1#fixed {
  position: absolute;
  top: expression(
      (d = document.compatMode == "CSS1Compat" ?
          document.documentElement : document.body) &&
      (eval(d.scrollTop))
  );
}
```

The `h1` element with ID `"fixed"` will remain at the top of the viewport even though the content of the main document scrolls up and away. The display is a little jerky, which exemplifies a drawback of using expressions: a considerable performance overhead incurred by doing so. As the values are being monitored constantly you may find that the performance of the page becomes slower, and the display isn't as smooth as usual when windows are resized or redrawn.

Expressions are a powerful feature, but they do blur the distinction between presentation and behavior. Think carefully before you use expressions, and assess whether the behavior you want could be implemented more cleanly via a dedicated script.

Summary

Vendor-specific extensions are proprietary properties implemented by browser vendors and were never meant for normal consumption by authors. They follow a pre-defined format that allows them to exist within the rules of CSS and to be protected from conflicts with existing and future properties.

Vendor-specific extensions allow you to experiment with properties that have not been fully implemented as standard CSS properties, and also allow you to apply proprietary properties specific to that vendor's implementation. They should be avoided in everyday applications, as there is no guarantee of consistency and they are not subject to the same rigor that applies to standard CSS properties.

In some cases, if there is no other solution, these extensions can be employed to good effect but there is always a risk involved in doing this. If you cater for the risks and craft your code carefully, there are occasions when these extensions can be used without too much danger. The onus as usual lies upon the author to make sure that the code used is as stable as possible by testing thoroughly before use.

Internet Explorer implements a wide variety of extensions that don't follow the CSS specifications and in most cases are unique to IE (as in the case of expressions, behaviors and filters). Some of these extensions can prove very useful and provide support for missing features, but as usual we urge authors to tread carefully and only use an extension as a last resort.

Workarounds, Filters, and Hacks

Unfortunately, as you deal with CSS you'll eventually discover differences in the way user agents apply and render CSS rules. These differences can be caused by the user agents' varying interpretations of, and levels of support for, the CSS standards, as well as rendering problems and bugs. But—luckily for us—they can be addressed using workarounds, filters, and hacks.

If you search the Web for "CSS hacks," you'll find numerous sites and articles from as far back as 2001 describing ways to tackle browser-related CSS problems. These problems were discovered once people started attempting to create completely CSS-based web design and layout. Happily, modern browser support for CSS is fairly good, so many of those old-school hacks are no longer needed. Older browsers have fallen into disuse and workarounds for problematic browsers that are still in use are well documented.

All software has bugs. Browsers are no exception to this rule, but some browsers are certainly buggier than others. In the past, some bugs related to browsers' CSS rendering caused web pages to become unreadable, and in some cases, they even crashed browsers. It's also true that browsers don't provide perfect support for CSS—a fact that's often the cause of much frustration. Of course, the situation was far worse in the past, when levels of support could differ wildly.

Workarounds, Filters, and Hacks Defined

Once CSS-based layout and design became popular, web designers and developers needed a way to supply different CSS rules to different browsers—a capability that's absent from CSS. A **hack** has typically been regarded as a temporary, inelegant, or unadvised solution to a problem. But in CSS terms, applying a hack generally means exploiting incorrect or buggy CSS features in order to target or exclude a browser, or group of browsers, so that alternative styling may be applied to them.

Other techniques—often called **workarounds** or **filters**—include targeting the proprietary features of a specific browser, or employing advanced CSS features to exclude older browsers that don't support the newer features. If all this jargon's getting a bit much for you, just remember that workarounds are CSS-oriented solutions to these problems, while filters and hacks are browser-oriented solutions.

The Problem with Workarounds, Filters, and Hacks

While it's often tempting to leap in and apply a complicated hack to force a particular browser to behave, a more careful approach is needed to address CSS problems efficiently. First, you need to make sure that the problem you're addressing is a real CSS problem—not just the result of incorrect CSS code or an incomplete understanding of CSS. If your web page looks as you intended in one browser but not another, you may be tempted to think that the browser that's not displaying your site properly has a CSS bug, but of course the exact opposite is equally likely.

Consider, for instance, the fact that different browsers apply varying default margin and padding values to HTML elements like headings and list items. You'll often see sites on which CSS hacks are used to apply particular rules to different browsers simply because the designers weren't aware of the variations in these values. The use of CSS hacks in these kinds of situations is redundant; simply spending a few minutes to gain an understanding of the margin and padding rules would negate the need to apply hacks.

If you're sure that you have a valid CSS rendering problem, and you're tempted to use a hack, first see whether a change of design could enable you to avoid the issue altogether. If you can design layouts that don't depend on problematic CSS features, in most cases you won't need hacks at all.

The Internet Explorer 5 box model (p. 156) problem is a famous example of the unnecessary use of hacks. Many complicated hacks (p. 405) were developed to solve this problem, but with a simple design change—the addition of padding to the parent of an element with a fixed width, instead of to the element itself—designers could have avoided the problem altogether.[1] This approach wasn't possible in every case, but the option was there.

Avoiding Implementation Pitfalls

If you find yourself in a position where you have no choice but to use a workaround, filter, or hack, be aware of the dangers involved. Your chosen hack may be unreliable—in the future, it may actually cause more problems than would have resulted had you not used it at all. As newer browser versions are produced, new features are implemented, and bugs are fixed, the hack mechanism you've been using may cease to work. Also consider the maintenance issues that can arise when many hacks are spread throughout a style sheet.

In reality, the only completely safe way to use a browser hack is to target **dead browsers**—those browsers that are no longer in development, like Internet Explorer 6—and target them in such a way that you can be sure the hacks you're using will continue to work in that browser.

Don't apply hacks to newer browsers, such as Firefox 2, and Opera 9—they're updated regularly, and new features and bug fixes are addressed relatively quickly. It's just not safe to use a hack for these newer browsers, and usually they don't need it anyway—even if they do need adjustment, a change of design will often accommodate any deficiencies you find. Finally, whenever you use a hack, you face the difficulty of finding one that will work on just the browser you're targeting

---

[1]   This fact was documented in Dave Shea's CSS best practice crib sheet
     [http://www.mezzoblue.com/archives/2003/11/19/css_crib_she/].

without affecting all the others. Let us tell you now: in the end, it's a fruitless pursuit. That's why the modern approach is to attempt to shun hacks altogether.

Using conditional comments (p. 394) is now the recommended way to target various versions of Internet Explorer; a number of workaround techniques (p. 400) that don't rely on ugly hacks are also available. Finally, we've included a list of popular CSS hacks (p. 404) here, not because they're recommended, but in case you come across them and need to understand what they attempt to achieve.

Internet Explorer Conditional Comments

Conditional comments[3] comprise a proprietary Microsoft extension to Internet Explorer that provides a mechanism to target each of the versions of IE either specifically, or as a group. This extension was introduced in IE5, so it can only be used in documents rendered in browsers from IE5 up on the Windows platform.

Conditional comments use a special syntax—HTML markup wrapped in a conditional statement—and are placed within an HTML comment. If the statement evaluates to `true`, the enclosed HTML is revealed within the HTML document. If the statement evaluates to `false`, the enclosed HTML remains hidden. Because conditional comments are placed with HTML comments, the enclosed HTML also remains hidden from all browsers that don't support conditional comments.

Conditional comments can be placed at any point in the document at which normal comments can be located. As such, you can't place them in external CSS files, or in between `<style>` tags. However, they can be used to link to specific files, or to provide specific HTML (or CSS) content for the IE versions specified within the conditional statement. It may seem odd to discuss HTML markup in a CSS reference, but conditional comments are Microsoft's recommended mechanism[4] for delivering targeted CSS to its browser.

---

[3] http://msdn2.microsoft.com/en-us/library/ms537512.aspx
[4] http://blogs.msdn.com/ie/archive/2005/10/12/480242.aspx

Conditional Comment Basics

The basic form of conditional comments is as follows:

```
<!--[if IE ]>
  <link href="iecss.css" rel="stylesheet" type="text/css">
<![endif]-->
```

The conditional statement is contained within square brackets, and begins with `if` followed by an expression. The enclosed HTML content is delimited by the opening `<!--[if]>` and a closing `<![endif]-->` statement.

In the example above, the enclosed HTML content—a `<link>` tag—will be revealed to all IE browsers that support conditional comments. It links to a style sheet that only IE will see. All browsers other than IE versions 5 and later will see the code above as one simple HTML comment. If we remove the brackets and text for the sake of clarity, we're basically left with a normal comment structure as follows:

```
<!--
  <link href="iecss.css" rel="stylesheet" type="text/css" >
-->
```

Conditional Comment Operators

As we mentioned already, we can use conditional comments to apply CSS rules to specific IE browser versions with the help of comparison operators that allow each version of IE to be targeted precisely. We can write complex expressions using one or more of the operators listed in Table 17.1.

Table 17.1: Conditional Comment Operators

Operator	Description
IE	represents Internet Explorer; if a number value is also specified, it represents a version vector
lt	less than operator
lte	less than or equal to

Operator	Description
gt	greater than
gte	greater than or equal to
!	the NOT operator
()	subexpression operator
&	the AND operator
|	the OR operator
true	evaluates to true
false	evaluates to false

So, for example, you'd use the following markup to target IE version 7:

```
<!--[if IE 7 ]>
  <p>Only IE 7 will see this</p>
<![endif]-->
```

Alternatively, if you wanted to target all IE browsers *except* IE7 and above (that is, versions prior to IE7), you could use this method:

```
<!--[if lt IE 7 ]>
  <p>Only less than IE 7 will see this</p>
<![endif]-->
```

If you wanted to include IE7 in that list, you'd use lte operator, which selects all version numbers that are less than or equal to 7.

The gt (greater than) and gte (greater than or equal to) operators work similarly. Have a look at this example:

```
<!--[if gte IE 6 ]>
 <p>Only  IE 6 and greater will see this</p>
<![endif]-->
```

This conditional comment will select all IE browsers with version numbers greater than or equal to 6, which will obviously include IE7 and even IE8—if it ever makes an appearance!

It should be noted that when you use a single digit to represent the version of IE you want to target (for example, `[if IE 7]`) that directive will be applied to all versions of that browser including those with version vectors. For example, if you used the conditional comment below, you'd be including all versions of IE5 including IE5.5:

```
<!--[if IE 5]>
 <p>This covers all versions of IE5 including IE5.5</p>
<![endif]-->
```

💡 Targeting Point Releases

If you want to target a specific point release, you'll need to specify the correct version vector.[5] You can specify a point release using a number followed by up to four decimal places. Even though this appears as a decimal number, IE doesn't see it that way: each individual digit is compared separately. For example, the expression `[if IE 5]` will have a broader match than `[if IE 5.0]`, even though they appear to be equal decimal number values. The expression `[if IE 5.0]` will not match IE5.5.

What this means is that you may need to check the version vector if you're aiming to target specific browser versions. For example, Microsoft points out that IE5 on the Windows 2000 platform has a version vector equal to 5.0002. This means that the expression `[if IE lte 5.0000]` would fail to target the release build of IE5.

You can also use the "not" operator, !, to exclude one of the IE browser versions. To exclude IE6, but not IE7 or IE5 (if ever you wanted to do such a thing), you'd use this expression:

---

[5] http://msdn2.microsoft.com/en-us/library/ms537512.aspx#Version_Vectors

```
<!--[if !IE 6]>
  <p>IE7 or IE5 only</p>
<![endif]-->
```

Downlevel-hidden Conditional Comments

More complicated expressions can be created using one or more of the available operators. For example, the following conditional comment targets IE6 and IE7 using subexpressions and the OR operator:

```
<!--[if (IE 6)|(IE 7)]>
  <p>IE6 or IE7 only </p>
<![endif]-->
```

Microsoft refers to the this style of conditional comments as **downlevel-hidden**, since browsers that don't support conditional comments (including IE4 and earlier) will interpret the conditional comment code as a standard HTML comment, and ignore it completely. And yes—Microsoft describes all browsers except IE5 and later as "downlevel" browsers!

There is, however, another version of conditional comments that will allow these downlevel browsers to be targeted; they're called **downlevel-revealed** conditional comments.

Downlevel-revealed Conditional Comments

In downlevel-revealed conditional comments, the HTML content inside the conditional statements is revealed to browsers that don't support conditional comments, because the conditional statements—and only the conditional statements—are ignored. If the statement evaluates to true (in a supporting browser), the content inside the conditional statements is also revealed.

Unfortunately, the syntax of these downlevel-revealed conditional comments will often cause HTML validation errors. Here's Microsoft's suggested syntax:

```
<![if !IE]>
 <p>This is shown in downlevel browsers, but is invalid HTML!</p>
<![endif]>
```

However, a better, valid version of the syntax is available.[6] It's been discovered that if you change the syntax slightly, the downlevel effect can be maintained *and* the HTML code will validate:

```
<!--[if !IE]>-->
  <p>This is shown in downlevel browsers.</p>
<!--<![endif]-->
```

Here, we simply wrap the conditional statements in HTML comments. It should be noted that this usage doesn't conform to Microsoft's specifications for these comments, but it presently works in all versions of IE5 and later (including IE7) and, more to the point, will also validate—unlike Microsoft's version.

That said, a problem exists with that approach should you wish to target downlevel browsers as well as a supporting Microsoft browser version. Take a look at this example, which attempts to target downlevel browsers and IE7 or later:

```
<!--[if gte IE 7]>-->
  <p>This is shown in downlevel browsers and IE7 or later.</p>
<!--<![endif]-->
```

This example uses valid HTML, but IE7 and later browsers will also reveal the --> after the opening conditional statement. The fix suggested by Microsoft is to add an extra <! just after the opening conditional comment:

```
<!--[if gte IE 7]><!-->
  <p>This is shown in downlevel browsers and IE7 or later.</p>
<!--<![endif]-->
```

Conditional Comments in Practice

If you want to use conditional comments in your approach to delivering targeted CSS, here's what you can do. First, link to your standard style sheet in the normal way (via a <link> tag, for example). Then, use conditional comments to link to one or more other style sheets that contain the CSS targeted towards IE. The IE-only style sheets should contain only the required CSS fixes. They shouldn't be a

---

[6]　http://www.456bereastreet.com/archive/200511/valid_downlevelrevealed_conditional_comments/

duplication of your standard style sheet—that would be a waste of bandwidth and completely redundant anyway. Here's an example of this approach:

```
<link href="main.css" rel="stylesheet" type="text/css">
<!--[if IE 7]>
<link href="ie7.css" rel="stylesheet" type="text/css">
<![endif]-->
<!--[if IE 6]>
<link href="ie6.css" rel="stylesheet" type="text/css">
<![endif]-->
<!--[if IE 5]>
<link href="ie5.css" rel="stylesheet" type="text/css">
<![endif]-->
```

main.css is the standard style sheet, while **ie7.css**, **ie6.css**, and **ie5.css** contain the CSS for specific IE versions. You may not need to be as version-specific as we've been in this example. Remember that the cascade will be in effect, and that the rules in the CSS files that are referenced lower down the page source will overrule any previously defined CSS rules.

Whether you like conditional comments or not, they do make it easy and safe to target versions of IE, and they're as future-proof as any of these tricks can be. The comments also provide a logical structure to your CSS management approach, and separate the targeted CSS from the standard CSS. At some time in the future when the targeted CSS is no longer required, the code, which is already separated, can easily be removed.

Workarounds and Filters

The art of selectively applying CSS to specific browsers probably began with the exclusion of Netscape Navigator 4. It was discovered that if you used a `media` value of anything except `"screen"` on a style sheet `link` element, Netscape 4 would ignore the style sheet. At the time, it was considered safer to avoid attempting to apply CSS to Netscape because it was so buggy that the CSS was likely to crash the browser.

Not long after that, it was discovered that Netscape didn't support the `@import` at-rule. Simply using `@import url(styles/main.css);` achieved the same result and had the added benefit of excluding all other browsers that provided poor CSS support, like Internet Explorer 4. Thus the concept of filtering out browsers through the use of more advanced CSS features gained popularity.

Before you dive into CSS filtering, however, you should take a considered approach to dealing with CSS rendering problems:

1. Ensure your CSS validates. CSS validation ensures a reliable baseline for dealing with CSS issues. Otherwise, you could waste you time chasing phantoms that turn out merely to be syntax errors.

2. Check the specifications. Make sure you're not imagining problems that don't exist. Some concepts like the box model, positioning, and floats are more complex than people realize, and problems may simply arise from incorrect assumptions about how CSS is supposed to work. This reference is an excellent place to start your research.

3. Check browser behavior. All browsers have CSS problems of one kind or another. What you're experiencing may be a rendering quirk or a bug. Researching the reason why the problem is occurring will better enable you to deal with it now and in the future. Web sites like Position Is Everything[7] and the Quirksmode Bug Report[8] are great resources.

Searching for a Workaround

Once you've been through that process, and have confirmed that yours is indeed a browser-related problem, your next step should be to search for a known workaround. Many CSS problems can be solved by adjusting your HTML markup or CSS. For example, a lot of Internet Explorer rendering quirks can be solved by either enabling or disabling the proprietary `hasLayout` property of a given element through the setting of specific CSS properties—read more about the topic in The Internet Explorer hasLayout Property (p. 158). Again, the web sites mentioned above, Position Is Everything and the Quirksmode Bug Report, are a great place to start this research as they often document usable workarounds for various problems.

[7] http://positioniseverything.net
[8] http://www.quirksmode.org/bugreports/index.html

Applying a CSS Filter

If no usable workaround exists for your problem, you may have to resort to applying a different set of rules for a specific browser. You may be able to use a CSS feature that's not supported by all browsers in order to direct CSS rules to particular browsers—a technique that's often referred to as using a **CSS filter**. In doing this, you're exploiting the feature of CSS error handling (p. 44) that specifies that user agents must ignore statements and declarations they don't understand.

Using a child selector (p. 76) is another common example of this kind of filtering technique. The child selector is 100% valid CSS—it's only a filter in the sense that it's only supported by modern web browsers. Internet Explorer versions prior to 7 have not implemented this feature, so it's a useful way to hide CSS rules from Internet Explorer 6 and earlier versions. The child selector is commonly used like this:

```
#test{
   position: absolute;
}
html>body #test{
   position: fixed;
}
```

The filter above is designed to address the fact that Internet Explorer 6 and earlier versions don't support the value of `fixed` for the `position` property. These browsers will only set the `position` of the #test element to `absolute`, and will ignore the second rule. Meanwhile, virtually all other modern browsers will set #test's `position` to `fixed`, because they apply the second rule and overwrite the property.

Though filters can work, you should be wary of rewriting CSS rules for good browsers in order to avoid problems with bad browsers—it just doesn't seem to be the right thing to do. It's preferable to target problematic browsers and keep your style sheets uncluttered.

The Star Selector Hack

The star selector hack,[9] also known as the star-HTML hack and the Tan hack, because it was first described in detail by Edwardson Tan, is the most widely used filter; it

[9] http://www.info.com.ph/~etan/w3pantheon/style/starhtmlbug.html

relies on a peculiar behavior in Internet Explorer 5.5 and 6. Even though it's often labeled a hack, I've included it in this section on filters because, despite the fact that it exploits a browser bug, it uses a valid CSS selector. The selector, however, should never match any elements; all browsers, except Internet Explorer 5.5 and 6, understand this fact and ignore the rule.

The technique is simply to apply a descendant selector that makes use of the universal selector. The universal selector is, of course, valid CSS, so don't be confused and start thinking that using the universal selector is bad news. The most common form of the technique (and the origin of its name) is to compose a rule with the `*  html` selector. This constitutes valid CSS, but it shouldn't match any elements. The selector should apply the rule to any `html` element that's the descendant of any other element and, as `html` is the root element, it's never a descendant of any other element.

However, while most other browsers ignore it, Internet Explorer 5.5 and 6 will interpret this selector as if there was no universal selector, like the rule below:

```
html {
    declarations
}
```

Thus, the star selector hack is a safe way of applying CSS rules to Internet Explorer 5.5 and 6 without affecting other browsers.

You'd use it like this:

```
.test {
  position: fixed;
}
* html .test{
  position: absolute;
}
```

Only Internet Explorer 6 and earlier versions will apply the latter rule; other browsers will ignore it.

The three selectors that function in this way are documented in Table 17.2.

Table 17.2: Internet Explorer's Star HTML Selector Bug

Selector	Internet Explorer 5.5/6 Interpretation
`* html`	`html`
`* * body`	`* body`
`* html body`	`html body`

CSS Hacks

CSS hacks have a long and colorful history. For a bit of historical perspective, some of the most popular CSS hacks are explained below. This is not an exhaustive list, and there's really no need to remember all the hacks and variations in detail, but you should be aware that they exist. For example, if you happen to inherit a site and discover some obscure CSS notation in an old style sheet, you'll be able to identify it and understand its purpose. If you can't find a particular hack in this list, look them up as required from the many resources around the Web, including Dynamic Site Solutions[10] and Centricle.com.[11]

The Backslash and Underscore Hacks

Numerous characters trigger non-compliant behaviors in different browsers. Both of the hacks we'll discuss in this section constitute legal CSS, but rely on specific browser bugs in order to work.

The first application we'll look at is the backslash hack, in which a backslash character is inserted into a property name. The backslash indicates a character escape in CSS escape notation (p. 43) and browsers that comply with the CSS specification should ignore the character in this context. However, Internet Explorer 5.5 and earlier versions will ignore the whole declaration when they meet a character escape in the middle of a property name. Here's an example:

---

[10] http://www.dynamicsitesolutions.com/css/filters/support-chart/
[11] http://centricle.com/ref/css/filters/

```
.test {
  height: 500px;
  he\ight: 400px;
}
```

Modern browsers will apply a height of 400px, but Internet Explorer 5.5 and earlier versions will retain the value of 500px, since they'll ignore the latter declaration.

📖 Positioning the Backslash

For this hack to work properly, the backslash must be positioned in the middle of the property, not at the beginning. Also, it shouldn't appear before the letters a to f, or A to F, or numerals 0 to 9—if it does, those characters will be treated as hexadecimal numbers according to CSS escape notation rules.

The second application we'll review is the underscore property hack, in which an underscore character is inserted at the beginning of a property name. This is valid CSS, and modern browsers will simply ignore the declaration because the property is unknown. However, Internet Explorer 6 and earlier versions ignore the underscore and apply the declaration. For example, in the following CSS, most modern browsers will ignore the second declaration, but Internet Explorer 6 and earlier versions will apply it:

```
.test {
  position: fixed;
  _position: absolute;
}
```

The Voice-family Hack

The most famous, and perhaps oldest, CSS hack is the voice-family hack, also known as the box model hack because it was specifically designed to work around the disparity in the implementation of the box model (p. 142) in Internet Explorer 5.x and other standards-compliant browsers. It's also known as the Tantek Hack—named after its inventor, Tantek Çelik.[12] It's an ugly and complicated hack that's virtually

---

[12] http://tantek.com/CSS/Examples/boxmodelhack.html

impossible to remember off the top of your head. Here's what the complete hack looks like:

```
.test {
  width: 500px;
  padding: 50px;
  voice-family: "\"}\"";
  voice-family: inherit;
  width: 400px;
}
html>body .test{
  width: 400px;
}
```

The hack worked thanks to a flaw in the CSS parser in Internet Explorer 5.x, and it effectively cut the declaration block short at the curly brace in the middle of this section of code: "\"}\"".

This flaw effectively made Internet Explorer 5.x see something like this:

```
.test {
width: 500px;
padding: 50px;
voice-family: "\"}
```

The browser ignored the width: 400px; declaration, and retained the 500px width value. Most other browsers will apply the 400px width instead.

Unfortunately, Opera 5, which was in use at the time, exhibited the same parsing bug as IE5 and IE5.5, so an extra rule needed to be added using the child selector. Opera 5 supported the child selector and applied the declaration:

```
html>body .test{
  width: 400px;
}
```

As I mentioned, it's an ugly hack, but it was necessary at the time. Eventually, it was surpassed by the simpler star selector hack. (p. 402)

The Commented Backslash Hack

This hack targets a CSS parsing bug in Internet Explorer 5 Mac. To hide rules from IE5 for Mac, simply place a backslash before the close of a comment:

```
/* begin hiding from IE5 Mac \*/
.test {
  color: red;
}
/* end */
```

IE5 for Mac won't see the close of the comment, so it'll ignore everything between the backslash and the end of the next comment.

You can also achieve precisely the opposite effect with the following CSS:

```
/* apply ONLY to IE5 Mac \*//*/
.test {
  color: red;
}
/* end */
```

The High Pass Filter

The High Pass Filter[13] was developed by Tantek Çelik in order to hide a style sheet from browsers that supported the @import method but didn't provide a decent level of support for CSS1. The hack looks like this:

```
@import "null.css?\"\{";
@import "highpass.css";
```

This actually constitutes valid CSS. The first statement attempts to import a file from the URI **null.css?"{**, which is an empty file, while the second statement imports the desired style sheet. Internet Explorer 6 and up, Internet Explorer 5 for Mac, Netscape 6 and up, and Opera 5 and up could read these two statements correctly, but older browsers got caught up on the escape characters and failed to load any style sheets.

---

[13] http://tantek.com/CSS/Examples/highpass.html

Summary

Coping with browser differences is a way of life for the CSS practitioner. Although filters should be avoided wherever possible, you may encounter situations in which a design change isn't possible or feasible, and a browser's behavior is so problematic that the only way you can solve the problem is to apply some sort of CSS filter. Hacks, however, should be avoided at all costs.

Remember to use CSS filters that only target dead browsers—then you won't be in the situation in which a bug gets fixed and stops your CSS from working as you expected.

Use CSS filters carefully and adopt a structured, logical approach to your CSS management. This way, you can ensure that you recognize where and why you have used the filters, and that you understand their implications.

Consider using conditional comments as a safe and future-proof way of addressing all Internet Explorer versions. Make sure that the CSS files are manageable and don't contain unnecessary code. Keep only the changed CSS in the Internet Explorer-only files and avoid duplicating CSS code unnecessarily.

Remember that, in most cases, workarounds, filters, and hacks can be avoided if you take a considered approach to the page architecture using valid CSS and HTML code. CSS is so flexible that it allows you to code the same layout in many different ways, and often a small change in design will obviate the need for any hacks at all.

Differences Between HTML and XHTML

Even though this is a CSS reference, we should spend some time talking about HTML and XHTML, because your choice of markup language will affect how CSS is applied in some instances. Moreover, in order to understand the variations in the way CSS is applied to HTML and XHTML, you need to grasp the fundamental differences between the two markup languages.

The most important difference between the two markup languages is that **HyperText Markup Language**, or HTML, is an application of SGML (Standard Generalized Markup Language),[1] and allows an author to omit certain tags and use attribute minimization.[2] The Extensible HyperText Markup Language, or XHTML, is an application of XML (Extensible Markup Language).[3] It doesn't permit the omission of any tags or the use of attribute minimization. However, it provides a shorthand

---

[1] More accurately, HTML has been an application of SGML since version 2.0.
[2] Attribute minimization is an SGML feature that allows us to omit the attribute name and use only the value; for instance, we could use `<input readonly>` instead of `<input readonly="readonly">`.
[3] XML is a subset of SGML.

notation for empty elements—for example, we could use <br/> instead of
</br>—which HTML does not. A conforming XML document must be well formed, which, among other things, means that there must be an end tag for every start tag, and that nested tags must be closed in the right order.[4] When an XML parser encounters an error relating to the document's well-formedness, it must abort, whereas an HTML parser is expected to attempt to recover and continue.

There are three areas in which the differences between HTML and XHTML affect our use of CSS:

- case sensitivity (p. 412)
- optional tags (p. 413)
- properties for the root element (p. 415)

Note, though, that these differences apply only when an XHTML document is served as an application of XML; that is, with a MIME type of application/xhtml+xml, application/xml, or text/xml. An XHTML document served with a MIME type of text/html must be parsed and interpreted as HTML, so the HTML rules apply in this case. A style sheet written for an XHTML document being served with a MIME type of text/html may not work as intended if the document is then served with a MIME type of application/xhtml+xml. For more information about MIME types, make sure to read MIME Types (p. 411).

This can be especially important when you're serving XHTML documents as text/html. Unless you're aware of the differences, you may create style sheets that won't work as intended if the document's served as real XHTML.

Where the terms "XHTML" and "XHTML document" appear in the remainder of this section, they refer to XHTML markup served with an XML MIME type. XHTML markup served as text/html is an HTML document as far as browsers are concerned.

---

[4] An XML document can be well-formed without being valid. Only well-formedness is a formal requirement of XML. (Browsers use non-validating XML parsers, anyway.)

MIME Types

When a web document is requested, the web server delivers an HTTP response comprising two parts: the headers and the body. The headers contain meta information about the body, while the body is the actual document (the HTML or XHTML markup, in this case).

One very important HTTP header is called `Content-Type`. This header specifies the MIME type, and though it can also contain information about the character encoding that's used in the file, this data shouldn't be included for XML documents. The MIME type tells the user agent what type of content it's about to receive.

A `Content-Type` header for an HTML document can look like this:

```
Content-Type: text/html; charset=utf-8
```

For an XHTML document, it should look like this:

```
Content-Type: application/xhtml+xml
```

It's primarily the MIME type that dictates how a web document's handled by a browser. For an XML MIME type, the `<html>` tag's `xmlns` attribute is what specifies a document as containing XHTML. The doctype declaration (p. 17) has nothing to do with this matter, except when it comes to validating the markup.

Internet Explorer doesn't support the MIME type `application/xhtml+xml`. Although it supports `application/xml` and `text/xml`, it'll treat the document as generic XML rather than XHTML. This is why most authors serve their XHTML markup as `text/html`, yet few realize that this causes browsers to handle their pages as HTML, rather than XHTML.

Serving XHTML as `text/html` is permitted by the W3C, provided that the markup complies with the guidelines in Appendix C of the XHTML 1.0 specification.[5]

---

[5] http://www.w3.org/TR/xhtml1/#guidelines

Case Sensitivity

CSS is case insensitive in all matters under its control; however, some things, such as the document markup language, are beyond its control. HTML is case insensitive in most respects, except when it comes to certain attribute values, like the id and class attributes. XHTML, being XML, is always case sensitive.

This means that the CSS element type selectors (p. 62) for an HTML document are case insensitive, though they're case sensitive for XHTML, as this example shows:[6]

```
h1 {
  font-size: 150%;
}
H1 {
  color: red;
}
```

The first rule will apply to all level-one headings in HTML (even if the tags are written as <H1>...</H1> in HTML) and XHTML.

The second rule will apply to all level-one headings in HTML, even if the tags are written as <h1>...</h1>. It won't apply to any heading element in an XHTML document.

In attribute selectors (p. 67) for HTML documents, attribute names and some attribute values are case insensitive, while other attribute values—most notably the attributes id and class—are case sensitive. As these attributes are case sensitive in HTML, ID selectors (p. 65) and class selectors (p. 63) must always match the case of the id and class attribute values in the document. To find out which attribute values are case sensitive and which aren't, consult the HTML specification[7].

This issue is further complicated by the fact that browser behavior is inconsistent. For example, in Internet Explorer 6, id and class attribute values are only case sensitive in standards mode. In Safari 3 and earlier versions, attribute selectors are always case insensitive for HTML documents.

---

[6]   All XHTML tags and attribute names (and some values) must be written in lowercase.

[7]   http://www.w3.org/TR/html401/types.html#h-6.1

Since all attribute names and values are case sensitive in XHTML, selectors are always case sensitive.

The simplest way to mitigate any potential issues surrounding case sensitivity is to always use lowercase for everything in your markup and CSS, where possible. If that's not possible, make sure the case you use is consistent between your CSS and your document markup.

Optional Tags

The HTML specification allows us to omit some tags. Several end tags are optional, for instance `<p>` and `<li>`, but they don't matter from a CSS point of view. What is important to consider is that in HTML 4, the start tags are optional in four instances: `<html>`, `<head>`, `<body>`, and `<tbody>`. The corresponding elements will exist in the document object model (DOM) tree whether or not the tags are present in the markup. It's now considered best practice to include these tags explicitly, but an HTML document can be valid without them.

The `<html>`, `<head>`, and `<body>` tags aren't optional in XHTML; they must be included explicitly in the markup. It's permissible, even in XHTML, to omit the `<tbody>` and `<tbody>` tags in simple tables, not because the tags are optional—there's no such thing as an optional tag in XML—but because XHTML allows two content models for the `table` element type.

Whereas HTML regards the `tbody` element tags as optional (thereby making them implicit), the XHTML specification states that a table must contain either one or more `tbody` elements, or one or more `tr` elements (after any optional `caption`, `col`, `colgroup`, `thead`, and `tfoot` elements).

The important difference is that, in an XHTML document, a `table` element that lacks `<tbody>` and `<tbody>` tags won't contain a `tbody` element node in the DOM tree. In HTML, the `tbody` element will be present in the DOM tree whether or not the tags are present.

This variation can affect our use of CSS in specific cases. Consider the following CSS rules, which set a medium font weight for header cells in the table body (presumably row headers), and a bold font for other header cells (for example, those in a thead element):

```css
th {
   font-weight: bold;
}
tbody th {
 font-weight: normal;
}
```

Now, let's look at two different ways to write the markup for a simple table:

```html
<table>
  <tbody>
    <tr>
      <th>Blue Widgets</th>
      <td>$12.95</td>
      <td>3 lbs</td>
    </tr>
    : more table rows
  </tbody>
</table>
```

For the table above, row headings like "Blue Widgets" will have a normal font weight, regardless of whether the document uses HTML or XHTML, since the markup includes explicit <tbody> and <tbody> tags.

Here's another example; this one omits the <tbody> tags:

```html
<table>
  <tr>
    <th>Blue Widgets</th>
    <td>$12.95</td>
    <td>3 lbs</td>
  </tr>
  : more table rows
</table>
```

The table above is a little different. In an HTML document, the row headings will have a normal font weight: because the tbody element will be present in the DOM tree, the second selector will match the th elements.

In an XHTML document, however, the row headings will be bold, because only the first selector matches any th elements. Omitting the <tbody> and <tbody> tags means that a tbody element won't appear in the DOM tree, so the second selector won't match the th elements in this table.

Root Element Properties

For HTML, but not for XHTML, the CSS2.1 specification[8] recommends that we specify the document background for the body element, rather than for the html element. If the computed value of the background property for the html element is transparent (the initial value), any background properties specified for the body element will be applied to the canvas (p. 141). This isn't the case for XHTML.

The CSS2.1 specification[9] also says that an overflow property declared for the body or html elements may be applied to the viewport, but only for HTML documents. In reality, though, browsers apply this property to the viewport for XHTML documents too.

---

[8] http://www.w3.org/TR/CSS21/colors.html#background
[9] http://www.w3.org/TR/CSS21/visufx.html#overflow

Appendix A

Alphabetic Property Index

This is a complete, alphabetical list of the CSS properties contained in this reference.

background 312

background-attachment 309

background-color 299

background-image 301

background-position 305

background-repeat 303

behavior 387

border 255

border-bottom 240

border-bottom-color 235

border-bottom-style 236

border-bottom-width 239

border-color 249

border-collapse 293

border-left 247

border-left-color 242

border-left-style 243

border-left-width 246

border-right 233

border-right-color 228

border-right-style 229

border-right-width 232

border-spacing 294

border-style 251

border-top 226

border-top-color 220

border-top-style 222

border-top-width 224

border-width 254

bottom 277

caption-side 297

clear 271

clip 283

color 315

content 348

counter-increment 352

counter-reset 354

cursor 358

direction 343

display 264

empty-cells 295

The expression Property Value 388

filter 381

float 269

font 325

font-family 318

font-size 320

font-style 323

font-variant 324

font-weight 321

height 188

left 278

letter-spacing 326

line-height 328

list-style 290

list-style-image 289

list-style-position 288

list-style-type 286

margin 209

margin-bottom 205

margin-left 207

margin-right 202

margin-top 200

max-height 192

max-width 198

min-height 190

min-width 196

-moz-border-radius 372

-moz-box-sizing 375

The display Property Value: -moz-inline-box 377

orphans 365

outline 261

outline-color 258

outline-style 259

outline-width 260

overflow 280

padding 218

padding-bottom 215

padding-left 216

padding-right 213

padding-top 212

page-break-after 364

page-break-before 362

page-break-inside 363

position 267

quotes 355

right 276

table-layout 292

text-align 330

text-decoration 332

text-indent 334

text-shadow 337

text-transform 335

top 275

unicode-bidi 344

vertical-align 338

visibility 273

white-space 341

widows 366

width 194

word-spacing 327

z-index 279

zoom 380

THE ART &
SCIENCE
OF CSS

BY **CAMERON ADAMS**
JINA BOLTON
DAVID JOHNSON
STEVE SMITH
JONATHAN SNOOK

CREATE INSPIRATIONAL STANDARDS-BASED WEB DESIGN

THE PRINCIPLES OF
BEAUTIFUL
WEB DESIGN

BY JASON BEAIRD

SIMPLY JAVASCRIPT

BY **KEVIN YANK**
& CAMERON ADAMS

EVERYTHING YOU NEED TO LEARN JAVASCRIPT FROM SCRATCH

THE CSS
ANTHOLOGY
101 ESSENTIAL TIPS, TRICKS & HACKS

BY **RACHEL ANDREW**
2ND EDITION

ESSENTIAL READING FOR ANYONE USING CSS